THE EIGHTH
COMMANDMENT

THE EIGHTH COMMANDMENT

Lawrence Sanders

New English Library

First published in the United States of America by
G. P. Putnam's Sons in 1986

First published in Great Britain in 1986 by
New English Library, Mill Road, Dunton Green, Sevenoaks, Kent.
Editorial office: 47 Bedford Square, London WC1B 3DP.

Typeset by Hewer Text Composition Services, Edinburgh.
Printed in Great Britain by St. Edmundsbury Press, Bury St. Edmunds, Suffolk.

British Library Cataloguing in Publication Data
Sanders, Lawrence
    The eighth commandment.
    I. Title
    813'.54[F]   PS3569.A5125

ISBN 0 450 39707 6

1

MEN TREAT me with amusement, women with sympathy.

My name is Mary Lou Bateson, but the nickname 'Dunk' followed me from Des Moines to New York City. I am almost six-two – in my bare feet. When I wear heels, I loom – or so a man once told me.

'Don't worry about it, Dunk,' Daddy advised. 'People look up to you.'

That will give you an idea of his quirky sense of humor. That, and the fact that he named my three brothers Tom, Dick, and Harry. I suppose that if I'd had two sisters, we'd be Faith, Hope, and Charity.

About that 'Dunk' . . . Both my parents were tall, and all my brothers were over six-six before they were fifteen years old. If you think that means basketball, you're right. We had a barrel hoop nailed to the garage as long as I can remember. Having no sisters, and, being too tall to have close girlfriends, I joined my brothers in their daily practice.

We divided into teams of two, Tom and Dick flipping a coin to decide partners. The loser got me. But I worked as hard as they. And after months of striving to master the dunk shot, I succeeded well enough to earn my nickname. Everyone called me Dunk.

My brothers were stars in high school, and I played center on the girls' team. We won all kinds of tournaments, and our home was filled with trophies. Mother kept an album of newspaper clippings about our exploits. The *Register* referred to me as 'the lofty, spindly Dunk Bateson.' I know they meant it kindly, but it hurt.

The same year that story appeared, I wore a bikini to a pool party and overheard a girl say, 'It looks like two Band-Aids on a broomstick.' And I endured the usual chaff: 'How's the weather up there?' and 'Do you get many nosebleeds?' Sometimes people can be cruel without really meaning to be.

I tried to grin my way through all this. Wore my flats and kept

1

telling myself not to slump. But it is difficult being a *very* tall girl. And the fevered attentions of *very* short boys are no help either. I didn't have a date for our high school prom. I went with my brother Harry and his date, a cute, cuddly blonde who came to his belt buckle. Everyone thought they made an adorable couple. If I had shown up with a male midget, we'd have been laughed off the dance floor. It's not fair.

My brothers got athletic scholarships to prestigious universities. I ended up at Chase, a small liberal arts college that had no organized women's athletic activities except field hockey. I had already decided that my competitive dunk shot days were over.

Chase was a four-year vacation from the realities of life. I breezed through the required courses, and in my last two years took a heavy dose of art history and appreciation. I hadn't the slightest idea what I wanted to do with my life. But just to be on the safe side, I learned how to type and operate a personal computer. You never know.

The high point of my career at Chase was losing my virginity. I must have been the only nineteen-year-old virgin in the state of Iowa. It happened in the grass under an old billboard that advertised: 'Coca-Cola: The Pause That Refreshes.' Daddy would have liked that.

Clutching my sheepskin, printed in Latin that I couldn't understand, I went home to Des Moines and played some lazy driveway basketball with my brothers. Late in August, with a cash graduation gift from my parents, I headed for New York City, determined to seek fame and fortune. Or at least find a man who might sweep me off my big feet. A *tall* man.

This was several years ago, but even then it was hard to find reasonable rental apartments. Now it's impossible. Anyway, I ended up in a closet on West 76th Street. It was before the West Side became Madison Avenue-ized, and there was a small-town flavor about Columbus and Amsterdam that I liked. Also, my apartment was so small that I could furnish it in Salvation Army Traditional for less than $500.

So there I was, living in glittery Manhattan, and too poor to do much else than sightsee, eat tunafish sandwiches, and agonize over the *Times* want ad pages as if they were reprints from *Remembrance of Things Past*.

I had a number of discouraging interviews, none of which led to anything much. For a while I sold men's gloves at Macy's, worked behind the counter at Chock Full o' Nuts, and addressed envelopes for a mail order company that sold a baldness remedy and a wrinkle remover.

My personal life during this period was something less than ecstatic. I met a few men, who seemed to be hungry and lecherous, in that order. We usually settled for tunafish sandwiches. I had no close women friends. I suppose I was lonely, but there was so much in Manhattan, so many things I wanted to see and do, I can't honestly say I was unhappy. I resolutely avoid self-pity.

I had a brief affair (about six weeks) with a man a few years older and a few inches shorter than I. He told me he wasn't married, but he had been out in the sun a lot the previous summer, and his hands were still tan. Except for a pale strip around his ring finger. He always took off his wedding band before he met me. I never told him I knew.

But he was handsome and amusing. I knew it couldn't last – but that was all right. I often wondered why he started up with me in the first place, and then decided it was for the same reason some men climb mountains: because I was *there*.

Also, there are certain men who seek the outré in their personal relationships: very tall women, very short, the very obese, those exceedingly ugly or, for all I know, the crippled and the blind. The whole subject is too depressing to think about.

Anyway, we broke up after six weeks (no tears), he went back to his wife, and I went back to the want ads. I answered a very short one requesting résumés be sent to a box number by anyone interested in becoming a secretary-assistant-salesperson for a numismatist.

As a kid, I had collected Indian head pennies and buffalo nickels in an empty pickle jar; that was the extent of my knowledge about coins. But nothing ventured, nothing gained, so I sent off my résumé with a covering letter. I remembered I answered a half-dozen ads in a similar fashion that weekend, and had no high hopes for any of them.

But two weeks later I received a letter from the numismatist asking me to come in for a personal interview. I was tempted to dash to the library and bone up on the history of coinage, but then decided it would be a waste of time. A few days of cramming would never convince him I was an expert. If he wanted to hire me, he'd have to live with my ignorance.

His name was Enoch Wottle, and he had a small, dusty shop on West 57th Street. It was really a hole-in-the-wall kind of place with one narrow, barred show window. The entrance was kept locked, and when I rang the bell, he peered at me from behind a torn green shade. I held up the letter I had received. He examined it carefully, then opened the door just wide enough for me to slip through.

He stared up at me, smiled, and said, 'You're hired.'

I worked for Enoch Wottle for almost three years, the two of us alone in that dim, cramped shop filled with locked glass cabinets and a safe in the back room as big and heavy as a bank vault. We started out as Mr Wottle and Miss Bateson. Within six months we were Enoch and Dunk.

He was the dearest, sweetest man who ever lived. Pushing seventy, with a nimbus of snowy white hair surrounding his skull like a halo. He was terribly afflicted with arthritis, could hardly handle the coin tongs, which was why he had advertised for an assistant after working by himself so many years.

He had been a widower for twenty of those years, and now lived alone in a dinosaur of an apartment house just a block from his store. His only child, a son, was married and lived in Arizona. He was constantly urging the old man to come out and spend his remaining days in a hot, dry climate.

But Enoch resisted. His shop was his life, he told me, and giving it up would be the final surrender to age and mortality.

'Don't you want to see your grandchildren?' I asked him.

'I see them,' he said. 'Occasionally. I talk to them on the phone. I carry their photographs in my wallet.'

I don't think he was a wealthy man, but I'm sure he was well-off. I know he was generous to me. I started out at just a little over minimum wage, but at the end of my three years with Enoch, I was doing very well indeed, had moved into a larger apartment with new furniture, and was buying my clothing and shoes at tall girls' shops. Expensive.

Wottle's was a strange sort of business. No off-the-street trade at all. But he had a faithful clientele, most of whom he served by phone or letter. So noble was his reputation and so trustworthy his judgment, that customers bought valuable coins on Enoch's say-so, without ever seeing their purchases until they arrived by mail or messenger.

He, in his turn, bought from collectors, other commercial numismatists, or at coin auctions all over the world. Most of this by phone, mail, or cable. After a while I started making weekly deposits at the bank for him and saw how profitable Wottle's Coin Shop actually was. He made no effort to minimize his success or hide it from me.

Although he dealt in all kinds of metal and paper money, tokens, and even a few medals, his specialty was ancient Greek coins, and most of his income was derived from buying, selling, and trading those little bits of minted gold, silver, copper, and bronze.

He taught me so much. I learned all about dekadrachms, tetrobols, and trihemitartemorions. (Try humming that last on your old kazoo!) I learned to distinguish electrum from purer forms of gold and silver. I even learned to judge between Extremely Fine and Very Fine, and between Fair and Mediocre. Close distinctions indeed.

Once Enoch tried to explain to me the fascination of those ancient Greek coins. It was a dusky November evening, and we were having a final cup of tea and a biscuit before closing up and going home.

He sat behind his battered desk in a wing chair so worn and burnished that the leather had a mirror gleam. He looked with quiet satisfaction at the glass cabinets containing his coins. The disks twinkled like imprisoned stars. He knew their history, and the men who had minted them, worked for them, fought for them, died for them. A wonderful people who lived short, harsh lives but never lost their capacity for joy or their love of beauty.

Those old bits of metal he loved were at once a link to the past and a promise of the future. In a way he could not define, Enoch Wottle saw his coins as proof of immortality. Not his own, of course, but of the human race. When great thoughts had been forgotten, great wars ignored, great art scorned, and monuments of stone crumbled to dust, money would survive.

That evening I think he infected me with his passion.

It couldn't last. His arthritis became progressively worse. And then came the summons from the landlord. The entire block, including Wottle's Coin Shop, was to be demolished so that a luxury high-rise could be erected. It was time to go. Enoch was not bitter – or claimed not to be.

'Off to Arizona,' he said, trying to smile. 'I'll close up and sell my stock to Fletcher Brothers on Lexington Avenue; they've been after me for years. The important thing is – what are we going to do with you?'

I kissed his cheek and held him tight.

What he did for me was beyond expectations, even my most fantastical hopes. Three months' salary as severance pay; a gift of his cherished library, including rare and gorgeously illustrated volumes on Greek coinage; all his catalogues of coin auctions of the past several years.

Best of all, he made several impassioned phone calls to old friends, and by the time I put him on the train to Arizona (he refused to fly), he had obtained a promise of a job for me with Grandby & Sons, the old, respected auction house on Madison Avenue. I was to work in the estate and appraisal department as resident numismatist.

And that was where my Great Adventure began.

2

'My name is Felicia Dodat,' she said, looking up at me in amazement. 'It is spelled D-o-d-a-t, but pronounced Do-day. Please remember that. I will supervise your work at Grandby and Sons.'

I nodded brightly. I loathed her on sight. She was everything I could never be: petite, shapely, and dressed with a careless elegance that drove me right up the wall. She was dark, with a bonnet of black hair as soft as feathers, olive skin, brilliant makeup. I could understand why men might drool over her, but I dubbed her a bitch from the start.

'You will be responsible for all coin appraisals,' she said sharply, tapping blood-red talons on her glass-topped desk. 'Occasionally it may be necessary for you to go out of town to appraise an estate. You understand?'

Again I nodded, beginning to feel like one of those crazy Chinese dolls with a bobbing head.

'Unfortunately, our space is limited, and I cannot assign you your own office. You will have to share with Hobart Juliana, who handles stamps, autographs, and historical documents. I should tell you at once that he is gay. Does that offend you?'

'Not at all.'

'Good. Then let's get you settled in so you can go to work at once.'

Sweet lady. I tramped after her down a long decorated corridor furnished with raddled settees, end tables with cracked marble tops, and oil paintings of dead fish. She stopped before a solid oak door equipped with a small judas window.

'This will be your office,' Felicia Dodat said severely. 'Since you and Hobart will be examining valuable consignments at your desks, this door is *always* kept locked. Is that clear?'

My nodding was giving me vertigo.

She rapped briskly. In a moment the judas was opened, an eye peered out at us. The door was unlocked, swung open.

'Hobart,' my boss said, smiling winsomely, 'this is your new roommate, Miss Mary Lou Bateson. I'm sure the two of you will get on just marvelously. Show her the ropes, will you, dear?'

Then she was gone, I was inside, the door locked again. He turned to me and said, 'My name is Felicia Dodat. It is spelled D-o-d-a-t, but pronounced Do-day. Please remember that.'

It was such a perfect impersonation in tone and manner that I cracked up. He smiled and held out his hand.

'Hobie,' he said.

'Dunk,' I said.

'Dunk? As in doughnut in coffee or basketball in hoop?'

'Basketball,' I said.

'Ah. Well . . . welcome to the zoo.'

He had a little coffee-maker next to his desk, and we each had a cup. Mine paper and his a porcelain mug with DOWN WITH UP printed on the side.

'You better bring in your own mug,' he advised. 'About the boss, she's a pain in the ass – as you've probably noticed – but she can be dangerous, too, so do try to get along. She handles estates and appraisals, so she's a power to be reckoned with. Got a lot of clout with god.'

'God?'

'Stanton Grandby. Who owns the whole caboodle. He and his multitudinous family. He's the great-grandson of Isaac Grandby, who founded the house way back in eighteen hundred and something. You'll meet him eventually, but Felicia Dodat is the one you've got to please. The office gossip is that dear Felicia has something going with Stanton Grandby. We all keep asking, "Does Felicia do dat?"'

He gestured about our office, which seemed enormous to me after three years in Enoch Wottle's cubby. Hobie pointed out that we'd each have a window, overlooking a splendid airshaft. Each a massive desk, pine worktable, wooden file cabinets, glassed-in bookshelves. All a wee bit decrepit, but serviceable nonetheless.

'What happened to my predecessor?' I asked.

'Fired,' Hobie said. He looked at me. 'I don't mean to put you down, Dunk, but I fear she was just a bit too attractive. God was showing interest, and Madam Dodat took offense.'

'Oh-ho,' I said. 'Like that, was it?'

8

'Just like that.'

'Well, Felicia has nothing to fear from me.'

'She would,' he said, 'if god had any sense.'

'That's the nicest compliment I've had in years,' I told him, and we smiled at each other, knowing we'd be friends.

Grandby & Sons dated from 1883 – and so did most of the furnishings. We may have been installed in an elegant town-house on Madison Avenue, just south of 82nd Street, but the place looked like a recently opened time capsule: velvet drapes, Tiffany lamps, Victorian love seats covered with moiré, and ornate clocks, chinoiserie, and mind-boggling objets d'art that had been purchased outright as part of estates and had never been sold.

Another office joke was that everything in Grandby's was for sale except the loo. Not true, of course. But I admit the surroundings were somewhat discombobulating. All that old stuff. It was like working in a very small Antwerp museum.

But I loved Grandby & Sons, and my career went swimmingly. I learned a lot about my new profession, didn't make any horrible mistakes, and was able to contribute my share to the bottom line by bringing to auction a number of coin collections from old customers of Enoch Wottle.

Although nowhere near as large and splendid as Sotheby's or Christie's, Grandby's really was a pleasant place to labor, especially for Hobart Juliana and me in our locked office. We were very *small* specialists, since most of Grandby's sales were paintings, sculpture, drawings, silver, prints, jewelry, antique weapons and armor – things of that sort. Coins and stamps came pretty far down on the list; there was no great pressure on us to show big profits.

So we were pretty much left with our tongs, loupes, magnifying glasses, and high-intensity lamps. A casual observer, admitted to our sanctum, would have thought us a couple of loonies: Hobie studying a scrap of gummed paper, and me examining a tiny chunk of bruised metal. Both of us exchanging muttered comments:

'Look at that watermark!'

'It's been clipped; what a shame.'

'Unperforated; that's a blessing.'

'Roman copy.'

'They *will* use hinges.'

'Silver hemidrachm of the Achaean League. Very nice.'

Occasionally we would get so excited with a 'find' that Hobie would summon me over to his worktable to take a look at an expertly forged signature of Herman Melville, or I'd call him to my side to admire the exquisite minting of a tetradrachm that dated from 420 BC and showed an eagle with wings spread, and a crab on the reverse.

I suppose we were a pair of very young antiquarians. All I know is that we shared an enthusiasm for the past, and liked each other. That helped to make our work pleasurable. Sometimes we went out to dinner together – but not often. Hobie's live-in lover was insanely jealous and suspected him of harboring heterosexual tendencies. He didn't.

Hobie was a slight, fair-haired lad with a wispy manner and a droll sense of humor. He dressed beautifully, and gave me some very good advice on clothes I might wear to minimize my beanstalkiness. I reckoned he and I got along so well together because the world considered us both bizarre creatures. For different reasons, of course. We had a kinship of discrimination – but our friendship was real.

I had been at Grandby & Sons for a little more than two years when one morning – late April, rainy and gusty: a portent! – I was summoned by Felicia Dodat. She was wearing a particularly oppressive perfume, flowery and sweet, and her office smelled like a greenhouse.

Following Hobie's advice, I had kept my relationship with dear Felicia on a cool, professional basis. We were warily cordial with each other, and if she was occasionally snappish, I laid that to the pressures of her job. She never joked about my formidable height, but she had a way of looking at me – her eyes starting at my feet, then slowly rising as if she was examining Mt Everest – that I resented.

'Do you know a man named Archibald Havistock?' she demanded.

'Havistock? No, I'm not familiar with the name.'

She gave me one of her dagger glances. 'He owns what seems to be a very large, valuable collection of antique coins. Almost five hundred items with an insured value of two million. I'm surprised you've never heard of him.'

'Miss Dodat,' I said, as patiently as I could, '*no* one knows the names of the world's biggest coin collectors. For security reasons they buy and sell only through agents, attorneys, or professional coin dealers. You never see their names mentioned at auction or anywhere else. Sometimes they're known in the trade by nicknames. "Midas," for instance, is a Saudi Arabian sheikh. Nobody knows who he is. A woman called "The Boston Lady" is reputed to own one of the finest collections of antique Greek coins in the country. "The Man from

10

Dallas" is another. These people work very hard to keep their names secret. When you possess that much wealth in portable property – a two-million-dollar collection of antique coins could be carried off in a small, brown paper bag – you don't wish to have your name and address publicized.'

'Why don't they put their coins in a bank vault?'

I looked at her in astonishment. 'Because they want to look at them, touch them, dream over them. Most of these people don't invest in antique coins for profit. They're hooked on the beauty, history, and romance of the mintage.'

She made a gesture, waving away everything I had said as of no importance. 'Archibald Havistock,' she repeated. 'He wishes to put his entire coin collection on the block or sell outright. I'm sure he has contacted Christie's and Sotheby's, and probably other houses as well. I have here a copy of his insurance inventory. I want you to go over it very, very carefully and give me an accurate estimate of what you feel Grandby's might earn if the collection was consigned to auction or whether we'd be better off buying outright.'

'Miss Dodat, I can't do that without making a physical examination of the coins. Even an insurance inventory can be inaccurate. Values in the coin market change rapidly.'

'Then make arrangements to see them,' she said crossly. 'He lives in Manhattan, so it shouldn't be difficult. Here – it's all yours. I'll expect your report within a week.'

She held a folder of documents out to me. I took it and tried to smile, wondering if I should curtsy. I started out.

'By next Friday!' she cried after me.

Hobie was down in Virginia, appraising the value of a stamp collection left to his heirs by a recently deceased nonagenarian. Grandby's provided this service to executors for a fee even though we might not be selected to offer the property at auction or be given the opportunity to buy outright.

So I had the office to myself that morning. I poured a mug of black coffee – my mug had I TAKE CANDY FROM STRANGERS printed on the side – and started going over the inventory of Archibald Havistock's coin collection.

In my business, there are collectors and there are accumulators. The former are people of taste and discernment, who have an educated knowledge of the history, provenance, and intrinsic value of what they acquire. Most of all, they buy through love. Accumulators are greedy addicts who buy everything, without regard to rarity

11

and condition, and are only concerned with the bottom line (catalogue value) of their collections. Which often turns out to be woefully inflated when they try to sell.

It was immediately obvious to me, studying the inventory, that Archibald Havistock was a very discriminating collector indeed. His list included some real beauties, but the insurance estimates were dated four years previously and did not allow for inflation or the recent runup in antique coin values.

The gem of the collection, a real museum piece, was a silver dekadrachm dating from about 470 BC. It was a famous coin, one of the great classics of Greek mintage. It was called the 'Demaretion' and judged as being in Extremely Fine condition. I consulted my catalogues and discovered the most recent Demaretion in similar condition to come on the market had sold for almost a quarter of a million dollars. The value in the insurance inventory was given as only $150,000. I felt Grandby's could auction this coin for a possible $350,000.

I read the covering letter addressed to Grandby & Sons, picked up the phone, and called Mr Archibald Havistock.

3

In my eager wanderings about Manhattan I had discovered it to be a
borough of neighborhoods, the most disparate side by side: poor and
wealthy, ugly and lovely, raucous and sedate. And within those
districts, even a single block could have a distinctive character that
set it off from its neighbors, a weed in a nosegay of posies or a rose in a
clump of nettles.

Archibald Havistock lived in a unique East 79th Street block that
had not yet been given a transplant of glass and steel high-rises. The
elephantine brick and stone apartment houses, all looking like
armories, seemed to have settled into the earth since they were built
fifty years ago. They gave the appearance of solid, dull permanence,
and one supposed the occupants of those seven-, nine-, and eleven-
room suites had taken on the character of their surroundings.

The lobby, paneled in varicose-veined marble, was a small Grand
Central Station, with a codger behind the desk as patterned as the
marble. I announced my name, he picked up a house phone and
announced my arrival to Mr Havistock, then announced the apartment number for me. It was all as formal as a court investiture.

The man who opened the apartment door didn't look like an
Archibald to me; he looked more like a Tony or a Mike. Actually,
he turned out to be an Orson. So much for my perspicacity. He
introduced himself as Orson Vanwinkle, Mr Havistock's nephew and
secretary. We shook hands. A damp experience.

He was a dark, saturnine fellow with a beaky nose: a perfect Iago
with that kind of menacing handsomeness I suppose some women
find attractive, but which makes me slightly queasy. Also, his cologne
smelled like Juicy Fruit.

I followed him down a muffled corridor, noting a series of etchings
on the walls. They all seemed to be of Liverpool at low tide. Not too
exciting. But then Vanwinkle ushered me into a chamber that *was*

13

startling: a den-library from another era. Slate-tiled floor almost hidden by a buttery Oriental rug. Walnut paneling. Heavy velvet drapes swagged back with cords as thick as hawsers with tassels. Oil paintings in gilt frames (including two original Hoppers). Crystal and silver on a marble-topped side-board.

And on deep, built-in oak shelves, a number of glass-topped display cases. The Havistock coin collection.

The man behind the enormous partners' desk rose to greet me with a wintry smile. A blocky figure draped in a gorgeous suit of dove-gray flannel with a hairline red stripe. White silk shirt with a bow tie: polka-dotted blue. His vest had white piping – the first time I had ever seen that. Hair silvered to a sheen, and eyes a cold, cold azure.

'Miss Bateson,' he said in diapason tones, holding out a mani-cured paw, 'I am Archibald Havistock. Delighted to make your acquaintance.'

I had an instant reaction: I was meeting a personage. Later, I tried to analyze my awe, and decided it was due to his carriage, voice, grooming, and his *presence*. He just gave the impression of being a very important man. In control. Even in less admirable surround-ings, I think he still would have conveyed the feeling of power and distinction. He was so *complete*.

And – as if he needed it! – he was beautiful, in the way certain older men sometimes are. A heavy face with crinkly laugh lines. Full mouth. Solid jaw. And, of course, the silvered hair and ice-cube eyes. He could have posed for Chairman of the Board of the Universe. His cufflinks were little enamel reproductions of a Picasso. I'm sure he thought them an amusing whimsy.

We all got ourselves seated. I was across that double-width desk from Mr Havistock. Orson Vanwinkle sat behind me on a straight-back chair near the door. Almost like a bodyguard or security agent.

I began to explain that before Grandby & Sons could make an estimate of what his collection might bring at auction, or was worth in an outright sale, I had to make a personal inspection and appraisal of the individual coins. He held up a pink palm and favored me with another cheerless smile. Something sad about that smile.

'I understand completely,' he said. 'As I'm sure you've guessed, I have contacted a few other auction houses, and they all work the same way. Would you like to get started now?'

I had brought along what I called my 'doctor's bag' – for out-of-the-office appraisals. It was a little black valise packed with a small high-intensity lamp, loupe, huge magnifying glass, silk gloves, tongs, a few of the latest catalogues, and a kit of chemicals in vials, used to test metal content. I spread all this paraphernalia on my half of the desk facing Mr Havistock. Orson Vanwinkle rose to his feet and brought the first display case, placing it gently in front of me.

Now I must describe in exact detail how the Havistock Collection was mounted since it led to such important and dramatic consequences.

There were 497 items in the collection, including the Demaretion. They were housed in display cases approximately 24 by 16 inches. Each case was divided into forty-two velvet-lined compartments, one coin to each. And every little topless box bore a small pasted number corresponding to the numbers on the insurance inventory.

If my arithmetic is correct, you will see that the 497 coins could be accommodated in twelve display cases, with seven empty compartments. Explanation of that in a moment . . .

The first display case Orson Vanwinkle placed on the desk before me was completely filled. I spent a moment examining the case, running my fingertips lightly over the oiled teak sides, the solid brass hardware: recessed hinges and lock.

'The case,' I said, looking up at Archibald Havistock. 'It's splendid!'

'Yes,' he said, and his smile had more warmth. 'Custom-made for me by Nate Colescui in Greenwich Village. The best man for that kind of work in the city. Orson, will you unlock, please.'

Vanwinkle took a ring from his pocket, selected a small, intricately tooled brass key, and unlocked the case in front of me. He raised the glass lid (framed in teak) and made certain the lid support was holding. I went to work, the copy of the inventory at my elbow.

It became quickly apparent that whoever had done the insurance appraisal knew the business: the condition ratings were, in my opinion, almost completely accurate. I disagreed on only 17 of the 497 items, and in 12 of them, the coin deserved a higher rating, and only 5, in my judgment, should have had a lower: from Very Fine to Fine, or from Fine to Fair. But at current values of antique coins, the whole collection was woefully under-insured.

I was there almost three hours, and it was a perfect delight. Only another numismatist could understand how I felt. The beauty of those coins! Miniature sculptures. Profiles of gods and goddesses. Horses and chariots. Birds and fish. Beasts and gargoyles. And so

15

many nameless young men with faces of such joyous hope that I almost wept from the sight of them. All gone.

During those three hours, Havistock or Vanwinkle occasionally left the room. But never both at the same time; one of them was always present during my appraisal. I didn't blame them a bit. With those display cases of treasures unlocked, I preferred to have a witness present to testify that I had not suddenly swallowed an exquisite silver obol.

And finally, the thirteenth case . . .

It was laid before me by Orson Vanwinkle as if it was the pièce de résistance of a cordon bleu chef. If he had popped off a domed cover and shouted, 'Voilà!', I wouldn't have been a bit surprised.

There it was, all by its lonesome, the Demaretion centered in its own case.

No mistaking it: a chunky silver dekadrachm, about the size of an American half-dollar. On the obverse, a trotting quadriga with a standing charioteer. Nike flies above, crowning the horses. Below, a lion springs. On the reverse, four dolphins swim about the profile of Artemis, who wears an olive wreath.

I am not going to tell you this is the most beautiful of all ancient Greek coins – in my opinion, it is not – but it is lovely enough, with crisp minting (the horses' legs are especially well done), and, of course, its rarity adds to its allure. That, and the romantic story of how the Demaretion came to exist. But I'll tell you about that later.

I looked up from my examination to find Archibald Havistock examining *me*. Again, that distant smile . . .

'Do you like it?' he asked in his deep rumble.

'It's splendid!' I burst out. 'Up to now I've only seen it in photos – but they don't do it justice.'

He nodded. 'It's perfection. I bought it thirty years ago, paying more than I could afford at the time. But I had to have it.'

Thus speaketh the true collector. They'll sell their mothers to possess something you or I might think a bauble or an incomprehensible daub of paint on canvas. But in this case I agreed with the owner; the Demaretion was a treasure.

I left shortly after, promising Mr Havistock he would have an appraisal from Grandby & Sons within a week, including recommended reserve values. (When the final bid is lower than these floor prices, the items are removed from auction.)

I was conducted down that gloomy corridor to the front door by Orson Vanwinkle, who insisted on shaking my hand in parting,

16

holding it just a wee bit too long in his clammy grasp. I will not say the man was slimy, but I believe he might have laughed at a homeless dog in the rain.

I went back to my office and set to work. I saw at once that attempting to auction 497 individual coins would be too time-consuming – and counterproductive. A better method would be to divide the coins into lots by period: Archaic, Classical, and Hellenistic, and by country of origin: Gaul, Spain, Sicily, Britain, etc. (Those ancient Greeks got around!)

After dividing the bulk of the coins into lots which I thought might attract specialized collectors, I withheld fourteen items to be sold individually. Including the Demaretion, of course. I then started estimating reserve and top values of each lot and the fourteen individual coins. It took me four days.

While I was laboring, Hobart Juliana returned to our lair from Virginia with fascinating tales of life amongst the gentry. We went out to lunch together, and I told him about the Havistock Collection, the biggest appraisal I had ever handled. Hobie was even more excited than I.

'Dunk, that's marvelous!' he enthused. 'If you can bring it off, it'll mean mucho dinero for the house and probably a raise for you.'

'Not a chance,' I said gloomily. 'If I can win it, Madam Dodat will take all the credit.'

'No way!' he said determinedly, shaking his head. 'You happen to be sharing an office with the best little rumormonger at Grandby and Sons. You bring in the Havistock Collection, and I'll make sure everyone in the place, including god, knows that it was due to your talent, intelligence, perseverance, and keen, analytical judgment.'

I laughed and gripped his hand. It was good to have someone on my side, rooting for me. In other circumstances we might have . . . Oh, well, why talk about it.

I went in early and stayed late every night. Then went home, thawed and ate a 'gourmet' dinner, and went to bed. I wrestled with the sheets, my brain churning, and finally fell asleep dreaming of drachms and trihemiobols, and a standing charioteer leaning forward to goad four elegant horses. What kind of dreams were those for a normal, healthy American female? Feh!

I met my self-imposed deadline, and delivered to Felicia Dodat a handsomely typed appraisal that included estimated reserve and top values on twenty-two lots and fourteen individual coins ($350,000 for the Demaretion). I left it up to Dodat, god, and the accountants

17

to figure out an offer to make to Archibald Havistock if he wanted to sell his collection outright.

'Thanks,' Felicia said briefly, tossing my manuscript aside.

'When do you think we might have an answer?' I ventured.

'When we get it,' she said shortly, and I had a brief, violent desire to wire-brush her seamed pantyhose. That woman brought out the worst in me.

Nothing happened for almost two weeks. I gloomed around the office, hardly able to answer my correspondence or do appraisals on the little bits and pieces of large estates that came across my desk. Hobie counseled patience, patience, and more patience.

'The one thing you don't want to do,' he told me, 'is to bug Madam Dodat. Treat it casually. Make her think that appraising a two-million-dollar collection is just routine, and you couldn't care less if Grandby's gets it or not. Play it cool, Dunk.'

But I couldn't play it cool; the Havistock coins meant too much to me. Especially that gorgeous Demaretion. I found myself gallivanting madly all over town for distraction, to movies, art galleries, new restaurants. Then coming home to sip a big shot of raspberry-flavored brandy so I could sleep at night.

Finally, into the third week, on a bright, sunshiny May afternoon, crisp and clear, I took Hobie's and my coffee mugs into the ladies' room, hoping to scour them clean of their accumulated crud.

Felicia Dodat was standing before one of the mirrors, preening, touching her raven hair, stroking her eyebrows with a fingertip.

I put the two coffee mugs into a sink and ran hot water into them. Soaked a paper towel and started to scrub them out.

'I understand they call you "Dunk," ' Felicia said, still staring at herself in the mirror, turning this way and that.

'That's right.'

'Dunk,' she repeated. 'What an odd name.'

I didn't say anything.

She raised her skirt to tug up her pantyhose. I would never do that in front of anyone, woman or man. Then she smoothed down her skirt and inspected herself again. I swear she nodded with approval.

'Dunk,' she said again, and laughed.

She started out, then paused at the door.

'Oh, by the way . . .' she said, as if she had suddenly recalled a detail of no importance. 'Did I tell you we got the Havistock Collection?'

4

NEW PROBLEMS never encountered before: the logistics of moving the Havistock Collection from the owner's apartment on East 79th Street to the basement vault of Grandby & Sons on Madison Avenue. Stanton Grandby had signed the auction contract, but I got the donkeywork.

I had met four times with Mr Havistock, Mr Vanwinkle, a representative of the insurance company carrying a policy on the collection, and a burly gentleman from the armored truck service that was to make the actual transfer. We finally agreed on a plan and assignment of responsibilities that seemed to please everyone.

The move would be effected in this manner:

Archibald Havistock would seal the thirteen display cases holding his collection with strips of masking tape on all four sides, plus a blob of sealing wax near the lock which he would imprint with a heavy silver signet ring he sometimes wore.

I made a mild objection to this form of sealing, fearing it would mar the surface of those lovely teakwood cases. But Mr Havistock stated he would have no need for the cases after his collection was sold, and in any event they could easily be refinished.

I would stand by, a witness to the sealing process to insure that each case contained the requisite number of coins. After sealing, each case would be slid into a protective Styrofoam outer container in which, I was told, Nate Colescui, the casemaker, had delivered his handicraft. Each container would be plainly marked with large pasted labels: Mr Havistock's name and address, ditto for Grandby & Sons, and heavy numerals, 1 to 13.

After I had witnessed the loading of the Styrofoam containers and *their* sealing with masking tape, the men from the armored van service would take over. With armed guards in attendance, they would take the thirteen containers down to ground level via the freight elevator. Once they were loaded into the truck, the driver would sign a receipt. A copy to Mr Havistock, a copy to the insurance company, a copy to Grandby & Sons.

I would then scurry back to my office – by cab, if I could find one; I was not allowed to ride in the armored truck. I would oversee the unloading of the thirteen containers and their safe storage in our vault. When all thirteen cases were accounted for, I would sign a receipt – copies to everyone – and the Havistock Collection became the responsibility of Grandby & Sons.

It all sounded so simple and logical.

I should mention at this time that during the planning sessions I met two more members of the Havistock family: wife, Mabel, and unmarried daughter, Natalie (called Nettie). In addition, I was told, the Havistocks had a married son and daughter-in-law, Luther and Vanessa Havistock, and a married daughter and son-in-law, Roberta and Ross Minchen.

But when the collection was moved, I was personally acquainted only with Archibald Havistock, nephew Orson Vanwinkle, wife Mabel, and daughter Nettie.

Mabel Havistock was a square, chunky matron with bluish hair and the jaw of a longshoreman. She was the sort of woman, I thought, who probably wore a brown corset with all kinds of straps, laces, buckles, and snaps. She looked somewhat ogreish, but I must admit she was civil enough when we were introduced, though her cold glance immediately pegged me as the costume jewelry type. Her pearls were real.

I liked Natalie, the unmarried daughter, much more. She was the 'baby' of the Havistock family, and a wild one. The T-shirt and stone-washed jeans type, with a mop of uncombed dirty-blond curls and an unbra-ed bosom that made me reflect once again that life is unfair.

Nettie and I spoke briefly, but really hit it off, discovering we were both pizza mavens. She asked to stop by Grandby & Sons to learn how the auction of her daddy's coins would be organized. I told her to come along anytime. I wanted to witness Felicia Dodat's reaction when this fast-talking, sandal-clad wildebeest descended on her.

Anyway, the date of the Great Move finally arrived: a rare Tuesday in June that only needed birdcalls on Manhattan streets to make the morning perfect. I took it as a good omen, that the day would end as splendidly as it began.

I alerted our vault manager and was happy to see he had already made space for the Havistock Collection. Then I sauntered over to East 79th Street and was delighted to find the armored truck had already arrived, right on schedule, and was parked in the service alley alongside the apartment house. A bored driver sat slumped behind the wheel.

The antique concierge knew me by now, and gave me a limp wave of a plump palm as I went directly to the elevator bank. I rode up to the 9th floor. In the corridor was parked a four-wheeled dolly from the armored truck. Two uniformed and armed guards were sitting on it, smoking, and looked up as I arrived.

'All set?' I asked brightly.

'We'll never be setter,' one of them said. 'Let's get this show on the road.'

I was admitted to the Havistock apartment by an employee I had never seen before: a stingy, dour-faced lady swaddled in black bombazine with white apron. Maid? Housekeeper? Cook?

'I am Mary Bateson from—' I started.

'They're in the back,' she growled, jerking a thumb over her shoulder.

So I walked down that depressing corridor by myself, wondering if I had announced, 'Hi! I'm Ma Barker, and I've come to steal the Havistock Collection,' would she have growled, 'They're in the back,' and shown me where to go? Probably. So much for tight security.

They were awaiting me in that splendid library, both busy sealing the thirteen display cases. Orson Vanwinkle was neatly cutting strips of masking tape, and his uncle was just as neatly applying them to sides and lids. If Archibald Havistock felt any sadness or depression at seeing his collection go on the block, he gave no sign. As I said, he was a very contained man.

I had brought along two inventories, the insurance company's and my own, and I checked carefully to make certain every coin was in its correct compartment in its correct case. As I okayed each case, Vanwinkle applied a thick blob of warmed sealing wax to the front junction of lid and case, and Mr Havistock pressed his signet ring firmly. Then Vanwinkle slid the sealed display case into its properly labeled Styrofoam box, closed that with masking tape, and the deed was done.

I lingered over case thirteen, staring through the glass at the Demaretion. It twinkled back at me.

'Aren't you going to miss it?' I asked Mr Havistock.

21

He shrugged and tried to smile. 'As someone said, you spend the first half of your life collecting things, and the second half getting rid of them.'

Then the Demaretion was gone, its own display case slid into the Styrofoam container marked thirteen, and sealed. I prepared to depart.

'I'll send in the armored truck guards,' I said. 'I want to get downstairs to make certain all the cases are brought down safely, and get my receipt.'

'I think I'll come along,' Orson Vanwinkle said, smiling thinly, 'to get *our* receipt.'

The two of us waited near the truck in the service alley. In about ten minutes the armed guards appeared, pushing the loaded dolly. The thirteen cases were put into the armored van. The driver ticked them off carefully on his loading list, then signed a receipt for the shipment. One copy to me, one copy to Orson Vanwinkle.

'See you at the auction,' I said to him blithely.

'Before that, I hope,' he said with a smarmy smile.

Boy, was he ever right!

I was lucky enough to grab a cab almost immediately, buzzed back to the office, and got things organized for the reception of the Havistock Collection. Grandby & Sons employed its own security force, and I recruited the Chief and two stalwarts to stand by for the arrival of the armored truck.

When it pulled up in front of the town-house, our guards did sentry duty as the Styrofoam containers were unloaded and carried down to the basement vault. I took up station at the opened vault door as they were brought in. Thirteen, tape unbroken. I counted them again. Thirteen, tape intact.

I then signed a receipt for Grandby & Sons and handed it to the driver of the armored truck. He and his two minions disappeared. The Havistock coins were now safely tucked away in our vault, the door thick enough to stop a cruise missile, but so perfectly hinged and balanced that I could move it with one hand.

Hobart Juliana came down, laughing, to bring me a mug of hot black coffee.

'Got 'em?' he said cheerfully.

'Safe and sound,' I said. 'Am I ever glad that's over. Look at my hands; I'm shaking.'

'Calm down, Dunk,' he advised. 'Your part of the job is finished.'

'I guess,' I said, just beginning to realize that my connection with

22

the Havistock Collection had ended. Now it was all up to the sales staff and auctioneer.

'Hobie,' I said, 'I want to show you something that'll knock your eyes out. The Demaretion. A work of art if ever there was one.'

I set my coffee mug aside. Slid container thirteen from the stack and pulled back the masking tape. Opened the Styrofoam box and gently withdrew the sealed teakwood case. I cradled it in my arms, held it out to Hobie.

'Just take a look at that,' I said.

He glanced down, then raised his eyes slowly to my face. Something happened to his expression. It congealed.

'At what?' he said in a low voice.

I stared at him for a second or two, then looked down at the sealed display case.

It was empty. The Demaretion was gone.

You know the opening words of Dickens' *A Tale of Two Cities*? 'It was the best of times, it was the worst of times . . .' That last part was written for me: it was the worst of times.

Later, Hobie told me that he was afraid I was going to faint when I saw the Demaretion had disappeared. He moved closer so he could grab me if I began to crumple.

'It wasn't that you turned white,' he said. 'You turned absolutely *livid*, as if someone had kicked you in the cruller.'

Disbelief was my initial reaction. Then bewilderment. Then anger. Then cold guilt when I realized what I had done: signed a receipt for a $350,000 coin that was not in Grandby & Sons' vault. Goodbye to job, career, reputation. I had visions of a lifetime in durance vile. Plenty of days, and nights, to try to solve the puzzle of how the Demaretion had been stolen from a sealed display case within a taped container.

When we sounded the alarm, everyone came running. That was all right; I wanted plenty of witnesses to the fact that the teakwood display case still had all its seals intact, including that blob of wax bearing the imprint of Archibald Havistock's signet ring. Then the question was asked: Was the Demaretion in the case when it was sealed?

I swore it was. People looked at me. I would not weep.

Stanton Grandby, god, was a plump, pouty man who dressed like a penguin. I could tell from his pursed lips and glittering eyes that he

23

was computing what this catastrophe was going to cost the family business.

Grandby & Sons carried heavy insurance, of course, to cover disasters of this nature. But the money loss didn't bother god so much as the damage done to the reputation of the house. Who would be eager to consign coins, stamps, paintings, and sculpture to Grandby's if it was bruited about that valuable antiques disappeared from the premises?

I was set to work examining the other twelve display cases, peering through the glass lids without disturbing the seals. The collection was complete – except for the Demaretion. Then god, in whispered consultation with Felicia Dodat, decided to inform Archibald Havistock of the loss, and the New York Police Department, Grandby's insurance company, Mr Havistock's insurers, and the armored truck service that had made the transfer.

'And we better phone our attorneys,' Stanton Grandby added, glancing at me wrathfully. 'This is a mess, and we need legal advice.'

The remainder of that day was horrid, a monstrosity I find hard to recall, it was so painful. A detective team from the NYPD was first on the scene, followed by the burly man from the armored truck service, followed by representatives from the two insurance companies involved. Last to arrive was Lemuel Whattsworth, junior partner of the law firm of Phlegg, Sample, Haw, Jugson, and Pinchnik, attorneys for Grandby & Sons.

I must have told my story at least a half-dozen times, relating the exact details of how the coins were inventoried, displayed in the compartments, and how I witnessed the sealing of the display cases, their packing in Styrofoam, and the taping of those boxes. Six times I vowed to high heaven that I had seen the Demaretion sealed in its own case and slid into container thirteen.

Curiously, this repeated recital of what had happened did not anger me or bore me or offend me. In fact, I welcomed going over the facts again and again, hoping I or someone else would spot a fatal flaw in the preparations for the move of the Havistock Collection and cry, 'Ah-ha! There's where you went wrong. That's how it was done.'

But I didn't see it, and neither did anyone else. It was impossible for the Demaretion to disappear. But it had.

Finally, dusk outside and streetlights on, all my interrogators departed, and I was left to ponder the enormity of what had befallen me. I wanted, more than anything, to call Archibald Havistock, apologize, and commiserate with him on the theft of that prize I knew he cherished. But Lemuel Whattsworth had told me, in no uncertain terms, to have no communication whatsoever with Mr Havistock or anyone else in his household.

Hobart Juliana – bless him! – refused to desert me during that dreadful day, and comforted me between my question-and-answer sessions with all those investigators. Then, the office lights being switched off by departing staffers and night security guards, he said:

'Dunk, have you got a couch in your place?'

'A couch?' I said dispiritedly. 'Of course I've got a couch. Why?'

'I don't think you should be alone tonight. Let me come home with you. I'll sleep on the couch.'

'Oh, Hobie,' I said, 'you don't have to do that.'

'I know I don't *have* to do it, but I *want* to do it. Please let me.'

'All right,' I said helplessly.

'Do you have anything to eat in the house?'

'Some frozen dinners.'

'That'll do splendidly. Anything to drink?'

'Some wine. Vodka. Raspberry brandy.'

'Loverly. Let me make one phone call, and then we'll take off.'

It was a long phone call in a low voice I couldn't overhear, but I knew he was explaining to his roommate why he wasn't going to be home that night.

Hobie was so good to me; I don't know how I could have endured that night without him. He prepared the Lean Cuisine, poured the wine, served me, and did the dishes. Later we sat quietly, sipped a little brandy, and without prompting I told my story once again, and we went over it all, step by step.

Hobie shook his head. 'I can't see anything you should have done that you did not do. It sounds absolutely foolproof to me.'

'But someone copped the Demaretion.'

'Yes,' he said sorrowfully, 'someone did.'

'What do you think will happen to me, Hobie? Am I the number one suspect?'

'Maybe not number one,' he said cautiously. 'But you better be prepared for some nasty digging into your private life. The insurance companies are not going to pay out without a very, very close investigation. And the New York cops will be just as thorough. You're in for a tough time, Dunk.'

'I didn't steal it, Hobie. You know that, don't you?'

'Of course I know it. And you couldn't even if you had wanted to. You never touched that damned coin today, did you?'

'Never. Not once. Just looked at it.'

'Well, there you are. But someone touched it.'

Then I began to weep. Hobie came over to the couch, sat close, put an arm about my shoulders.

'Come on, Dunk,' he said. 'You're a strong lady, I know you are. You'll survive. Those smart cops will find out who did it, and you'll be completely cleared.'

'You really think so?' I said, snuffling.

'Absolutely.'

He was such a sweet man. A wraith, with his fair hair and pale skin. So slight and frail. But when it came to the bottom line, he was a substantial man, a mensch, sympathetic and understanding and offering support at the moment in my life when I needed it most.

The day had been a trial for both of us, and after a while I brought out sheets, a pillow, blanket, and made up the couch.

'You're going to wake up with a sore back,' I warned.

'Not me,' he said. 'I can sleep anywhere. That's what comes from having a pure heart.'

I took him into my arms. He barely came up to my chin.

'You do have a pure heart,' I told him. 'Thank you for all you've done for me. I love you, Hobie.'

'And I love you, Dunk. Try to sleep. Things will look better in the morning.'

I hoped, but I doubted. We exchanged a chaste kiss, and I went into the bedroom. I don't know whether it was the strains of the day or the raspberry brandy, but I fell asleep almost instantly. A dreamless sleep. But when my alarm went off and I awoke, things seemed no brighter, and I dreaded what shocks the new day might hold for me.

5

LEMUEL WHATTSWORTH, the attorney, was a thinnish man: thin face, thin body, thin voice. Even what he had to say was thin, being composed mostly of *whereas, heretofore, notwithstanding*, and similar expressions designed to make the eyeballs glaze over.

There we were, gathered in the conference room: Whattsworth, Stanton Grandby, Felicia Dodat, and me, awaiting judgment. The lawyer was attempting to explain the possible results (the *ramifications*) of the loss of the Demaretion.

Trying to follow his crazy lecture, I gathered that no lawsuit had yet been filed, but he guessed *(intuited)* that Archibald Havistock would not claim the $150,000 for which he had insured the Demaretion, but instead would demand $350,000 from Grandby & Sons, since that was the estimated value of the coin stated in the auction contract Havistock had signed with Grandby's.

'Naturally,' Whattsworth said, 'in fact, indubitably, his insurer will heartily concur with this course of action. The receipt for the coin was signed by a representative of Grandby and Sons' – here a cold stare in my direction – 'so legally this house is responsible. Grandby's, in effect, stated an item of value was on the premises when, in fact, it was not.'

A little more of this, I thought, and I'd go bonkers.

'Investigations are under way,' he droned on, 'and we can but hope this grave offense will be satisfactorily resolved with the perpetrator of the theft brought to justice. Until that eventuality is finalized, it is my considered judgment that Miss Mary Lou Bateson be granted an indefinite leave of absence, without salary, until this distressing matter is explicated. Such a course of action will, in some small way, serve to protect the professional reputation of Grandby and Sons.'

'And make me look like a thief,' I said hotly.

27

'Not at all,' he said in his tinny voice. 'It is merely a temporary measure designed to avoid the rumors and confusion that would inevitably result from your continued employment. After all, Miss Bateson, you *are* deeply involved in this sad incident, and I am sure you can appreciate the need for Grandby's to, ah, distance itself from your involvement.'

I looked at god and Felicia Dodat, hoping to find support and encouragement. Nothing. Stanton Grandby stared back at me blankly, and Madam Dodat was busy examining the vermillion lacquer on her talons.

So that was that. I was cast adrift, and went back to my office to pack up my coffee mug and few other personal possessions. I was scribbling a short note to Hobart Juliana, telling him of my expulsion, when there was a hard rap on the corridor door. I peered through the judas and saw, held up for my inspection, the gold shield and ID of a New York Police Department detective. I unlocked.

He was about my height, which made it easy to look into his startling electric blue eyes.

'Al Georgio,' he said. 'Can I come in and talk to you a few minutes about the theft?'

'I've already talked,' I said. 'Yesterday. At length. To two of your men.'

'I know,' he said. 'I have their reports. But this thing was dumped on me, and I have a few questions I'd like to get cleared up before we prepare a statement for you to sign. Okay?'

'Sure,' I said, 'come on in. Coffee? In a plastic cup.'

'That would be great,' he said. 'Sugar and milk if you've got it.'

I poured us coffee and gave him packets of Sweet 'n' Low and some non-dairy creamer we kept around for visitors.

'You just caught me,' I told him. 'Another five minutes and I'd have been gone. I've been canned.'

'So I heard,' he said. 'But not canned; just a leave of absence.'

'Without pay,' I said bitterly.

He shrugged. 'Such is life in the great city.'

He was a big, rumpled man who looked like he had been sleeping in his clothes. About thirty-seven to forty years old, I guessed – around there. A face like a punched pillow, except for those sharp eyes. And a smile of real warmth. I thought he was a charmer. Also, I thought he might be hung over.

'So,' I said, 'what can I tell you?'

28

'Who was in the Havistocks' apartment when you witnessed the packing of the coins?'

'Mr Archibald Havistock and his secretary, Orson Vanwinkle, who is also Havistock's nephew. And a woman let me into the apartment. I had never seen her before, but she was dressed like a maid or housekeeper.'

Detective Georgio took out a little pocket notebook and flipped a few pages. 'Housekeeper,' he said. 'Ruby Querita. Her brother's in the slammer on a drug bust.'

I looked at him in astonishment. 'You guys do move, don't you?'

'Occasionally,' he said. 'You saw no one else on the premises?'

'Only the two guards from the armored truck service. They were waiting in the outside corridor. I never saw more of the apartment than the hallway and the library where the coins were kept. But I got the impression it was an enormous place.'

'It is,' he said. 'Eleven rooms, three bathrooms. And there were a lot of people there you didn't see.'

'I met Mrs Mabel Havistock and Natalie, their younger daughter. But I didn't see them yesterday.'

He consulted his notebook again. 'They were there. And the son, Luther Havistock, and his wife, Vanessa. Also the older, married daughter, Roberta Minchen and her husband, Ross. The whole family was going to have lunch together.'

'An occasion?'

'Sort of. It was Mrs Havistock's birthday.'

'Oh, God,' I said despairingly. 'The burglary must have put a damper on the festivities.'

'Robbery,' he said. 'Yes, I guess it did. When Havistock put the Demaretion in the display case, did he—'

I held up a palm. 'Whoa. He didn't put the coin into the case. It was already in there when I inspected it.'

'So there was no possibility of sleight of hand? A little juggling?'

'Absolutely not. The Demaretion was in its case. I examined it through the glass lid.'

'It was the real thing? Not a counterfeit?'

'It was the real thing.'

'And you saw the case sealed?'

'I did.'

'And the case put into the Styrofoam box?'

'I saw that, too. Then the container was closed with masking tape. That tape was still intact when I opened it in our vault.'

29

'The container was already labeled? Marked with the number thirteen?'

'That's correct.'

He looked up suddenly from the jottings he had been making in his notebook. 'Who do you think did it?'

I was startled. 'I haven't the faintest idea.'

'That makes two of us,' he said, giving me that melting smile again.

He really was a most attractive man. A little frazzled around the edges, like a worn French actor, but all the more comfortable for that. I mean he wasn't trying to be anything he wasn't. His heavy face, wrinkled clothes, his slouch, the way he moved – everything about him said, 'What you see is what you get.'

He finished his coffee and stood up. He looked at the catalogues, books, knitted cap, a pair of snow boots, etc., all piled on my desk.

'Hey,' he said, 'you clearing out? Going to take all that stuff home?'

'That's right.'

'Where do you live?'

'Isn't that in your little black notebook?' I asked.

'Sure,' he said cheerfully. 'West Eighty-third Street. I've got a car outside. Can I give you a lift to your apartment?'

I was wary. 'Detectives aren't mad rapists, are they?'

'Not me,' he said. 'I haven't got the energy.'

He helped me down to the street with all my junk, got it stowed in his double-parked, faded blue Plymouth, and drove me home. Then he helped carry everything inside.

'I have some vodka,' I offered.

'I'll pass,' he said. 'But I could stand another coffee – if it's not too much trouble.'

'All I've got is instant. Black.'

'My favorite vintage,' he said.

When Hobart Juliana had left my apartment early that morning, I had folded his sheet and blanket and stacked them atop his pillow on the couch. They were still there, and I knew Detective Al Georgio noticed them. But he didn't say anything.

I made him a cup of instant decaffeinated. He blew on it to cool it. My father used to do that.

'Tell me about the coin,' he said. 'Please.'

I described the Demaretion, and then showed him an exact-size photograph in one of my catalogues.

30

'Doesn't look like much,' he said.

'It is much,' I said indignantly. 'A beautiful example of classic Greek minting.'

'How come it's worth so much?'

'Rarity. It's a real museum piece. And the quality of the minting. Also, there's a story connected with it. It was made in Sicily when the Greeks occupied the island. Gelon, the Greek commander, defeated attacking Carthaginians at the battle of Himera in Four-eighty BC. I guess Gelon was going to cut off all their heads, or something – he was supposed to be a genuine bastard – but his wife, Demarete, interceded on behalf of the Carthaginians, and Gelon softened the surrender terms. In gratitude, the Carthaginians gave Demarete a gold wreath in the value of a hundred talents. From this, she had minted a series of big coins, dekadrachms, that were named for her. How do you like that romantic tale?'

He looked at me thoughtfully. 'I thought this coin was silver.'

'It is. Not pure silver, of course. That would be too soft for a coin. But an alloy with a high silver content.'

'Well, if this Demarete got a gift of gold, how come she had silver coins made? Why didn't she have the wreath melted down and have gold coins minted?'

I laughed. 'You really *are* a detective, aren't you? A lot of numismatists have asked the same question. Some of them think the story is pure hogwash. Some keep looking for a gold Demaretion. But no such animal has ever turned up. Just the silver variety.'

'How many are there?'

'In the world? Maybe a dozen. Possibly fifteen. Those are the known ones. There may be others in private collections no one knows about.'

He shook his head. 'Crazy business. What's a talent of gold worth?'

'About six thousand drachms. Ask what an ancient Greek drachm is worth in today's money – or an ancient Syrian shekel – and you'll get a million guesses. But no one really knows exactly.'

He sighed. 'I suppose all I've got to know is that the missing Demaretion was insured for one-fifty big ones and valued by Grandby's at three-fifty. That's grand larceny no matter how you slice it.'

I stared at him. 'You don't think I stole it, do you?'

He stared back at me. 'I'm just starting on this thing,' he said quietly. 'I'd like to be able to tell you, No, I don't think you did

31

it. But I can't say that. Right now everyone in the Havistock family and everyone connected with the transfer of the coins is a possible perpetrator. Including you. You can understand that, can't you?'

'I guess,' I said miserably. 'But for what it's worth, I didn't do it. I could never do anything like that. I love coins too much.'

He threw his head back and roared with delight. 'That's one hell of an alibi,' he said.

Then I laughed, too, realizing what I had said.

'Where do you go from here?' I asked him. 'What's the next step?'

He sobered. Frowned. 'I think I better meet with Havistock and the secretary, Vanwinkle, and get their story on how the transfer was made.'

'They'll verify everything I've told you.'

'Will they?' Then, suddenly: 'I'd like you to be there. If they say something that doesn't check with your recollection of what went on, I want you to speak up in their presence. Sometimes a confrontation of witnesses can help.'

I considered that for a moment. 'Grandby's attorney told me to have absolutely no contact with Havistock, but that was when I was an employee. I'm on leave of absence now, without pay, and I want more than anything else to clear my name. All right, I'll go along with you.'

'Good,' he said. 'I'm glad you feel that way.'

'Listen,' I said, 'apparently we'll be seeing more of each other, so what do I call you? Detective Georgio, Mr Georgio?'

'Al will do fine,' he said. That smile again.

'Al? For Albert?'

He may have blushed. At least he looked up into the air over my head.

'Alphonse,' he said in a low voice.

I didn't laugh. 'People call me Dunk,' I told him.

'Dunk? For baseball?'

I nodded.

'That's cool,' he said. 'I follow the Nets.' He stood up to leave. 'Thanks for the coffee. I'll give you a call when I set up a meet with Havistock and Vanwinkle. Okay?'

'Fine,' I said. 'I can make it anytime. I've got nothing else to do.'

He moved to the door.

'Al,' I called, and he turned back. 'Have you got any idea at all how someone got the Demaretion out of that sealed display case within a taped box?'

He grinned without mirth.

'Dunk, my old man was with the Department all his life. Mostly on what they called the Bunko Squad in those days. Scams and cons and the Gypsy Handkerchief Drop, and a hundred other tricky swindles. He taught me a lot. Everyone wants to know how it's possible to steal a coin from a sealed case within a taped container. It's not possible. No one copped that coin by itself. The whole box was switched.'

6

THAT AFTERNOON, about two o'clock, I got a phone call that added another potato to the stew.

A man's voice: 'Miss Mary Lou Bateson?'

'Yes,' I said. 'Who is this?'

'My name is John Smack. I'm with Finkus, Holding, Incorporated. We're the—'

'I know who you are,' I interrupted. 'You handle the insurance for Grandby and Sons. I spoke to a man from your company yesterday, Mr Smack. I told him all I know about the theft of the Demaretion.'

'Uh-huh,' he said. 'That was Ed Morphy, the salesman who services Grandby's account. I'm an investigator, and I'd like to ask you a few more questions, if I may. At your convenience, of course.'

I sighed. No end to it. 'I'm just as anxious to get this cleared up as you are,' I told him. 'When and where do you want to meet?'

'I'm calling from Grandby's. I was hoping to catch you in your office, but I understand you're on leave of absence.'

'Not through choice,' I said, and he laughed.

'Only temporary, I'm sure. Any chance of my coming up to your place right now? I have the address. I could be there in twenty minutes.'

'All right,' I said, 'come ahead. I hope you have some identification.'

'A business card,' he said. 'But if you have any doubts, please call Stanton Grandby or Felicia Dodat; they'll vouch for me.'

But instead, after we hung up, I phoned Hobart Juliana, having no great desire to chat with god or Madam Dodat. I asked Hobie to check and find out if John Smack really was an investigator for Finkus, Holding, Inc. Hobie called back in five minutes and said Smack was legitimate.

'They call him Jack Smack,' he said. 'How do you like that?'

'Unreal,' I said.

'I miss you already, Dunk,' Hobie said sorrowfully. 'The place isn't the same without you.'

'And I miss you, too, dear,' I said. 'Maybe if all these hotshot detectives get results, I'll be back before you know it. I like that job, Hobie, and I want to keep it.'

'I know.'

'And besides, I need that paycheck – even with all the deductions.'

'Listen, Dunk,' he said anxiously, 'if you get the shorts, don't be bashful about asking me for help. I have a few dekadrachms I can lend you.'

'Wise guy,' I said, laughing, and hung up.

Jack Smack turned out to be a very elegant young man indeed. About thirty-five, I judged, and a few inches taller than me. His suit of raw black silk showed Italian tailoring, and he was wearing Aramis, which always turns me on.

I offered him refreshments, and he opted for a vodka on the rocks with a splash of water. I didn't have a drink, figuring I better keep a clear head.

'No doubt about the coin being the genuine Demaretion when the case was sealed?' he asked me.

'No doubt whatsoever.'

'You saw the case sealed, and then you saw it put into the box, and *that* was taped?'

'Correct.'

'And the next time you saw container thirteen was when the armored truck delivered it to Grandby's?'

'Correct again.'

He uncrossed his knees, crossed them in the other direction. He fussed with the hanging trouser leg to make certain the crease was unwrinkled. Then he sipped his vodka reflectively, tinking the rim of the glass gently against his white teeth.

Really a beau ideal: slender, graceful, with all the right moves. A wry smile – but that may have been part of his act. There *was* a certain theatricality about him; I had the sense of his being always *on*. But that didn't diminish his attractiveness. He was possibly, I thought, the handsomest man I had ever seen – except for my oldest brother, Tom, who could have been minted on the obverse of a Greek drachm with a laurel wreath around his head.

'I understand Al Georgio is handling the case for the cops,' he said suddenly.

35

I nodded. 'You know Detective Georgio?'

'We've worked on a few things together,' he acknowledged.

'Do I detect a slight note of hostility in your voice?' I asked him.

'Slight,' he admitted, coming down hard on the irony. 'But it's got nothing to do with Al personally. I really like the guy. It's just that he's police, and I'm insurance, and sometimes the two don't see eye-to-eye.'

'I can't understand that,' I said. 'Both of you want the same thing, don't you? To catch the crook.'

'Sometimes,' he said, 'but not always.' He leaned forward, forearms on his knees, holding his drink with both hands. Very serious, very intent. 'Look,' he said, 'here's how it works: Say a goniff steals something. Call it a painting we've insured for a hundred grand. The cops go to work trying to find out who did it. Now the guy who stole the painting will be lucky to get ten percent from a fence. That's ten thousand dollars. So he contacts us and makes a deal. We pay him say, twenty thousand, and he returns the painting to us. He gets double what a fence would pay him, and were out twenty grand – which is a hell of a lot better than paying out a hundred grand in insurance.'

I stared at him. 'How long has this been going on?' I demanded.

He laughed. 'Since property insurance was invented. Actually, the thief isn't stealing something of value; he's kidnapping it and holding it for ransom. The cops hate it, because when we pay ransom, the crook strolls away whistling a merry tune.'

'I can see why the police would dislike deals like that,' I said. 'But doesn't it cost insurance companies a bundle?'

'So we raise premiums,' he said, shrugging.

'You think that's what might happen with the Demaretion?'

'It could.'

'Has anyone called you, offering to sell back the coin?'

'Not yet,' he said. 'Hey, I came here to ask you questions, and it seems to me you're doing all the asking.'

'Go ahead,' I said. 'Ask away.'

He grinned ruefully. 'Can't think of anything else. We seem to have covered all the bases. At Grandby's, they told me you're called Dunk.'

'That's right.'

'May I call you Dunk?'

'Sure.'

'Only if you call me Jack. I admit Jack Smack sounds like caramel

36

popcorn, but I've learned to live with it. I hope we can work together on this thing, Dunk. I know you've been put on unpaid leave of absence – which was entirely unfair and unwarranted in my opinion – and you'll want to clear your name. So maybe if the two of us can put our great brains together on this, you'll be back at work before you know it.'

He smiled winsomely. A hard guy to resist. Al Georgio was charming, too, but Jack Smack was charming *consciously*. Every woman over the age of four is able to spot the difference. Which doesn't mean we're able to resist the deliberate charmer.

He got up to go, then paused for a moment. Dramatic effect.

'By the way,' he said casually, 'no one lifted a single coin from a sealed display case within a taped container. I think the container itself was switched.'

After he was gone, I reflected that I had met two tall, handsome men in the last few hours – so the day wasn't a total loss. But I recognized angrily my own stupidity at not seeing that stealing container thirteen and substituting a similar box (sans Demaretion) in its stead was the only way the robbery could have gone down.

Two male investigators, Georgio and Smack, had seen it at once. And I, witness and participant, had been racking my poor, feeble brain trying to imagine how it had been done. It was humiliating.

I have always been a competitive type; I suppose those driveway basketball games with my brothers contributed to that. Anyway, I was determined to show Georgio and Smack that I wasn't just another pretty face; I had brains. Feminism had nothing to do with it; it was *personal*.

I reasoned this way:

I accepted their theory that container thirteen had been switched. It was the only way the Demaretion could have been stolen. But when I exhibited the empty display case to Hobie in Grandby's vault, it was absolutely identical to all the other teakwood cases with glass lids that housed the Havistock Collection. I was willing to swear to that.

Which meant there had to be at least fourteen display cases – right? And an empty extra, sealed, was substituted for the one containing the Demaretion.

Now then . . . what was the name of the guy Archibald Havistock said had made the cases? 'The best man for that kind of work in the city,' he had told me. First name Nate – that I remembered. But the last name? Calesque? Colliski? Callico? – something like that. And he worked in Greenwich Village. I grabbed up the Manhattan telephone directory and Yellow Pages, and started searching.

It took me about fifteen minutes, but I found him: Nathaniel Colescui, custom carpentry, with a shop on Carmine Street. I pulled on beret, suede jacket, shoulder bag, and rushed out. Practically sprinted over to 86th Street and Broadway. Took the downtown IRT. All the short people in the subway car stared at me, but I was used to that.

I got off at Houston Street and walked back to Carmine. Colescui's shop wasn't hard to find. It was right next to a pub-type restaurant that had a legend gold-leafed on its window: FOUNDED IN 1984. That tickled me – but I guess when a restaurant lasts two years in Manhattan, it's something to brag about.

Colescui's window didn't brag, it just said: CUSTOM CARPENTRY. EVERYTHING TO ORDER. Inside, it smelled pleasantly of freshly sawed wood, and there was a fine mist of sawdust in the air. The middle-aged black woman pounding away at an ancient typewriter at the front desk was wearing a hat, and I could understand why.

She stopped her typing when I came in. 'Help you?' she asked.

'I'd like to inquire about having a display case made,' I said. 'For coins.'

She swung around on her swivel chair and yelled into the back room. 'Nate!' she screamed. 'Customer!'

I heard the diminishing whine of a power saw switched off. Then a twinkly gnome of a man came out of the back, pushing goggles up onto his bald skull. He was wearing a leather apron over what looked like a conservative, three-piece business suit, plus white shirt and jacquard tie. And all of him – scalp, eyebrows, suit, apron, shoes, everything – was coated with sawdust, as if someone had gone over him with a shaker, sprinkling vigorously.

He couldn't have been more than five feet tall. He looked up at me, smiled, and said, 'Now if you and I had a son, he would be just right.'

'Great idea,' I told the old man. 'When do you want to start?'

'Oh-ho,' he said. 'A fresh lady. I like fresh ladies. Clara, did you hear that? When do you want to start, she asks me.'

'I heard,' the typist said, then addressed me. 'Don't listen to him; he's all talk and no do.'

That made the little guy laugh. His method of laughing was to clamp his dentures, press his lips tightly together, close his eyes and shake. His whole body bounced up and down.

When the seismic disturbance was over, I said, 'Mr Colescui?'

38

'The same,' he said, 'but a fresh lady like you can call me Naté.'

'Nate,' I said, 'I came to ask about having a display case made for my coin collection. Do you do things like that?'

'Everything I do,' he said. 'Display cases, tables, chairs, bookcases, picture frames – whatever. What size display case you thinking of?'

'I was at a friend's house the other night,' I said, faintly ashamed of myself for scamming such a nice man in this fashion, 'and he kept his coin collection in beautiful cases he said you had made for him. I was wondering if I could get one case like those he had.'

'Oh-ho,' Nate Colescui said, head tilted to one side. 'And what was this customer's name?'

'Havistock. Archibald Havistock.'

He went to a battered file, pulled open the top drawer, began rummaging through folders. 'Habley, Hammond, Harrison . . . Yes, here it is: Havistock.' He withdrew the file, opened it, began reading, holding it close to his nose. 'Oh my yes, I remember this now. Several years ago. A *big* order. The finest teak, tempered glass lids, velvet lining, recessed brass hardware. Everything the best.' He peered up at me in a kindly way. 'And expensive.'

'How expensive?' I asked him.

'Mr Havistock paid four hundred dollars a case. But as I say, that was several years ago. I'm afraid it would be considerably more today. Say six hundred a case.' He must have seen my shock, for he added, 'Of course I could make the same size case in pine, maybe maple or cherrywood. Put the hardware on the outside. Skimp a little here and there. Make it affordable.'

'But it wouldn't look like Mr Havistock's cases.'

'No,' he said, with an understanding smile, 'it wouldn't.'

'Well, that's that,' I said, sighing. 'I had no idea they cost that much.'

He shrugged. 'A lot of work. Dovetail joints. Everything just so.'

'How many cases did Mr Havistock have made?' I asked casually.

He consulted the file again. 'Fifteen.'

'Wow,' I said. 'My poor little coin collection isn't worth that much. Well, thank you for your time and cooperation, Nate. If I ever decide to have a case made, I'll bother you again.'

'No bother,' he protested. 'It's always a pleasure to talk to a fresh lady like you. Stop in anytime.'

I left the shop and tramped north to Sheridan Square. The day had started out balmy, but now there was an edge to the wind, and the blue had disappeared behind a screen of muddy clouds. Pedestrians were beginning to hustle, and I noticed several were carrying furled umbrellas. That always amazed me about New York: It can be a perfectly clear day, then clouds come over, it begins to drizzle, and suddenly everyone has an umbrella – except me.

But the possibility of getting caught in a shower, and having my suede jacket spotted, didn't concern me half so much as those fifteen display cases Archibald Havistock had purchased. Thirteen of them housed his original collection. That left two empty extras, presumably stored in the Havistock apartment.

If one of the extras was missing, it would be proof positive that it had been substituted for the case containing the Demaretion. I was gloating over my newly discovered talents as a detective when I stopped abruptly in the middle of the sidewalk, stunned by the realization that the thief might have removed the Demaretion and left its case with the other extra. Result: two empty cases, just as there should be.

But then, resuming my brisk walk to the subway station, I reflected that if the crook had done that, the case he replaced would show signs of having been sealed: the residue of sealing wax and masking tape. Unless the thief had been clever enough to have the case refinished.

Groaning, I began to appreciate the complexity of the detective's art. All those imponderables, what-ifs, and possibilities. I felt a grudging admiration for Al Georgio and Jack Smack. But then, if they could pick their way through a thicket of facts, fantasies, and suppositions, so could I, and I resolved to continue my new career as Girl Detective.

It turned out to be the most important dunk shot I ever tried to sink.

7

AL GEORGIO picked me up in his grungy blue Plymouth. He waited until we were in traffic, heading for the Havistock apartment on East 79th Street, then he let me have it.

'What the hell do you think you're doing?' he demanded.

'What?' I said, startled.

'Why did you go down to see Nate Colescui yesterday?'

'Oh . . .' I said confusedly. 'Oh, that. Well, I wanted to find out how many display cases Havistock had. Because that empty case was the real thing. So if it was substituted . . .' My voice trailed away.

'Leave the detecting to the professionals, will you?' he said angrily. 'I go down to Carmine Street this morning and find you and Jack Smack have been there before me. Colescui doesn't know what the hell is going on. He gets three people asking about Havistock's cases.'

'I'm sorry,' I said humbly. 'I just wanted to find out where the extra came from.'

'Ahh . . .' he said disgustedly, 'I'm not sore at you. It's my ego that's suffering. Because you and Smack thought of it first and got there before me. No harm done. I called Havistock. Yes, he bought fifteen cases. He had two extras, kept in a closet in his bedroom. I asked him to check. He came back on the phone and said there's only one extra case now. One is missing. That was the empty switched for the Demaretion case.'

I thought about it for a while.

'That clears me, doesn't it?' I asked him. 'I couldn't have known about the extra cases. And even if I had, how would I know he kept them in his bedroom closet? He never mentioned them.'

'Oh, you're clean,' he said. 'As of now. And, for the same reasons, so are the guys on the armored truck.'

'Well, then . . .' I said, trying to puzzle it out, 'who does that leave?'

'The family,' Al Georgio said. 'As they say in dick shows on TV, it was an inside job.'

We drove through Central Park in silence for a while. Then:

'I'm sorry I yelled at you, Dunk,' he said.

'That's all right, Al,' I said. 'I really didn't mean to interfere with your job. I was just so anxious to clear myself.'

'Sure, I can understand that. But don't do any more prying on your own. Someone committed a crime. I don't want to scare you, but when you're dealing with big bucks like this, anything can happen.'

'You mean I could be in danger?'

'People do wacky things when a lot of money is involved. And a lot of years in stir.'

I didn't believe him. Was I ever wrong!

'When we talk to these people,' he went on, 'let me carry the ball. You tell your story as honestly and completely as you can. Then I'll see how they react and take it from there.'

'Whatever you say, Al,' I told him.

We all met in the living room of the Havistock apartment, a cavern I had never seen before. I mean the place was a mausoleum, swaddled in brown velvet, and I had to resist an impulse to take off my beret and look around for the open casket. If an organ had started to boom 'Abide with Me,' I wouldn't have been a bit surprised.

Awaiting us were Archibald Havistock, wife Mabel, married daughter Roberta Minchen with husband Ross, Orson Vanwinkle, and a lady introduced as Lenore Wolfgang, Mr Havistock's attorney. She was almost as tall as I, but blockier: a real linebacker wearing a black gabardine suit that looked like it had been hacked out of a hickory stump.

We all shook hands, showed our teeth, and got seated on those horrendous velvet couches and obese club chairs. Not at all daunted by the crowd, Detective Georgio took charge immediately, and orchestrated the entire interview. I had to admire his stern, no-nonsense manner.

'I'm going to ask Miss Bateson,' he said, 'to relate in detail, to the best of her recollection, exactly what happened on the morning the coin collection was packed and shipped to Grandby's. Please do not interrupt her. When she has finished, I will ask you, Mr Havistock, and you, Mr Vanwinkle, if your memories of that morning differ in any appreciable degree from her account. Miss Bateson?'

So I began my recital again, as familiar to me now as 'Barbara Frietchie,' which I memorized in the 5th Grade: 'Up from the meadows rich with corn, Clear in the cool September morn . . .' As I spoke, almost mechanically, I looked from face to face, zeroing in on daughter Roberta Minchen and hubby Ross.

She was a dumpling, swathed in a high-collared, flowery chiffon, loose enough to hide the bulges. A florid face with popping eyes and pouty lips. Her hair was cut short, which was a mistake. I thought she had a kind of blinking, rabbity look. Maybe that was due to her incisors: big and glistening.

Husband Ross was one of those solemn young men, prematurely bald, who comb their thinning locks from one side to the other. Awfully pale, with the grave look of a professional mourner. I remember that he cracked his knuckles until his wife reached out to stop him. While I was delivering my spiel, I had a sudden, awful vision of those two in bed together, and almost lost the thread of my discourse.

I finished and looked brightly at Al Georgio.

'Thank you, Miss Bateson,' he said. 'Very complete.' He turned to Archibald Havistock. 'Now, sir, does your recollection of the events differ from what you've just heard?'

Havistock stared at me, expressionless, heavy jaw lifted. 'No,' he said decisively. 'Miss Bateson has given an accurate account.'

'Mr Vanwinkle?' the detective asked. 'Any corrections or additions?'

'Oh, I don't think so,' the secretary said, with a languid wave. 'It happened just as she says.'

Al Georgio took out his pocket notebook, a ballpoint pen, and made a few jottings. It seemed to impress everyone – except me. Then he sat back, crossed his knees, took a deep breath.

'All right,' he said. 'Now we're at the point when Miss Bateson and Mr Vanwinkle leave the library and the taped cases and go out into the corridor to send in the armored truck guards. Correct?'

'Yes,' I said, 'that's how it happened.'

'You showed them where to go, and then the two of you went down to the street to supervise the packing of the armored van?'

'Not exactly,' Orson Vanwinkle said. 'Miss Bateson was outside when I conducted the two guards into the library.'

43

'Oh?' Georgio said. 'And when you brought the guards into the library, was Mr Havistock still there?'

The attorney, Lenore Wolfgang, spoke up: 'What is the purpose of this line of questioning?' she demanded.

Georgio looked at her stonily. 'The purpose of this line of questioning is to find out who stole the Demaretion. Mr Vanwinkle, when you accompanied the guards to the library, was your uncle there?'

'Ahh . . . no,' the secretary said. 'He was not.'

The detective turned to Havistock. 'Is that correct, sir?'

'Yes, yes,' he said, somewhat testily. 'The whole family had gathered, so I came into the living room, here, to see how everyone was getting along.'

'It was my birthday,' Mrs Havistock said. 'We were going to have a little party.'

'In other words,' Georgio said, 'no one was in the library with the coins until Mr Vanwinkle returned with the guards to start them loading the boxes. Is that right?'

He looked at them all. No one answered.

'Mr Havistock, how long were you gone from the library?'

'A minute or two. No more than that.'

'Mr Vanwinkle, from the moment you left the library until you returned with the guards, how much time elapsed?'

'Couldn't have been more than two minutes. Then my uncle reentered the library. He supervised the loading of the dolly. I went back to the outside corridor, rejoined Miss Bateson, and we both went down to the street to oversee the loading of the armored van.'

Georgio was jotting furiously in his notebook. Then he looked up. 'In other words, the packed coins were unattended in the library for a period of approximately two minutes?'

'I regret to say,' Archibald Havistock declaimed in his resonant voice, 'you are correct. It was my fault. I should never have left them alone.'

The detective ignored that. 'When you came into the living room, sir, who was present?'

Havistock frowned. 'Hard to remember. People were milling about. Some going into the kitchen to sample things the caterer had brought.'

'The caterer?' Georgio said sharply. 'When did the caterer arrive?'

'Oh, that was at least two hours previously,' Mrs Havistock said.

44

'All cold dishes. The delivery men were long gone before Miss Bateson arrived, and they started packing the coins.'

'Okay,' the detective said. 'Scratch the caterers. Let's get back to who was here, in the living room, when Mr Havistock came in from the library. Were you here, Mrs Havistock?'

'I was,' she said firmly. Then, hesitant, 'I think I was. Part of the time. I may have stepped into the kitchen to see how Ruby was getting along.'

'Mrs Minchen, were you here?'

'Right here,' she said in an unexpectedly girlish voice. 'Exactly where I'm sitting now.'

'Well, not exactly, darling,' her husband said. 'We were both sitting on the chocolate couch – remember?'

'And where was young Miss Havistock during the two minutes her father was in this room?'

'She was here,' Mrs Havistock said.

'And where were your son and his wife – were they also in this room during that two-minute period?'

They all looked at each other helplessly.

'Look here,' Archibald Havistock said angrily. 'I told you we were all milling about. People were sitting, standing, moving to the kitchen, mixing a drink for themselves. I deeply object to your line of questioning. You're implying that a member of my family might have stolen the Demaretion.'

Al Georgio slapped his notebook shut with a smack that startled us all. He glared at them. 'The armored truck guards couldn't have done it,' he said, addressing Havistock. 'Miss Bateson couldn't have done it. Who do you want me to suspect – the man in the moon?'

'I resent that,' Lenore Wolfgang said.

'Resent away,' the detective said, standing up. 'This is only the beginning. I'll be back.'

He started out, then stopped suddenly and turned back to Havistock. 'Who knew you kept the two extra display cases in your bedroom closet?' he demanded.

For the first time Mr Havistock appeared flustered. He could hardly get the words out. 'Why . . .' he said, almost stammering, 'I suppose everyone did. All the family.'

Georgio nodded grimly and stalked out. I rose hastily and ran after him.

When we were back in his car, he said, 'How about some lunch, Dunk? A hamburger?'

'Fine,' I said. 'I'll pay for my own.'

'Okay,' he said cheerfully. 'I know a good place over on Lex. They make British burgers. With bacon.'

So that's what we had. Sitting at a minuscule table for two alongside a tiled wall, munching burgers, popping French fries, and sipping tea out of glasses.

'I think it went good,' Al Georgio said. 'I shook them up, got them looking at each other. They're beginning to wonder: Which one did it?'

'Orson Vanwinkle did it,' I said.

'Why do you say that?'

'I don't like him.'

Al almost choked on a piece of bacon, he laughed so hard. 'Beautiful. I take that to the DA, and he kicks my ass out the window. Why don't you like Vanwinkle?'

'He's a snaky character.'

'How could he have pulled it? He was never alone with the sealed cases.'

'Somehow he did it. I'll find out.'

'Who the hell are you – Nancy Drew?' Then, suddenly, surprising me, 'How about dinner tonight?'

I stared at him. 'Are you married, Al?'

'Divorced,' he said. 'Almost two years now.'

'Children?'

'A girl. Sally. Would you like to see her picture?'

'Of course.'

He dug out his wallet, showed me a photo in a plastic slip-case.

'She's a beauty,' I said. And that was the truth.

'Isn't she?' he said, staring at the photo. 'She's going to break a lot of hearts.'

'How old is she?'

'Going on twelve.'

'Do you see her often?'

'Not as often as I'd like,' he said miserably. 'I have the right to two weekends a month. But this lousy job . . . That's why my wife divorced me. It's not easy being married to a cop. The job comes first.'

'All right, Al,' I said, 'I'll have dinner with you tonight. Do I have to dress up?'

He laughed. 'You kidding? Look at me. Do I look like a dress-up

46

kind of guy? The place I'm taking you to isn't fancy, but they've got the best linguine and clams in New York.'

So I wore my usual uniform: pipestem jeans, black turtleneck sweater, suede jacket and beret. Al said I looked like a Central American terrorist; all I needed was a bandolier. He was wearing one of his rumpled suits with all the pizzazz of a bathrobe. I had never met a man so completely without vanity. I found it rather endearing.

It was a scruffy trattoria he took me to, in Little Italy, but after I got a whiff of those marvelous cooking odors, I knew I had found a home. The moment we entered, the owner came rushing over to embrace Al, and the two men roared at each other in rapid Italian. Then the owner, a man with a white mustache big enough to stuff a pillow, turned his attention to me.

He kissed his fingertips and started chattering away again. All I caught were two 'bella's' and one 'bellissima!'

'He says,' Al translated, 'that if you are willing to run away with him, he will desert his wife, six children, and eleven grandchildren.'

'Tell him not before I eat,' I said.

Al relayed the message, and the old guy slapped his thigh, twisted the curved horns of his mustache upward, and rolled his eyes. Forty years ago he must have been a holy terror with the ladies.

We finally got seated, and even before we ordered, the owner brought us glasses of red wine.

'Homemade,' Al told me. 'In the basement. It's got a kick.'

It did, but was so smooth and mellow, I felt I could drink it all night. 'How did you ever find this place?' I asked.

'I was born two blocks away. It was here then. Same wine, same menu. Even some of the same waiters. It hasn't changed a bit, and I hope it never does.'

We had a memorable meal: a huge platter of seafood linguine, with clams, baby shrimp, slivers of crabmeat, and chunks of lobster. I could have filled a bathtub with that sauce and rolled around in it. The fresh, crunchy salad was special, too, and afterwards we had cappuccino with tortoni, and Al taught me how to float a spoonful of the ice cream atop the coffee. Heaven!

The owner brought us two little glasses of Strega, and after a taste I was ready to move into that restaurant and never leave. I told Al how much I enjoyed the dinner, and he nodded absently.

'Listen, Dunk,' he said, 'you met that Natalie Havistock, didn't you?'

'Nettie? Sure, I met her.'

'What was your take?'

'A wild one. The hippie of the family. She just doesn't fit in with the others. But I like her.'

'You get along with her okay?'

'Of course. She came up to the office one day to learn how the auction would be organized. Then we went out for pizza together.'

'Uh-huh,' he said, looking over my head. 'I should tell you she runs with a rough crowd. Some of them are into drugs and some into guns. We've got a special unit that keeps an eye on gangs like that, hoping to grab them before they do something stupid – like blowing up the Statue of Liberty.'

'Nettie?' I said, shaking my head. 'I can't believe it.'

'Oh, yes. She and her pals are a bunch of fruitcakes.'

'You think they could have stolen the Demaretion?'

'Possible, but I doubt it. It's not their style. They'd go for a bank or armored van – something where they could wear ski masks and wave submachine guns around. How about you giving Nettie a call. Maybe having lunch with her.'

'What for?'

'Pump her. I got nowhere with her. She's a throwback to the nineteen sixties; I'm a cop so therefore I'm a pig. But you say the two of you hit it off. So maybe she'll talk to you. About her family. The conflicts and so forth. In a family that big there's got to be jealousies. Grudges. Undercurrents. I'd like to know about them.'

I stared at him, trying to smile. 'And all the time I thought you invited me out to dinner to enjoy the pleasures of my company.'

He leaned toward me. 'That's the truth, Dunk. That's exactly why I asked you out. If you don't want to brace Nettie, just tell me, and we'll forget about the whole thing.'

'You're something, you are,' I said. 'Well, you warned me – with you the job comes first. All right, I'll try to see Nettie. Only because I'm as anxious and curious about this thing as you are.'

'Fine,' he said. 'Try to meet her tomorrow if you can.'

'What will you be doing?'

'I've got an appointment to talk to Luther and Vanessa Havistock.'

'If I tell you how I make out with Natalie, will you tell me what you learned from Luther and Vanessa?'

He held out a big, meaty hand. 'It's a deal,' he said, and we shook on it. 'I've got some reports to do tonight,' he continued. 'I better get you home. Look, Dunk, I was being honest when I said I invited you out just to enjoy your company. I like being with you. You believe that, don't you?'

'I guess.'

'Can we have dinner again, or lunch, or whatever?'

'Sure,' I said. 'I'm a forgiving soul. Just keep feeding me like to night and I'm all yours.'

That charming smile again. 'And I'll bet you didn't gain an ounce. I envy people like you. Look at my gut. Isn't that disgusting?'

He double-parked in front of my brownstone and we sat a few minutes, talking about the Havistocks.

'Right now it's a can of worms,' Georgio said. 'But within a few days I hope we'll be able to eliminate a few possibles, and things will look simpler.'

I stared at him in the gloom. 'Why are you doing this, Al?'

He was astonished. 'It's my job.'

'I know that, but I think there's more to it. It's almost like a crusade with you.'

He shrugged. 'I just don't like wise-asses who think they can get away with murder – or even get away with copping an antique Greek coin. I hate people like that – the ones who go elbowing their way through life, thinking the laws are for other people but not for them.'

'You get pleasure from putting them behind bars?'

'Not pleasure so much as satisfaction. It just seems right to me.'

'You're a deep, deep man,' I told him.

'Me? Nah. I'm just a cop running to suet. You'll see Nettie tomorrow?'

I sighed. 'Yes, I'll see Nettie tomorrow. Thanks for the marvy dinner.'

I leaned forward and kissed his cheek. I think it shocked him. But he recovered fast enough.

'Thank you,' he said. 'You're a sweet lady, Dunk.'

I stood on the sidewalk until he pulled away. We both waved. I turned to the doorway of my brownstone. A man came out of the shadows. I took a deep breath and opened my mouth, prepared to scream.

'Hi!' Jack Smack said. 'Have a pleasant evening?'

'You bastard,' I said wrathfully. 'You scared the hell out of me.'

'Did I?' he said, grinning. He held up a brown paper bag. 'Look what I've got – a glorious bottle of Finlandia vodka. For you. How's about inviting me in for a nightcap?'

8

JACK SMACK lounged on my couch, one arm extended along the back, his legs crossed. That night he was wearing a Norfolk suit of yummy gray flannel, soft broadcloth shirt with a silk ascot at the open neck. Tasseled loafers buffed to a high gloss. What a nonchalantly elegant man!

'Where do you buy your clothes?' I asked him.

'Thrift shops,' he said, with a snort of laughter.

He was working on a double vodka on the rocks. After all I'd had to drink at dinner, I settled for a cup of black coffee. He didn't scare me, but I recognized a kind of wariness in my feelings toward him. I wasn't sure what he wanted, and decided not to listen to his pitch with a muzzy mind.

'I don't suppose,' he said with a lazy smile, 'you'll tell me what Al Georgio said about the Havistock case tonight.'

'You're right. I won't tell you.'

He uncrossed his legs, leaned forward, suddenly serious and intent.

'I'm glad to hear that, Dunk,' he said solemnly. 'Glad to hear that you're discreet. Can I depend on you not to repeat to Al what I tell you?'

'Of course,' I said. 'But I think it's silly. The two of you should be working together. Exchanging information and all that.'

'Mmmm,' he said. 'Sometimes it doesn't work out that way. Sometimes it's best that we do our own thing. My company got an anonymous letter this morning. Typewritten on cheap bond. Postmarked Manhattan. The writer wants to know if we'd be interested in buying back the Demaretion.'

I sat up straight, excited. 'My God, Jack, do you think it's legitimate?'

He shrugged. 'Seems to be. The forensic lab we use went over it.

The typewriter was an Olympia standard. No usable prints on the letter. They think it was written by a man.'

'How do they know that?'

'Wording. Phrasing.'

'How much does he want for the Demaretion?'

'Didn't say. Just asked if we'd be interested in buying.'

'Well, if you are, how do you get in touch with him?'

'Cloak-and-dagger stuff. We occupy the ninth floor of a building on Third Avenue and Eighty-third Street. If we're interested in buying, we're to close the venetian blinds on the entire floor. If the writer of the letter sees them closed any working day within the next week, he'll send us another letter stating his price.'

'Are you going to do it?'

He shrugged again. 'Maybe, maybe not. Right now it's being debated by the top brass. It could be a fake, you know. A colossal con. So meanwhile I'm to continue my investigation.'

'And how are you coming along with that?'

He flipped a palm back and forth. 'Bits and pieces. A little here, a little there. The brother of the housekeeper, Ruby Querita, is in the pokey on a drug charge. That could be something. And the youngest daughter, Natalie, runs with a bunch of wild-assed loonies. That could be something.' He turned on the charming smile. 'And I know you found out about those two extra display cases Archibald Havistock had made.'

I nodded, figuring he heard about my visit to Nate Colescui.

Suddenly he was serious and sincere again. 'That was good thinking on your part, Dunk. You were ahead of me and Al Georgio.'

His quick switches of mood, levity to solemnity, were confusing. I wondered if he was doing it deliberately, to keep me rattled and unsure. I wanted to prove to him that he wasn't succeeding.

'Is there a typewriter in the Havistock apartment?' I asked him.

He smiled coldly. 'That's a sharp brain you've got there, kiddo. Your mama didn't raise you to be an idiot. Yes, there's a typewriter in the Havistock apartment. But it's an IBM Selectric, not an Olympia. Vanwinkle uses it for correspondence. So the letter we got must have been typed somewhere else. That would be easy; there are hotels in the city where you can rent a desk and typewriter by the hour.'

I saw his glass was almost empty and took it from his hand. I brought it into the kitchen, refilled it with ice cubes and a really stiff jolt of Finlandia. If he was trying to unsettle me with his mercurial

51

changes of mood, I could play my own game – get him befuddled enough to tell me more than he intended.

'Jack,' I said, handing him the bomb, 'when you're assigned to an investigation like this, where do you start? What's the first thing you look for?'

'Motive,' he said promptly. 'Somebody needs money – right? So they steal something of value.'

I shook my head. 'Not necessarily. Not when you're talking about antique coins or paintings or rare documents. Sometimes they're stolen not from greed, but because the thief wants to *own* them. It's the collector's instinct: to possess an object of great rarity and beauty. He doesn't want to make a profit from it; he just wants to look at it, devour it with his eyes, and think, "Mine, mine, *mine!*"'

'You think that's what happened to the Demaretion?'

'It's possible. A private collector may have hired a thief, for a fee. Then the coin disappears into his safe. I mean, what else are you going to do with it? Jack, it's so *rare*. No reputable dealer is going to handle a Demaretion without wanting to know where it came from and how the would-be seller came into possession.'

He stared at me thoughtfully. 'That's an angle I hadn't considered: a contract theft engineered by a private collector with a mad desire to own the coin. But that anonymous letter we got knocks that theory into a cocked hat, doesn't it?'

'Not necessarily. Suppose a rich collector pays a professional thief ten thousand to lift the Demaretion. The crook succeeds, but then he finds out what the coin is really worth. So he says to himself, Why should I take all the risk for this piddling fee when I can get five or ten times as much from the insurance company? So he double-crosses the guy who hired him and contacts you.'

'Dunk,' he said admiringly, 'you have a devious mind. I like that. I hope we can work closely together on this. I need the benefit of your expertise.'

'What's in it for me?' I said boldly.

'The sooner we get it cleared up, the sooner you go back to work at Grandby's, with maybe a fat raise in gratitude for the help you provided. Isn't that enough for you?'

I thought a moment. Then: 'Yes, it's enough.'

'Then we can work together?'

I nodded.

'The first thing I'd like to get from you,' he said, 'is a list of coin dealers all over the world. We want to get letters out to them to be on the lookout for someone trying to peddle a hot Demaretion. Can you provide a list like that?'

'Sure,' I said. 'No problem. I'll just lend you the most recent directory of the Association.'

'Fine,' he said, then hesitated a moment. 'Something else I'd like you to do – if you're willing.'

'What's that?'

'Have a private meeting – a talk, lunch, dinner, whatever – with Orson Vanwinkle, the secretary.'

'Why him?'

Jack Smack sat back, frowning. 'I don't really know, except that there's something cheesy about the man.'

'I agree. I don't like him.'

'I can't see how it's possible that he could have lifted the coin, but I get bad vibes from that guy. There's something phony there; he doesn't ring true.'

'I can't just call him and ask him to take me out to lunch.'

'I know that,' Smack said, 'but there must be some way you can work it; you're a brainy lady. Think about it and see if there's any way you can talk to him in private. Did he come on to you?'

'Maybe,' I admitted. 'But maybe that's the way he treats all women.'

He nodded. 'Think about it,' he repeated. 'If you decide to do it, give me a call, and we'll talk about what we want to get out of him.' Then, out of the blue: 'Would you like me to stay the night?'

I glared at him. 'No, I would not like you to stay the night.'

'Okay,' he said equably. 'If you don't ask, you'll never know – right? You got a guy, Dunk?'

'Several,' I said, lying in my teeth.

'I wish you'd add me to the list,' he said. 'I'm single, own a Jaguar, and know how to make Beef Wellington.' Again that warm smile that melted my knees. Oh, God, he was so handsome! 'This has nothing to do with our business, Dunk. This is between you and me.'

'Oh, sure,' I said.

He drained his drink and stood up – steadily. So much for my plot. Did I want him to leave? Did I want him to stay? If he planned to confuse me, he was doing one hell of a job.

'I'll get your bottle,' I told him.

'Oh, no,' he said, 'that's for you. Maybe you'll invite me in again for a drink.'

'Anytime,' I said. Was that me talking?

At the door, he turned and kissed me. On the lips. It was nice.

'Out you go,' I said, gasping.

'Sure,' he said, staring into my eyes. 'Don't forget about Vanwinkle. I've got a feeling there's something there.'

Then he was gone. I locked, bolted, and chained the door. I was still shaken by that kiss. The swine! The lovely swine!

Undressing slowly, I pondered all the happenings of that eventful day: the meeting at the Havistocks', lunch with Al Georgio, dinner with Al in Little Italy, and finally the set-to with Jack Smack.

I found myself grinning. Because I had been living such a placid existence and hadn't realized how lonely and bored I had become. Now I was meeting new people, becoming involved with strong passions – and I loved it. Suddenly my life seemed cracked open, full of emotions I had never felt before. I suppose it was the normal process of learning, but at the time it seemed to me a delightful revelation – like tasting caviar for the first time.

Before I went to bed, I had a little bit of Jack Smack's vodka with grapefruit juice. Just what I needed, because later, warm and snug, waiting for sleep, I reflected, giggling, that with two tall, good-looking New York guys wanting to jump on her bones, little ol' Mary Lou Bateson of Des Moines was doing okay.

9

THAT MORNING with Nettie Havistock was one of the most discombobulating experiences of my life. When I finally got through (her private number at the Havistock apartment was busy for more than an hour), she said she'd be 'charged' to see me, and suggested we do some shopping together and then have lunch. She told me to meet her at the toiletries counter of Saks 5th.

She showed up in a costume that threw me for a loop. From bottom to top: scruffy Adidas running shoes, heavy knitted leg warmers over baggy jeans, a T-shirt with SLIPPERY WHEN WET printed on the front, and over that a denim vest festooned with ribboned military medals. A man's fedora, sweat-stained, was crammed atop her fuzzy blond curls. And over her shoulder hung a leather, Indian-type bag with buckskin fringe, decorated with beads and shells.

'Hi, hon,' she said blithely, ignoring my wide-eyed stare. 'I'm not looking for anything in particular. Just thought we'd mooch around and see what's new.'

So I tagged after her, all over the main floor of Saks. It took me about five minutes to realize she was shoplifting. Small stuff: bars of imported soap, silk scarves, a man's tie, a gold-plated chain. She was so casual and practiced that I knew she had been at it a long time. She slid the stuff inside the waistband of her baggy jeans or just scooped it into her capacious shoulder bag. Wandering, smiling, chatting over her shoulder at me . . .

I was terrified. I wanted to turn and bolt. I just couldn't believe it. I knew she could easily afford all those things she was boosting. Kleptomania? Was that a legal defense? I looked about nervously, certain that at any moment we would be apprehended by store detectives and marched off in shame.

'That should do it,' Nettie said brightly. 'Let's go get something to eat.'

We walked over to Madison, Nettie nattering on and on. But I wasn't listening; I was debating with myself whether or not to mention her criminal behavior, what my reaction should be, how it might affect my relations with her and the investigation of the Demaretion theft.

'That stuff I lifted,' she said with a roguish smile. 'Want any of it?'

'No, thanks,' I said hastily.

She laughed. 'I don't need that crap,' she said. 'It's just a game. I give it all away.'

'What if you get caught?'

'Daddy will pay off,' she said confidently. 'He always has.'

I felt sorrow for Archibald Havistock, that complete man. His solid manner concealed what must have been harrowing family problems.

We had lunch in a crowded luncheonette on Madison Avenue, pushing our way to the rear past the cashier's desk, a take-out counter, and a jumble of little tables. We finally found seats in the rear, close to the kitchen doors, waitresses rushing in and out.

'This is a new place,' Natalie Havistock said, looking around. 'It's a setup.'

That comment made me uneasy, but I didn't dare ask what she meant. We finally ordered chicken salad plates with iced tea, and while we were waiting for our food, Nettie fished a crimped cigarette from her shoulder bag.

'My first today,' she said, holding the cigarette up for my inspection. 'Want one?'

'I think I'll pass,' I said.

'Good stuff.'

'Nettie, do you know what you're doing?'

'Nope,' she said cheerfully. 'Do you know what you're doing?'

'Not really,' I confessed.

'Well, then . . . there you are.'

She lighted her homemade cigarette, and when I got a whiff of that sweetish smoke, I hoped none of the nearby diners would start a ruckus. None did.

'Nettie,' I said, 'I feel terrible about your father losing that coin.'

'He can afford it,' she said casually. 'Besides, he'll collect from the insurance company, won't he?'

'I suppose so. But the insurance value is outdated. Today the coin would be insured for much, much more.'

'Then it's no big deal. The cops think someone in the family lifted it, don't they?'

I nodded.

'Not me,' she said. 'What would I do with that stupid coin?'

I just couldn't understand her. One minute she's showing no remorse for her shoplifting pranks, and the next minute she's shrugging off her father's loss of the Demaretion. I didn't know what she was revolting against. Family? Society? Or maybe herself.

But then our food arrived. Nettie handed the stub of her cigarette to the waitress.

'A little tip for you, luv,' she said, smiling.

The waitress took the roach, sniffed it, and said, 'Thank you, dear. Just what I need.'

That could never happen in Des Moines. Or could it?

I looked at her as we ate our salads. A thin, nervy young girl (twenty-two? twenty-four?) with brittle energy: sharp movements, quick gestures. I got the impression of unhappiness there, some deep despair cloaked by a bright smile and brisk manner. But sadness in her eyes that all the blue eyeliner couldn't conceal.

'Ruby Querita?' I asked. 'Could she have done it?'

'Ruby? Not a chance. Her brother's a doper, but she's a straight arrow. Works her ass off to keep her boy in private school. The kid's a mathematical whiz.'

'Who then?'

Nettie shrugged. 'Ross Minchen, my brother-in-law, is a wimp. I can't see him lifting anything more valuable than an ashtray from McDonald's. Roberta is just as dreary.'

'Certainly not your mother.'

Nettie laughed. 'Don't be so sure. Don't let the blue hair fool you; there is one tough lady. But why should she steal the coin? The way I hear it, most of what Daddy owns is in her name already.'

I realized how little I knew about the source of the Havistocks' wealth.

'Your father is retired?'

'Semi. He owned a textile company. Knitting mills and things like that. Then he sold out to a bigger outfit. But he's still on salary as a consultant. And Luther works for them. That was part of the deal.'

'What about Luther. Could he have done it?'

She paused, fork halfway to her mouth. 'Possibly,' she said thoughtfully.

'I've never met your brother.'

'He's got problems. Mainly his wife, Vanessa. She's a barracuda. Lives up to and beyond his income. Runs him ragged.'

'I gather you don't like her.'

'You gather correctly, Dunk. She's a real bitch.'

'Could she have stolen the coin?'

'Wouldn't put it past her. She loves money. But she wouldn't do it herself; she'd get a man to do it for her. She's got eyes for anything in pants, with a fat wallet in the hip pocket. She was coming on to Ross Minchen, and it got so bad that finally Daddy had to tell Vanessa to lay off. It's a fun thing with her. She likes to stir guys up. Gives her a feeling of power, I guess.'

'Is she attractive?'

'Like a snake. Yes, I suppose you could call her attractive. I can't see it – I think she's chromium-plated – but men take one look at her and unzip their flies.'

I laughed. 'What about Orson Vanwinkle? Did he unzip his fly?'

She drained her iced tea before she answered. 'Orson is a shmuck. He thinks he's God's gift to women, but he's a shmuck. He came on strong with me once – I mean really physical. But I gave him a knee in the balls, and that was the end of that. You know, in a lot of ways he's the male equivalent of Vanessa. I think they're both a couple of hustlers.'

'You think there's something between them?'

'Vanessa and Orson? I doubt that. He's got no money, so Vanessa wouldn't be interested. I've seen them together many times, and never noticed anything going on. Mutual suspicion, maybe. They both know what they are; it takes one to know one. A couple of cruds. Well . . .' she said, pushing her plate away and sitting back, 'how do you like that rundown on the Havistocks? Just your average, normal, well-adjusted American family – right?'

'Nettie,' I said, feeling guilty, 'I really didn't mean to pry. But I'd like to get this whole thing cleared up so I can get my job back.'

'Sure, sweetie, I can understand that.'

'If you had to name someone in the family as a prime suspect, who would it be?'

She thought a moment, digging with a fingernail at a fragment of chicken caught in her teeth. 'Orson Vanwinkle,' she said finally. 'Or my brother, Luther.'

'Why them?'

'They're both hurting for money,' she said.

Then the waitress brought our bill. 'Thanks for the roach, honey,' she said to Nettie. 'It hit the spot.'

Natalie Havistock grabbed the check. 'You leave,' she told me. 'Go out to the street; I'll be along in a few minutes.'

'I want to pay my share,' I said, fumbling with my purse.

'Forget it,' she said. 'Just go!'

So I went, past the tables, the take-out counter, the cashier's desk. I waited on Madison Avenue. It was almost five minutes before Nettie came out. She was carrying a white paper bag. We walked a half-block, and she dumped the bag in a refuse basket.

'Coffee and bagel,' she said. 'Who needs it?'

'Nettie,' I said, 'what *are* you doing?'

'Our lunch bill came to almost fifteen bucks,' she said. 'So I stopped at the take-out counter, bought coffee and a bagel for two bucks. I palmed the lunch bill and gave the cashier the take-out check for two bucks and paid that. No strain, no pain. Lousy organization in that place.'

'What about a tip for the waitress?'

'She got the roach, didn't she?'

'Nettie,' I said, 'you're awful.'

'That's right,' she said, grinning. 'And I love it.'

We kissed cheeks, promised we'd stay in touch, and she popped into a cab on Madison. I wondered how she was going to con the driver. I shouldn't have laughed, but I did. I decided to walk all the way home. I had a lot to think about.

It was a dynamite day in Manhattan: a velvety June afternoon with a muskmelon sun in a washed sky and a breeze just cool enough to tingle. It was a long hike back to West 83rd Street, but I still had calf and thigh muscles from my dunk shot days, and it felt good to stretch them.

I had now lived in New York for several years, but never ceased to marvel at how thronged the city was. Mobs of people! I saw Manhattan as one big, overcrowded basketball court. The only way for a pedestrian to make progress on those jammed sidewalks was by bobbing, ducking, weaving. I was good at that, and went dancing home, darting and spinning, imagining I was dribbling an inflated spheroid all the way.

59

But that was physical and mechanical. While I played games on the ganged sidewalks, my mind was wrestling with the Havistock family and what Natalie had told me. Her frankness was amazing; I could never be that open about *my* family to an acquaintance. And I certainly had less dramatic revelations to divulge.

I couldn't decide whether Nettie's casual disclosures were motivated by rancor toward parents, siblings, and in-laws, or whether she had a more devious reason. Perhaps she was trying to direct guilt elsewhere — her own guilt. I found that hard to believe, but it was possible.

I finally decided that her lack of discretion might be (probably was) due to an abiding hatred and disgust of hypocrisy. So open and forthright herself, she could not endure dissembling in others. She really was an idealist — or at least a romantic.

Al Georgio had accused me of acting like Nancy Drew. Now I was making like Sigmund Freud!

I stopped at a neighborhood grocery and picked up a blueberry yogurt and a plastic container of fresh salad. Also, on impulse, two cans of Schaefer beer. I toted my purchases home, kicked off my shoes, and popped one of the beers.

Slumped on the couch, I went over again what Nettie had told me about the Havistocks. A rogue's gallery! But in all honesty, I could not see any one of them as the Demaretion thief.

I was debating whether or not I had the energy to wash my hair when the phone rang. It was Al Georgio. He sounded harried and tense.

'Listen,' he said, 'you see Natalie Havistock today?'

'Yes, we had lunch together.'

'Good. I'm seeing Luther and Vanessa at six o'clock. He gets home from work then, and I want to catch the two of them together. I figure it'll take about an hour; no more than that. You said you're a pizza maven — right? How's about I pick up a pepperoni and maybe a jug of red ink, and I'll show up at your place around seven-thirty or eight — like that. You tell me about Nettie, and I'll tell you about Luther and Vanessa. Okay?'

'Sure,' I said, 'come ahead. But make the pizza half-anchovy; that's my favorite.'

'All that salt isn't good for you.'

'And all those garlicky spices aren't good for *you*.'

'All right, all right,' he said, laughing. 'You get the heart attack, I get the ulcer. See you later, Dunk.'

He showed up a little before eight, lugging a big pizza box and a

60

half-gallon of Chianti in a raffia cozy. As usual, he looked lumpy and disheveled. And weary. His heavy face sagged, but those electric blue eyes were sharp enough.

'Tough day?' I asked him.

'They're all tough,' he said. 'But I didn't come here to whine; let's eat.'

We sat on the couch and pulled the cocktail table close. I provided wineglasses and paper napkins. We gobbled and we swigged. Not an elegant dinner, but I loved it.

'You first,' he said. 'About Nettie . . .'

So, between chomps of pizza and gulps of Chianti, I told him the whole story, not omitting the shoplifting spree and the scam in the luncheonette. He laughed at that.

'What a character she is,' he said. 'A real flake.'

'She is that,' I agreed. 'But I don't think boosting in Saks means she lifted the Demaretion.'

'Mmm,' he said. 'Maybe, maybe not. What else?'

I repeated everything Nettie had told me about the Havistock family. Al listening carefully, not interrupting me and not interrupting the destruction of his half (pepperoni) of the pizza.

'You've got good recall, Dunk,' he said, sitting back and swabbing his mouth with a paper napkin. 'And everything you've told me ties in pretty much with what I've picked up about the Havistocks. You think Nettie is clean?'

'I think she is, Al. She may be a nut, but I just can't see her stealing from her own father.'

He brooded awhile. 'Maybe it wasn't her idea,' he said finally. 'I told you about the gang of crazies she runs with. Her lover is a black stud who wears a red beret and one gold earring. He might have pushed her into it.'

I sighed. 'She's a mixed-up kid.'

'Oh, sure,' he said. 'So am I. So are you. But we don't rip off Saks Fifth Avenue. The first thing you learn in the detective business, Dunk, is not to let your personal likes or dislikes influence your thinking. Nettie could be guilty as hell. Will you buy that?'

'All right,' I said shortly, certain he was wrong. 'Now tell me about Luther and Vanessa.'

'They're just about what Nettie told you. Luther is a victim. A loser. Vanessa is a real femmy fa-tally.' He said that with wry, deliberate mispronunciation. 'She even came on to *me*, for God's sake. A slob like me.'

61

'You're not a slob, Al,' I said.

'No,' he said, 'and I'm not Cary Grant either. I knew what she was doing, Dunk, but I've got to tell you, there is one exciting woman.'

'Beautiful?'

'Different. Striking. She just gives the impression of being available. She's not obvious about it. Doesn't show her thighs or flash her boobs – nothing like that. As a matter of fact, she was dressed conservatively. But she just exudes sex. I think what Nettie told you was right: Vanessa gets her jollies from teasing. I felt sorry for her husband.'

'What kind of a man can he be to let her get away with that?'

'He's defeated. But so much in love with her – or infatuated, or obsessed, or whatever you want to call it – that he'd never think of dumping her.'

'Al, do you think if she told him to steal the Demaretion, he'd do it?'

'If she told him to slit his throat, he'd do it. Dunk, you've got to meet this woman. She's something, she is.'

'When I asked Nettie to name who she thought stole the coin, she said Luther or Orson Vanwinkle. She said they were both hurting for money.'

'I can believe it about Luther. You should see their apartment. Park Avenue and Sixty-fourth. And the jewelry she was wearing! She had one ring that could feed a Puerto Rican family for ten years. He works for the conglomerate that bought out Archibald Havistock's textile company. If Luther makes seventy-five grand a year, he's lucky. But believe me, Dunk, a hundred grand a year wouldn't cover that apartment and Vanessa's jewelry and all the paintings and the Mercedes and the summer house in Montauk. Unless Daddy is helping him out, I think the guy is overextended. He's got that bankrupt look about him: pale, tremors of the hands until after the second drink, lips pressed together, high-pitched laugh. I've seen it all before in people trying to hang on to their style of living when they haven't got two nickels to rub together.'

'So maybe copping the Demaretion could be the answer to all his troubles.'

'It sure as hell would help,' Georgio said, nodding. 'He's got the motive, all right. But I haven't figured out yet how he could—'

The phone rang and he stopped talking. I have a wall phone in my kitchen, and an extension on a table in the bedroom. Like a complete idiot, I went to the kitchen. Al could easily overhear.

'Hello?' I said.

'Hi, luv,' Jack Smack said breezily. 'Can you talk?'

'Not very well,' I said.

'Oh-ho,' he said, 'company. Al Georgio?'

'I'm busy,' I said.

'Call you tomorrow,' he said, and hung up.

I went back to the living room.

'Jack Smack?' Al asked.

I couldn't lie to him. I nodded miserably.

'That's okay,' he said. 'You're entitled. I know you're not carrying tales.'

'I'm not!' I said hotly.

'I *know* that,' he repeated patiently, trying to smile. 'Jack has got his job to do, too.'

Still, there was constraint.

'So . . .' I said, 'where do you go from here?'

He shrugged tiredly. 'Dig deeper. Try to find out who would profit most. This thing is a can of worms. And I'm getting a lot of flak. You've been reading the papers? The tabs love it. Who stole the priceless Greek coin? The Department is leaning on me.'

'I can imagine,' I said. 'Have some more wine; there's plenty left.'

'Splendid idea,' he said, and this time his smile was warm and charming again. He topped off my glass and filled his.

'Where do you live, Al?' I asked him.

'Queens,' he said. 'Basement apartment. My ex got the house. But I'm not complaining; I've got a place to sleep.'

'You cook for yourself?'

'Of course. When I get the chance. I happen to be a good cook.'

'I'll bet you are,' I said. 'Italian stuff?'

'Mostly. I can gussy up chicken breasts until you'd swear you were eating veal.'

'Stop it,' I said. 'I'm gaining weight just listening.'

He looked at me. 'If I invited you out, would you come for dinner?'

'Just try me,' I said.

'Thanks, Dunk,' he said. 'You're good people.'

I took the empty pizza box and used napkins out to the kitchen and dumped them in the garbage can. I couldn't have been gone more than a minute. When I went back to the living room, Al Georgio was fast asleep; it happened that quickly. His chin was

63

down on his chest, he was breathing deeply, and the wineglass he was holding was tilting dangerously.

I lifted the glass gently from his fingers and set it aside. I turned off the overhead light and switched on a table lamp next to the only comfortable chair I owned: an oversized wing with enough soft pillows to make snuggling easy. I put on my half-moon reading glasses and dug out the needles, wool, and the Afghan I had been working on for the past four months.

I enjoyed needlework. Great therapy. Once you learn how, grasp the basic pattern of what you're doing, your hands fly, almost of their own volition. It's a pleasure to be creating something, and it's so automatic that your thoughts can soar. I've heard of women who knit sweaters while they watch TV soap operas. I believe it.

The Afghan I was working on was just a big shawl in an open, boxy pattern. Light blue. Not as deep as Al Georgio's eyes – more of a sky blue, an azure. So while Al dozed, my needles went clicking quietly away, and I could think about the lives of the Havistocks, much more tangled than my skeins of wool.

The complexities of that one family amazed me. And fascinated, too, I admit. My life, so far, had been simple and straightforward. Problems and troubles, of course, but nothing cataclysmic. Not even very dramatic. Now I was plunged into the operatic existence of the Havistocks – or so it seemed to me. I was playing a small role – extra or walk-on. But I found it exciting.

I called to mind all the members of the Havistock ménage, trying to decide which one was the thief, because Georgio and Jack Smack both thought the crime had been committed by a family member, and I agreed. Al had told me not to let my personal likes or dislikes influence my thinking – but he was a man, and I was a woman, and I wasn't certain he was correct. Men have this big love affair with logic, but cold reason can't explain everything.

So I just let my instincts roll, and decided Orson Vanwinkle did it. Or if he didn't steal the Demaretion personally, he was involved in the theft. Why did I believe that? Because he had a clammy handclasp and treated me in a lewd, insinuating manner. That was enough to condemn him. He was what my grandmother used to call a lounge lizard.

I was working on the puzzle of how Vanwinkle might have switched display case number thirteen, when Al Georgio roused. His head snapped up, he looked about, stupefied with sleep.

'My God,' he said. 'What's the time? How long have I been out, Dunk?'

'About a half-hour.'

'Sorry.'

'Don't apologize,' I said. 'You obviously needed it.'

'Where's the john?' he said. 'Maybe some cold water on my face will help.'

He came out of the bathroom shaking his head ruefully. 'I don't know what happened to me.'

'The wine,' I said.

'Nah. We didn't even put a dent in the bottle. I think I better get home and sack out for about eight hours.'

'You're sure you want to drive?' I asked anxiously. 'You can sleep here on the couch if you like.'

That melting smile again. 'Thanks, Dunk, but I better not. You may never get me out of the place.'

'I'll take that chance.'

He laughed and came over to kiss my cheek. 'I like you in glasses,' he said.

'You do?' I said, astonished, peering up at him over my half-moons. 'Why do you say that?'

'I don't know,' he said, shrugging. 'Somehow they make you look more sexy.'

'Then I'll wear them all the time,' I said. 'Al, most of your wine is left; take it with you.'

'No way. You keep it. It'll give me an excuse to come back.'

'Anytime,' I said, and remembered I had told Jack Smack the same thing. Dunk Bateson – the femmy fa-tally!

At the door, Al said, 'Thanks for the hospitality. And the nap. Next time I'll try to be a little more alert.' Then: 'Why are you looking at me like that?'

Sometimes, I had learned, you can stagger men with complete honesty.

'I was wondering,' I told him, 'if you had asked to spend the night, not on the couch but in my bed, what I would have said.'

He took me in his arms, pressed. He was very warm, solid, comforting. He touched my hair.

'When you decide,' he said, 'may I be the first to know?'

'Absolutely,' I promised.

'Ah, Dunk,' he said, almost groaning, 'what the hell is going on here?'

'I'm not going to worry about it,' I said. 'Are you?'

He moved away and stared at me. 'There's more to you than meets the eye,' he said.

'That's right,' I agreed. 'I'm not just another pretty face.'

We both broke up and, like imbeciles, shook hands firmly before he left.

10

HAVE YOU ever had an experience like this:

You're trying to remember the name of an old friend, or the title of an old tune, or who played the male lead in an old movie – and you can't recall no matter how much you worry it, no matter how many names and titles your mind suggests. You go to sleep, still stymied.

Then you wake up in the morning – and there it is! Your brain worked while you slept and dredged up the recollection you sought.

I had related the details of the packing and transfer of the Havistock Collection from East 79th Street to Grandby & Sons on Madison Avenue at least a dozen times, to various people. And I had gone over the sequence of events in my own mind another dozen times. In all those retellings, I had searched for something missed, something that I, and everyone else, had overlooked that might provide a vital key to the mystery.

I sat up in bed the next morning, wide-awake, knowing what had been missed, and furious with myself for not having seen it before. But then, as far as I knew, no one else had either.

I showered, washed my hair, and wondered for the hundredth time what I could do with my mop. It wasn't short and it wasn't long; it just sort of hung there with no wave, no curl. And for the hundredth time I vowed that as soon as I got a few bucks ahead, I'd surrender myself to a hairdresser – someone named Louis or Pierre – and let him do with me what he would.

I looked at my Snoopy watch, but it was too early for Hobart Juliana to be in the office, too early for me to confirm the Great Revelation that had brought me sitting upright in bed that morning. So I went out, bought a buttered bagel and the *Times*, came back and made a cup of instant decaf.

I kept watching the kitchen clock, and at 9:30 I called Grandby & Sons, hoping Hobie wasn't off somewhere on a field appraisal. But

67

he was there and sounded delighted to hear from me. We chatted and laughed for almost ten minutes, and I got caught up on all the latest office gossip at Grandby's, including the rumor that Felicia Dodat had been to a plastic surgeon and was contemplating a fanny lift.

Then I turned serious and got down to the reason for my call.

'Hobie,' I said, 'something has come up, and I need your help.'

'Of course,' he said immediately. 'Anything.'

'On the day the Havistock Collection was shipped, I came back to Grandby's to accept delivery. I stood in the vault and signed a receipt for the thirteen cases. Then you came down, bringing me a coffee. Remember? I wanted you to see the Demaretion, so I opened the thirteenth container and slid out the display case. That's when we saw the Demaretion was missing. Is all that correct, Hobie?'

'Exactly,' he said, picking up on my earnestness and not joking anymore. 'That's just how it happened; I'll swear to it.'

'All right. Now, when I held the empty case out to you, do you remember how it was sealed?'

'Sure. There were strips of masking tape on all four sides, overlapping the glass lid. And in front, near the lock, there was a blob of sealing wax on the junction of lid and case. The wax had an imprint. You said it had been made by Havistock's signet ring.'

'You're positive of that, Hobie? You saw the wax seal and you saw the imprint?'

'Absolutely.'

'Thank you, darling,' I said. 'I saw it, too. I just wanted confirmation.'

Silence. Then . . .

'And that's all you're going to tell me, Dunk?' he said, disappointed.

'For the time being. Until I check it out.'

'You're onto something, aren't you?'

'I think so. I think I've found something important. Talk to you later, dear, and thanks for your help.'

I hung up before he could ask more questions. I sat back, sipped the tepid remains of my coffee, and went over again what I had discovered.

That thirteenth display case I had shown to Hobie in Grandby's vault had been sealed in just the way he recalled. And the patch of wax had been imprinted with Mr Havistock's signet ring, in exactly the same manner the wax seals on the other twelve cases had been imprinted. I would testify to that in a court of law.

Going by masculine logic – I admit it comes in handy, occasionally – that meant:

1. Archibald Havistock had used his signet ring to seal an empty display case.

Or 2. Someone had stolen or 'borrowed' the ring to seal an empty display case.

Or 3. There was a duplicate, one or more, of the signet ring, and the copy had been used to seal the empty case.

And Al Georgio hadn't seen it! And Jack Smack hadn't seen it! I confess I laughed aloud with delight. The great detectives! And knew immediately I wasn't going to tell either of them. Not yet. I had the ball now, and I remembered the feeling: rush down the court, timing, lift, and the slam-dunk. When everything went perfectly, there was no thrill like it.

And best of all, I now had a reason – my reason – for calling Orson Vanwinkle: I had to find out about that stupid signet ring. I thought a long time about how I should handle it. I didn't want to *lie* to anyone, exactly, but I didn't want to blab either.

The first thing I did was hunt up Jack Smack's business card. I called, but a secretary with an English accent said he was out of the office, but if I'd leave my number, she'd have 'Mr Smeck' – that's how she pronounced it – get back to me as soon as possible. He called two minutes later, so he must have been in the loo – right?

'Dunk!' he said. 'Good morning. Sorry I disturbed your tête-à-tête last night.'

'That's all right,' I said. 'No harm done. Jack, I've decided to try to have a meeting with Orson Vanwinkle.'

'Good,' he said. 'Glad to hear it.'

'I figured I'd call him and say how devastated I am by the loss of the Demaretion – which I am – and be very apologetic, and ask him to convey my regrets to Mr Havistock. How does that sound?'

'He won't believe a word of it,' Smack said promptly. 'He'll think you're warm for his form and just called to set up a meet. That guy's got an ego that doesn't end. But that's okay; we can use that.'

'Well, what do you want me to get out of him? I'm not going to enjoy this.'

'I know that, Dunk, but if I didn't think you could handle it, I wouldn't have suggested it. If he comes on too strong, just tell him to get lost. I'd like to learn two things: One: Have there been any other thefts from the Havistock apartment, like silver, plate, cash, pieces of art – small things that could easily be carried out. I'm thinking of Natalie now; she's capable of lifting stuff like that to keep her sewing circle in grass. Two: Are Ross Minchen and Vanessa Havistock having a thing? I picked up some scuttlebutt that suggests they might be making nice-nice together. If anyone would know, it would be Orson Vanwinkle. He's the kind of guy who gets pleasure from knowing everyone is as rotten as he is.'

'All right, Jack,' I said, 'I'll try to find out. No guarantees.'

'I understand that. And I want you to know that I appreciate what you're doing to help me. Can I call you later, Dunk?'

'No,' I said, 'I'll call you. After I see Vanwinkle – if I do.'

'Maybe we can have dinner tonight.'

'Maybe,' I said.

In for a penny, in for a pound; so I called Orson Vanwinkle, determined to be sorrowful and regretful. I asked timidly if he would convey my apologies to Archibald Havistock on the loss of his Demaretion.

'Sure, doll,' Vanwinkle said, with what I can only describe as an Evil Chuckle. 'I'll tell the old man. Hey, how's about you and me getting together?'

As my grandmother said – a lounge lizard.

'Such as?' I asked.

'Let me take a look at my schedule. Ah, yes, I have a business lunch at the Four Seasons at one o'clock today. Silly things: tax shelters and all that. I should get them off my back in time to meet you at the Four Seasons' bar at three o'clock. We'll have a drink or two and tell each other the stories of our lives. How does that sound?'

'Sounds fine,' I said faintly. 'All right, I'll be there. You will tell Mr Havistock how sorry I am?'

'Trust me, babe,' he said, and hung up.

In that short conversation I had been 'doll' and 'babe.' Could 'sweetie' and 'chick' be far away?

Now's a good time to tell you something about the geography of my apartment, because it has a lot to do with what transpired in the next few weeks.

It was a basement (or ground floor) apartment that you entered by coming down three steps from the sidewalk (past the plastic garbage cans) in a short hallway. A staircase led to the upper five floors of the brownstone. My pad was at the end of the ground-floor corridor.

70

It was called a 'garden apartment' (ha-ha), but it did have a back door giving access to a small patch of desert shaded by one noble ailanthus tree. I had tried to grow other things in that sad, scrabbly scrap of earth. Forget it.

You came into my place via a short hallway, just wide enough for a narrow sideboard and two nothing chairs. The bedroom was on your right. Straight ahead was the living-dining room area: large enough, I admit, but with a ceiling so low I was always afraid of scraping my scalp. The little john was to the left of that, and to the right was the compact kitchen with a barred door that led to my 'garden.'

I'm not complaining, mind you. It was rent-regulated; I was lucky to have it, and I knew it. In Des Moines, we had a three-story detached house with five bedrooms, three bathrooms, and a kitchen almost as large as my entire West 83rd Street manse. Plus a two-car garage. Plus a front lawn and a backyard. But I tried not to think of all that.

Anyway I had three or four hours to kill before my date with Orson Vanwinkle, so I decided to spend them cleaning. Housework is just as mechanical as needlework, but not nearly as rewarding or creative. Because you have to do it over and over; it's never finished.

I stripped to bikini briefs, covered my hair with a plastic shower cap, and set to work. Straightening. Washing. Vacuuming. Dusting. What a drag! Is there anything duller? I've heard that some women enjoy it. Nuts. The only good thing about it is that it's brainless; you can slave away while your thoughts and dreams take off.

I didn't spend those three hours puzzling the conundrum of the missing Demaretion; I spent them comparing the personalities and physical attractions of Al Georgio and Jack Smack. I even went so far, I confess, to say aloud 'Mary Lou Georgio' and 'Mary Lou Smack.'

But you must understand that I was unmarried, pushing the Big Three-Oh, and beginning to wonder where I'd be in five or ten years. Still manless with only an ailanthus tree for company? So sure I fantasized, imagining all kinds of crazy scenarios.

It seemed to me that Al was a true-blue kind of guy, solid and steady. I knew I could trust him, and, if I needed anything, he'd be there. But his job! He told me it came first; it was the reason for his divorce. How could any woman deal with that kind of competition?

Jack was a tap dancer, slight and debonair. The only way a wife could keep him from straying would be to nail him to the bed. The

71

guy was a conscienceless Romeo; I just knew it. But still, he was *soo* handsome and had so much sex appeal it was coming out his ears. You couldn't fault him for that; it's the way he was.

So I spent those housecleaning hours in silly reveries, enjoying every minute. You must realize that having one man in my life to daydream about was an Event. Two men were a Blessing. I didn't count Orson Vanwinkle; he was a Disaster.

It came time for me to shower (again) and get ready for my meeting with the Disaster. I won't bore you with the problems women of my height have in dressing attractively. Hobart Juliana gave me the best advice: Keep it simple. Solid colors. No plaids, no patterns. Avoid ruffles, ribbons, bows, and little girl fanciness. Stick to a chemise silhouette that hints of what's underneath but doesn't reveal. And if you've got no boobs (I hadn't – to speak of), show your back. I had a good strong, muscled back; I knew it. Sometimes I wished I could go through life in reverse.

Anyway, for my cocktail date with Vanwinkle, I wore a loose sheath of black silk crepe. Cut high in front and low enough in back so that a bra strap would have shown if I had worn one – which I didn't. Also, black lace pantyhose, and a single strand of carved wooden beads I had bought in a Mexican place in Greenwich Village. They were kitschy, but I liked them.

I must have done something right, because when I showed up at the Four Seasons' bar (fifteen minutes late – deliberately), Orson Vanwinkle almost fell off his barstool to greet me.

'Hey, hey,' he said, with a lip-smacking grin, 'you look ravishing – and if there weren't any people around, I would.'

He leaned forward and upward to kiss my cheek while I wondered how many times he had used that line.

It didn't take me long to realize he was smashed: eyes slightly out of focus, speech a bit slurred, tottery on his feet – and even wavering when he was sitting down. That must have been some business lunch.

He was working on a big drink: dark brown liquid on the rocks. I didn't know what it was, but it looked lethal. I decided that if I was going to get any information out of him, I better do it quickly before he became comatose.

'What'll you have, sweetie?' he asked, putting a heavy hand on my knee. 'I'm having a double cognac to settle the old tum-tum. Join me?'

'Just a glass of white wine, please.'

He snapped his fingers at the bartender. I hate it when men do that.

When my drink was served, he insisted on clinking his glass against mine. 'Here's to us,' he burbled. 'I have the feeling this is going to be the beginning of a beautiful friendship.'

He was such an *oozy* character I could hardly stand it.

'Mr Vanwinkle—' I started, but he interrupted by putting a finger on my lips. That was nice. I wanted to run out immediately and get a shot of penicillin.

'Orson, chick,' he said. 'Call me Orson. Or better yet, Horsy. That's what my best friends call me.'

'Why Horsy?'

He giggled. 'It's a long, dirty story. I'd tell you, but I don't know you well enough – yet.'

I stared at him, thinking he wasn't a *bad*-looking man, despite that beaky nose. He was beautifully shaved – something I always noticed about men – and his olive skin looked like felt. He dressed expensively, with a lot of gold glitter. Actually he would be a reasonably attractive package – if only he could learn to keep his big fat mouth shut.

'Orson,' I said, 'the theft of the Demaretion has really upset me, and I'd like to see it cleared up. I've been put on leave of absence until the crook is caught, so I have a personal interest in getting the case solved. The detectives seem to think someone in the household might be responsible. I wanted to ask you: Have there been any other robberies? Like silver, plate, cash, bric-à-brac – things like that?'

He bleared at me a moment, then squinched his eyes as if he was thinking deeply. 'Noo,' he said finally, 'can't recall anything recent. About five years ago a temporary maid lifted fifty bucks from Mama Havistock's purse, but there haven't been any rip-offs since then that I know about.'

I shook my head in mock amazement. 'That's a very unusual family.'

'Unusual?' he said, and moved his lumpy hand on my knee a little farther up. 'Bunch of wackos. I'm related, you know, but not on *that* side of the family, thank God. They should all be going to a shrink. Maybe they could get a wholesale rate. Ready for another drink?'

'Not yet, thank you. But you go ahead.'

He snapped his fingers again, and when the bartender turned, pointed to his empty glass. He watched the brandy being poured

73

with the careful attention of the serious drinker. Then he picked up the filled glass and sipped delicately, demonstrating that he was an epicure and not a boozer. Hah!

'Oh, I don't think the Havistock family is *that* bad,' I said. 'Of course, I haven't met all of them. Vanessa, for instance.'

'A slut,' he said darkly. 'She is not one of my favorite human beings.'

'I've heard some wild stories about her.'

'You can believe all of them, honey. Did you know she's got a tattoo?'

'You're joking?'

He held up a palm. 'Scout's honor. I haven't seen it myself, but I have it on *very* good authority. An informed source, you might say. I won't tell you where it's, uh, located; you wouldn't believe it. Slut. She thinks she invented sex and has a patent on it. She leaves me cold.'

Which meant, I supposed, that at some time in their relationship Vanessa Havistock had rejected Orson Vanwinkle. He reminded me of men who, when a woman rebuffs their advances, assume the woman is a lesbian. Of course. The fact that the guy has bad breath, a complexion like the surface of the moon, and wears white socks has nothing to do with it.

'Yes,' I said thoughtfully, 'I heard she comes on strong.'

'To men, women, doorknobs, and cocker spaniels,' he said with a nasty laugh. 'She even came on to Ross Minchen, who could be president of the International Association of Nerds. But the old man soon put an end to that.'

It was the second time I had heard that story; Nettie had told me the same thing at lunch.

'So there's nothing between them now?' I asked. 'Vanessa and Ross Minchen?'

'*Nada*,' he said. 'At parties he still sniffs around her like a yak in heat, but she won't give him a tumble. Listen, the old man told her to lay off, and he controls the bucks. She's smart enough not to cross him.'

So now I had discovered what Jack Smack had asked me to find out. It was time to do some sleuthing on my own – before the blitzed Horsy Vanwinkle fell off his barstool.

But I had waited too long. He stood suddenly, swaying, and drained his new drink, just chugalugged it straight down. I thought, next stop Intensive Care.

74

'Let's go,' he said thickly.

'Go?' I said, Little Miss Innocence. 'Where?'

'My place,' he said with a wolfish grin. 'We'll listen to some Sinatra tapes and let nature take its course.'

'Don't you have to get back to work?'

'I work when I feel like it,' he said, boasting, 'and I play when I feel like it.'

Dunk, I told myself, you've got problems.

I won't tell you all the aggravations of the next hour. Well, yes, I will tell you: Getting him to pay the bill at the Four Seasons' bar – with a credit card, of course; I was a business expense. Then half-supporting him down the stairs to the street. His Juicy Fruit cologne overwhelmed me.

Then, outside, it took forever to get a cab, while Horsy leaned against the Seagram Building and sang 'My Way' in a froggy tenor to the great amusement of passersby. And then in the taxi, he refused to tell the driver, or me, where he lived. I finally had to pluck his wallet from his inside jacket pocket as he giggled and tried to embrace me. I got his address from a card that testified he was a paid-up member of Club Exotica – whatever that was.

When I told the driver our destination, on East 85th Street, he said, 'You sure you want to go there, lady? I think I should deliver this nut to Bellevue.'

There wasn't enough cash in the wallet to pay the cab fare, so I had to make up the difference. I wasn't in a happy mood when I dragged him out of the taxi and implored him to straighten up and fly right. As a matter of fact, I came close to leaving him in a collapsed heap on the sidewalk and letting him survive on his own. But I was determined to find out about Archibald Havistock's signet ring.

He lived on the third floor of a six-story gray stone town-house. Getting him to fish out his keys from his trouser pocket was a Keystone Kops comedy in itself, with grapplings, staggerings, and foiled embraces.

I finally got the keys, opened the front door, and wrestled us both inside. There was an elevator, thank God, and I propped him against one wall while we went up. More strugglings and fumblings outside his door, but at last we were inside and I had succeeded in getting this calamity safely home and still conscious.

'Got to see—' he said with a glassy grin, and went rushing for what I hoped was the john. Maybe, I prayed, the idiot would

75

upchuck the business lunch and all that brandy and would return to me sober and chastened. No such luck.

Meanwhile I looked around at a trendy pad right out of *Playboy*. Stainless steel, glass, director's chairs in blond leather, imitation Motherwells on white walls, zebra rugs, enough electronic equipment to blow a dozen fuses, a fully equipped bar with wet sink – well, you get the picture. I didn't peek into the bedroom, but if it had mirrors on the ceiling I wouldn't have been a bit surprised.

It wasn't the glitz that shook me so much as the cost of all that flash in a townhouse on East 85th Street. Either Vanwinkle was making a giant salary as secretary to Archibald Havistock, or he was independently wealthy, or he had a secondary source of income that paid very well indeed.

And yet, when I asked Natalie Havistock if there was anything doing between Vanessa and Orson Vanwinkle, she said she doubted it. 'He's got no money, so Vanessa wouldn't be interested.' That's what Nettie had said.

Jack Smack had been right: there was something cheesy about the man.

Mr Roquefort himself came staggering out of the bedroom, and I didn't know whether to laugh or to cry. He had put on a red velvet smoking jacket with black satin lapels and sash, a silk ascot clumsily knotted at his throat, a paisley square spilling out of his breast pocket. I suppose it was his seduction uniform, but with his loopy smile and shambling gait, he looked like a clown.

'Now then . . .' he said, 'first things first . . .'

I thought he might fall over at any moment, but he navigated his way to the bar without bumping into any of the furniture. He poured himself a tumbler of brandy and a beer stein of warm white wine for me. If he had any ice available, he either forgot it or didn't want any dilution.

He collapsed on a couch shaped like two enormous red lips and patted the cushion beside him. 'You sit here, babe,' he said.

I took my schooner of wine and sat on the lips – at a wary distance. Sitting on that crazy couch was an unsettling experience. I expected the mouth to open up at any moment and swallow me down.

'Music,' he said, looking about vaguely. 'Sinatra tapes.'

'Later,' I said. 'Why don't we just talk for a while.'

'About what?' he said, looking at me blearily.

I told you he wore a lot of gold glitter, and he did. Chunky little ingot links on his cuffs, a Piaget Polo with gold strap, a gleaming

76

identification bracelet on the other wrist – the chain heavy enough to anchor the *QE2*. And on the third finger of his right hand, a square gold ring set with a sparkling diamond.

That was my cue.

'What a beautiful ring you have,' I said.

He looked down at it. 'Two carats,' he said, nodding. 'Flawless.'

'You do all right,' I said, laughing lightly. 'And all Mr Havistock has is that sad little signet ring.'

'Oh, hell, he doesn't *wear* that. It's a clunker. A piece of junk. I think Mama gave it to him when they got married. He just keeps it around.'

'Keeps it around?' I said. 'Where? If it has such sentimental value for him, you'd think he'd wear it or keep it locked up.'

'Nah,' Orson Vanwinkle said. 'It's either on his desk in the library or maybe in his jewelry box in the bedroom. He's not *that* sentimental.'

Which told me what I hadn't wanted to hear: anyone in that freaky family would have easy access to the signet ring.

'Listen,' Horsy said, 'you're not drinking. You still have your drinkee-poo. Come on, let the good times roll. Let's have a party.'

'Sure,' I said, 'why not? But let me take a look at your marvelous apartment.'

I rose, wandered behind him, and succeeded in dumping half my wine in the planter of an inoffensive ficus tree. I figured that within a day or two the poor thing would be dead – or maybe it would be twice as tall.

'Beautiful apartment,' I said. 'Just splendid.'

'You like it?' he said, beginning to mumble. 'Wanna move in – temporarily?'

'Oh, Horsy,' I said, 'you sweep a girl off her feet.'

I glanced at him to see how he was taking this bit of mild whimsy and to my horror I saw he was listing badly. He was slowly, slowly slumping sideways, his whole body leaning limply. I hastily came around in front of him and lifted the glass of brandy from his fingers.

I watched, fascinated, as he became hors de combat – you should excuse the expression. Within a moment he was completely out, eyes closed, breathing stertorously. His upper torso had fallen sideways onto the crimson lips. I lifted up his legs, made him as comfortable as I could, and looked down at him.

'Oh,' I intoned aloud, 'how have the mighty fallen.' But he didn't stir.

I cabbed home, and had just enough money to pay the driver, though I had to undertip him.

'Sorry about that,' I said, 'but it's all I have.'

'That's okay, lady,' he said cheerily. 'Give us a kiss and all is forgiven.'

'Catch you next time,' I said hastily, and scurried into my sanctuary, locking, bolting, and chaining the door behind me.

I slumped into my favorite chair, brooding about the last few hours. I was surprised to find I felt a little more kindly toward Orson Vanwinkle. Sympathy, I guess. The poor poop. Trying so hard to be something he could never be. But pity didn't stop me from wondering about his flashy wealth. Where *was* his money coming from?

That was exactly the same question Jack Smack asked when he called a few hours later. I gave him a rundown of my afternoon with Orson Vanwinkle, leaving out only the business about Havistock's signet ring. That was *my* baby. But I told Jack everything else, including Horsy's fervid pantings and grapplings.

Smack totally disregarded that. 'Where *is* the guy getting his loot?' he said. 'Not from his secretarial job. I can't believe dear old Uncle Archibald pays that much. I'll have to look into it.'

'Will you tell me what you find out?' I asked him.

'Sure, Dunk,' he said. 'We're partners, aren't we? And there's nothing between Vanessa and Orson?'

'No romance, if that's what you're thinking. He kept calling her a slut, and I think he was sincere.'

'Curiouser and curiouser,' Jack said. 'By the way, we closed all the venetian blinds on our floor like the anonymous letter writer wanted, signaling our willingness to make a deal, but we haven't heard anything more from him. Not yet. Hey, Dunk, how about some dinner tonight?'

'No,' I said promptly, 'thank you, but I can't make it.'

'Sure,' he said, not at all put out. 'We'll make it another time. Have a good evening. I'll be in touch.'

A minute later I was wondering why I had rejected him. I was all dressed up with no place to go, and he was a handsome, dashing guy. Considering the state of my checking account, I could have used a free dinner.

I think my quick decision had something to do with that afternoon with Orson Vanwinkle. I'd had enough of men for one day. I was tired of the hassle. I suppose that sounds stupid, that a brief encounter with a drunken idiot could sour me on the entire male sex, even for one evening, but that's the way it was.

So I got out of my silk sheath, Mexican beads, and black lace pantyhose, and pulled on my ratty flannel bathrobe with the frayed cord. I had a can of Campbell's chicken soup and a salami sandwich. *Bas cuisine.*

And spent a lonely and forlorn evening. Sometimes I don't understand myself.

11

THEY SAT as solidly as Easter Island statues – Mr Archibald
Havistock and Mrs Mabel Havistock – grim-visaged monoliths
glowering at me. I won't say I was frightened, but I was awed.

Both were stiffly erect, and I wondered if, in private, they ever
allowed themselves the pleasure of slumping. Probably not. In their
world it simply wasn't *done*. She so hard, square, and chunky; he so
impeccably groomed and complete. They could have posed for 'Urban
American Gothic'; both had steel in them, and not a little arrogance.

I had received a phone call from Orson Vanwinkle about ten
o'clock that morning. No indication of hangover, no apologies. And
he spoke in such circumspect tones I was certain someone was
standing at his elbow.

'Miss Bateson,' he said, 'Mr and Mrs Havistock would like to
meet with you here at their apartment at eleven-thirty this morning.
Will that be satisfactory?'

'Meet with me?' I said, startled. 'What for?'

'Ah . . . to discuss a matter to your advantage. Will you be able to
make it?'

'Okay,' I said breezily, 'I'll be there.'

I was greeted at the door by housekeeper Ruby Querita, dour as
ever, and ushered into that Frank Campbell living room. And there
sat Archy and Mabel, planted, as if they had grown to their velvet
club chairs, unable or unwilling to rise and greet me.

They wasted no time getting down to business. Mrs Havistock
carried the ball. I admired the way she lifted her chin as she spoke. It
almost smoothed out the wattles. Almost.

'Miss Bateson,' she said crisply, 'you impress me – you impress *us*,
my husband and me – as an intelligent and alert young lady.'

She paused, and I didn't know whether to simper or dig a toe into
their Aubusson and mutter an 'Aw, shucks.'

'I am sure,' she continued, 'you are aware of the activities of Detective Georgio of the New York Police Department and Mr John Smack, who represents the insurance company covering the loss of the Demaretion by Grandby and Sons.'

'I know both men,' I said cautiously.

'Then I am sure you are aware that both feel the theft was committed by a member of my – by a member of our family.'

'Ridiculous!' Archibald Havistock said angrily.

I said nothing.

'There are two factors to be considered . . .' Mrs Havistock went on. 'First, while any member of this family is under suspicion, recompense for the loss of the Demaretion will be delayed. Second, we deem it a personal insult that a family member should be suspected. All that dreadful publicity! I was brought up, Miss Bateson, to believe that a lady's name appeared in the public print only three times: when she was born, married, and died. I absolutely deny that any Havistock could be capable of such a crime. Archibald, do you agree with me?'

'Absolutely,' he boomed out in his resonant voice.

'What I – what we would like to propose,' Mrs Havistock said, 'is that we employ you in a private capacity. To investigate the robbery of this valuable piece of property.'

It took me a couple of ticks to realize she was talking about the Demaretion. It was like calling the Mona Lisa 'a valuable piece of property.'

Then as my resentment faded, astonishment set in. They wanted to hire *me* to find out whodunit! I was as shocked as if I had been floored under the basket while going up for a dunk shot. Apparently she took my shaken silence for doubt or rejection because she started the hard sell:

'We know that you are on leave of absence from Grandby's, so your time is your own. We can promise you complete cooperation – not only from my husband and myself, but from all the members of our family. Naturally, we expect to pay for your services. We feel that neither of the two official investigators has your knowledge of the inside world of numismatics.'

By that time my wits had settled back into place. 'Mrs Havistock,' I said, 'if you wish to hire me to investigate the theft of the Demaretion, I'd be happy to take the assignment, and be very appreciative of your trust in me. But if you're hiring me to give your entire family a clean bill of health, that I cannot do. I would like the

81

job – but with no guarantees that I won't find a family member guilty.'

They turned slowly to stare at each other. If a signal passed between them, I didn't see it.

'Look, Mrs Havistock,' I argued, 'you and your husband have complete faith in the loyalty of your family. That's very commendable, but you can't expect me to become a partner in any cover-up, if one becomes necessary. That I won't do, and the deal is off. But if you're willing to give me carte blanche, tell me to try to find out who stole the Demaretion, and let the chips fall where they may, then yes, I would accept – but only under those conditions.'

'Archibald,' she said, troubled, 'what do you think?'

'Let's do it,' he said. 'I think Miss Bateson's conditions are reasonable.'

'Very well,' she said, lifting her heavy chin again, 'we will employ you with the understanding that there will be no restrictions on your investigation. We will pay you four hundred dollars a week, plus expenses, for a period of one month. At the end of that time we will meet again to review your progress and determine whether your investigation should continue under the same terms, or whether your employment should be terminated. Is that satisfactory?'

'Yes, it is,' I said promptly, 'as long as you can promise me the cooperation of all the members of your family.'

'I can promise you that,' Archibald Havistock said grimly. 'In return, I ask only that in the unlikely event you discover a member of the family is the thief, I will be told before you take your information to the authorities.'

I nodded, never imagining the horrendous results of my casual agreement.

So we settled things, and he went into his den-library and returned with a check for four hundred dollars, which I accepted gratefully. We then decided it would be best if they reported to Al Georgio and Jack Smack that I had been employed as their private snoop, and ask both men to cooperate with me fully.

'How do you intend to start?' Mr Havistock asked curiously.

I didn't have to ponder that. 'I think I've met all your immediate family except for Mr and Mrs Luther Havistock. I would like to talk to your son and daughter-in-law this evening, but it would help if you'd call them first, explain who I am and what my job is. Then I'll call for an appointment.'

'I'll arrange it,' Mrs Havistock said decisively. 'You'll have no problem there. They will see you.'

What a gorgon! But I hadn't the slightest doubt that she would deliver. This was one grande dame, and when she said, 'Jump!' the other Havistocks asked only, 'How high?'

They both had the decency to rise when I departed. We shook hands formally, and I promised to deliver periodic verbal reports on my progress. We all agreed it would be best to put nothing in writing.

When I exited from the living room, Orson Vanwinkle was waiting for me in that muffled corridor. He might have been listening at the living room door or peering through the keyhole; I wouldn't have put it past him.

He conducted me to the outside door, looked about warily, then clamped a hot hand on my shoulder, leaning forward to whisper:

'Was it as good for you as it was for me?'

'Unforgettable,' I told him.

He gave me a smarmy smile.

I hadn't been home more than an hour when the phone calls started coming in. The first two were from Al Georgio and Jack Smack. I thought both men would be outraged at my accepting employment as a private detective to inquire into a crime they were investigating, but they seemed to accept my new job with equanimity.

'Look,' Al said, 'you'll be able to get closer to the family than I can with a badge. We'll trade information, won't we?'

'Of course,' I said. 'I'm counting on it.'

'We're still partners, aren't we?' Jack Smack asked. 'I'll keep you up to speed on what I'm doing, and you tip me on anything you dig out. Okay?'

'Of course,' I said. 'I'm counting on it.'

Their reasonableness surprised me. Until I decided that neither of them considered me a threat. What investigative experience did I have? I was just a long drink of water with a passion for pizza and more energy than brains. They might use me, but I don't think either of them took me seriously. That was all right; if they wanted to believe me a lightweight, I'd go along with that. It had something to do with catching more flies with honey than you can with vinegar.

The third phone call was from Vanessa Havistock, and it wasn't as pleasant. As a matter of fact, it was downright snarly.

'I have been informed,' she stated in icy tones, 'that my husband and I are expected to meet with you this evening and answer your questions about the burglary.'

'Robbery,' I said. 'I hope it won't be too much of an inconvenience, Mrs Havistock. I can make it at any time you suggest, and I promise you it shouldn't take long.'

'We have already answered endless questions by the New York City detective and that man with the odd name from the insurance company. How much longer are we to be harassed in this manner?'

I could feel my temper beginning to simmer, but I was determined to play it cool. Making an enemy of this woman would get me nowhere.

'I know how distressing it must be for you, Mrs Havistock,' I said meekly. 'But really, no one wishes to harass you. All we're seeking is information.'

'But I know nothing about it. Absolutely nothing.'

'You were there when the coin was taken,' I pointed out. 'At the birthday party planned for your mother-in-law. It's possible you noticed something that made no impression on you at the time, but which might provide a vital clue in solving the crime.'

A two-beat pause, then . . .

'You really think so?' she said thoughtfully. 'That I might know something I don't know I know?'

'It's quite possible,' I said earnestly. 'That's why I'm so anxious to talk to you and your husband. To refresh your memories and see if we can uncover something that will help end this dreadful affair.'

'It's been a nightmare. All those tabloid stories . . . Even my hairdresser wants to talk about it. Oh, very well,' she said, reverting to her petulant tone, 'we'll see you at six-thirty this evening. We'll give you an hour. No more.'

She hung up abruptly. I was looking forward to meeting that vixen. I decided to dress in my dowdiest, like Eliza Doolittle, the guttersnipe, before Professor Higgins converts her to a grand lady. I wanted Vanessa Havistock to feel immediately superior to me, to underestimate me and believe she had nothing to fear.

I made the fourth telephone call. Because the Havistocks were paying expenses, I called Enoch Wottle in Tucson, Arizona. Since he left New York, we had corresponded frequently, exchanging letters at least once a month. I often asked his advice on numismatic matters, not so much that I needed it, but because I wanted him to feel his perception and experience were still valued.

But this was the first time we had talked together in almost three years, and it was a touching experience for both of us. I know I cried a little, and I think he was similarly affected. We spent the first few minutes getting caught up on personal matters: his arthritis, my lack of suitors, his son's home and the grandchildren.

'Enoch,' I said, 'tell me the truth: how do you like Tucson?'

He sighed. 'Manhattan it ain't,' he said with heavy good humor. 'You want a hot pastrami sandwich at two in the morning, where do you go?'

I laughed. 'Enoch, you never in your life ate a hot pastrami sandwich at two in the morning.'

'I know,' he agreed, 'but in New York you know it's *there*.'

Then I got down to business. I had already written him about the loss of the Demaretion, and he had read about it in the newspapers and numismatic journals to which he still subscribed. Now I brought him up to date on recent happenings, including my employment by the Havistocks. He cautioned me about that.

'Dunk, darling,' he said, 'you are dealing here with someone who took the risk of stealing something worth a great deal of money. That can only mean someone desperate. I beg you, be very, very careful. People stupid enough to commit such a crime may do even more reckless things. Do not endanger yourself.'

'Don't worry about me, Enoch,' I said. 'I can take care of myself.'

Ah, the optimism of the innocent!

Then I told him I had supplied Jack Smack with a list of coin dealers all over the world, and his insurance company was getting out letters of warning, asking for information on anyone trying to peddle the stolen Demaretion.

'Now you know that's not going to do much good,' I said. 'There are some dealers who'll do anything to turn a buck, especially if they're buying for a client. The Demaretion could disappear into a private collection and never be seen again.'

'I'm afraid you're right,' he said mournfully.

I told him that I knew he had many old friends in the trade, and asked if he could call or write the most knowledgeable of his contacts and see if he could pick up any information, or even gossip, about a Demaretion coming on the market.

'The Havistocks will pay all expenses,' I said, 'but I admit it'll be a lot of work for you.'

'Work?' he said. 'Not work but a pleasure. Of course I'll do it. I'll get started today. You know, by now that dekadrachm could be in Sweden, Saudi Arabia, Iceland – anywhere. Smuggling a single coin across borders is the easiest thing imaginable. You put it in your pocket with your other coins. What customs inspector wants to look at small change? Of course, Dunk, I will be happy to see what I can find out. It will give me something to do. My son insists I play shuffleboard. I *hate* shuffleboard.'

Then I told him of the anonymous letter Finkus, Holding, Inc., had received, purportedly from the crook, asking if they'd be interested in a buy-back. They had signaled an affirmative but, as far as I knew, had not yet received a second letter.

'I don't know,' Enoch Wottle said dubiously. 'It sounds like a con game to me. After a major theft like this by some big shark, the barracudas gather around, hoping to pull a smaller swindle. But you never know. Dunk, this is a fascinating chase. I will do what I can to help. Please call me as often as you like. And reverse the charges.'

'Nonsense,' I said airily. 'I'm on an expense account. Goodbye, Enoch, dear, and stay well.'

'I survive,' he said philosophically. 'At my age that's an accomplishment.'

I spent the remainder of that afternoon mentally drafting the questions I wanted to ask Luther and Vanessa Havistock. Actually, I had little hope of learning anything startling from either of them, despite what I had told Vanessa of the possibility of her knowing something vital she didn't realize she knew.

What I wanted, most of all, was to meet them personally and get a splanchnic reaction. I had done the same thing with Roberta and Ross Minchen, and temporarily decided they were the wimpiest of wimps. But from what I had heard about Vanessa Havistock, she was cut from a different bolt of cloth. Gold lamé.

Natalie had called her a bitch. Al Georgio said she exuded sex. Orson Vanwinkle had insisted she was a slut. With a tattoo. Location not specified. And, from all accounts, father Archibald Havistock had to intervene to forestall a family scandal when rapacious Vanessa came on to Ross Minchen.

(But could she sink nine out of ten foul shots with one hand? I could.)

So I dressed like a ragamuffin for my meeting with Mr and Mrs Luther Havistock, feeling in a merry mood and wondering if I should take along a pen and pad and take notes as they answered my questions. I decided against it, figuring they'd speak more freely if they knew their words weren't being recorded for posterity.

Also, they'd think I was a complete incompetent. Let them.

12

Al Georgio had given me a hint of the richness of that Park Avenue apartment, but I wasn't prepared for its *splendor*. It made my modest pad look like a subway locker, and completely outclassed the Havistock home on East 79th Street and Orson Vanwinkle's *Playboy* spread on 85th. As Al had wondered, where *was* Luther's wealth coming from?

A panic sale of the stolen Demaretion?

A little gink greeted me at the door, dressed in a kind of uniform, combination chauffeur-houseman. It was deep purple whipcord with a starched white shirtfront and lilac bow tie. Different. I think he was from India, Thailand, Korea, Cambodia, Vietnam, or possibly Detroit – someplace like that. I know he had a purple eyepatch and hissed.

He ushered me into a living room that wasn't as large as Grand Central Station. Not quite. Very plushy, and so big I couldn't take it all in at one glance. I just had an initial impression of money, money, money. Original paintings, leather, glass, chrome, ankle-deep rugs, concealed lighting, crystal, brass, porcelains – it was a stage set, designed to accommodate a dozen actors.

They were standing when I entered, each with a glass in one hand, a cigarette in the other. Hi, there, Noel Coward! But they were affable enough, not bothering to shake hands but offering me a martini (Stolichnaya in Baccarat crystal, I noted) which I declined, and got me seated in an enormous pouf of buttery suede about ten feet away from where they took their seats on a couch upholstered in zebra skin – or maybe it was giraffe. Anyway, it was exotic as hell.

'I'm sorry to intrude upon you like this,' I began humbly, 'but I'm sure Mr Havistock has informed you that—'

'Mabel,' Vanessa interrupted sharply.

'Mrs Havistock has informed you that I have been employed to try

87

to discover what happened to the Demaretion, and in the process, hopefully, to clear members of the family of any complicity in the theft.'

'It's ridiculous!' Luther burst out. 'No one has accused any of us. It's an insult. Just because Father can't collect on the insurance . . .'

His voice trailed away, and I had a moment to take a close look at him. Not very prepossessing. A tall, attenuated man who seemed to have lost weight since he had that pinstripe tailored for him; it hung as slackly as a wet tent. Thinking it might be his first preprandial drink, I looked for the tremor Al Georgio had mentioned, and saw it.

Al thought Luther Havistock was a man teetering on the edge of economic disaster. That wasn't my take. I saw a man sliding into emotional collapse: vague stare, uncontrollable tic at the left corner of his mouth, endless crossing and recrossing of his knees, that high-pitched laugh Al had heard, and a broad, pale forehead slick with sweat that he kept swabbing with a trembling palm.

In better condition, he would have been presentable. Not as handsome as Archibald, but pleasant enough. He had a small echo of his father's firm jaw, full mouth, and ice-blue eyes. But all in a minor key, reduced and brought low. I had an absurd notion of a stalwart house, buffeted by the elements and allowed to molder and decay. No maintenance. That was Luther Havistock's problem: no maintenance.

I took them through that morning and afternoon when the Havistock Collection was packed and the Demaretion disappeared. They answered all my questions readily enough, and substantiated what Al Georgio, and I, had already learned from Mr and Mrs Archibald Havistock.

'You must realize,' Vanessa said, staring with amusement at my denim muumuu, 'it was a party day. The whole family was there. People were standing, sitting, mixing drinks, milling about. It's impossible to remember where any one person was at any particular time.'

'But do you remember your father-in-law coming into the living room for a few moments before the shipment of the collection began?'

'That I remember very well. He asked if everyone was present and having a birthday drink. Then he went back to the library.'

'I remember it, too,' Luther said. 'Father came in to play the host for a few minutes.'

'Did either of you see Mr Vanwinkle conduct the armed guards

88

into the library to start loading the coin collection for the transfer to Grandby's?'

'No,' Vanessa said. 'The living room door to the corridor was open, but I didn't notice anything. Did you, dear?'

'No.' Luther said. 'Nothing.'

I wasn't willing to give up. 'Did either of you, at any time, notice anything odd or out of the ordinary that morning? Anything that you might have shrugged off at the time, but could have some bearing on what happened?'

They looked at each other.

'Not me,' Luther said, wiping his damp brow. 'I didn't see anything.'

'Nor did I,' Vanessa said. 'Unless— No, it's too silly.'

'What was it, Mrs Havistock?'

'Well, as you probably know, the party was catered. The food had been delivered a few hours previously. All cold things. I remember wandering into the kitchen to see what we would be eating. I expected Ruby to be there, preparing the buffet. But she wasn't there. Some of the caterer's platters had been unwrapped, and some had not. As if she had left the kitchen in the middle of getting things ready.'

'Do you recall when this happened – your visit to the kitchen? Was it before or after Mr Archibald Havistock came into the living room?'

She looked at me directly, not blinking. 'I honestly can't recall.'

'And what did you do after you noticed that Ruby Querita was not there?'

'I took a piece of divine Brie from one of the uncovered platters and went back into the living room nibbling on it.'

'And was Mr Archibald Havistock in the living room when you returned?'

'I honestly don't remember. Oh, I don't suppose it means anything at all. Ruby could have gone to the front door to let someone in, or maybe she was in the john – there are a dozen innocent explanations of why she wasn't in the kitchen. But you said you wanted to know *everything*,' she added brightly, 'so I thought I'd mention it.'

Quite a woman. She was wearing a Halston sheath that would have paid my rent for two months: a tube of shimmering bottle-green satin that hung from a single shoulder strap and touched her body lightly at bosom and hip. Nothing raunchy about it, but it hinted.

She was almost as tall as her husband, but while his shrunken frame spoke of desiccation, drained of vitality, she was bursting with vigor. I could understand why men found their senses reeling and eyeballs popping. As Detective Georgio had said, she exuded sex. But there was nothing obvious about her, nothing of the hooker.

She sat demurely, ankles crossed, hands clasped in her lap. But there was no missing the ripe curves of her full body. She was not beautiful. 'Striking' is the word, with long, gleaming black hair parted in the middle, falling close in raven wings. Witchy. A coffin face saved from hardness by full, artfully colored lips. She made Felicia Dodat look like a Boy Scout.

It may have been pure bitchiness on my part, and envy, but I found her a little vulgar. There was a looseness about her that's hard to explain. She was certainly not blowsy, but I could see why men might immediately imagine her naked. Animal! That was it! She had an animal quality. In bed she might be a voracious tiger. In anger, I could see her snarling, spitting, clawing.

'Mrs Havistock,' I said boldly, 'would you say that yours is a happy family?'

'Oh, my,' she said, laughing lightly, 'that *is* a personal question. All families have skeletons in the closet, don't they? But generally speaking, I'd say yes, ours is a happy family. Wouldn't you say so, Luther?'

'Yes,' he said, busy refilling his martini glass from a crystal pitcher.

My ploy of arousing her disdain and contempt, of getting her to underestimate me, seemed to be getting nowhere. She could not have been more gracious or cooperative. Why did I have the feeling she was at least one step ahead of me?

Perhaps it was her jewelry that numbed me. With that bottle-green Halston sheath, she wore matching diamond choker, earrings, and bracelet. Nothing garish or ostentatious, mind you, but absolutely overwhelming. And she wore all that ice casually, as if each glittering stone was a merit badge.

Before I was rendered dumb by jealousy, I tried once more to get through that chromium plating Natalie had mentioned.

'Mrs Havistock, can you think of anyone, within or outside the family, who might be capable of stealing the Demaretion? Either from need of money or from motives of revenge or whatever.'

She frowned for a moment, considering. 'I honestly can't,' she said finally. 'Can you, Luther?'

'No,' he said.

It suddenly occurred to me that in the past fifteen minutes she had used the adverb 'honestly' at least three times. Maybe that was her way of talking, an affectation. But mother taught me to be suspicious of people who keep assuring you how honest they are. 'I wouldn't lie to you' and 'To tell you the truth . . .' Hang on to your wallet then, mother had said, and count your rings after you shake hands.

I knew I wasn't going to get anything more from Vanessa and Luther. I rose, thanked them for their kindness and cooperation, and moved toward the door. Then that woman did surprise me. She came close, took my arm, gave me a smile that gleamed as brightly as her diamonds.

'I like you,' she said. 'Could we have lunch?'

'Thank you,' I said, shocked. 'I'd enjoy that very much.'

'I'll give you a call,' she said, squeezing my bicep, and the purple eyepatch with the hiss showed me out.

I had Lean Cuisine spaghetti dinner that night, with some greens picked up at the salad bar at my local deli. I also had two glasses of red wine from the jug Al Georgio had left. So when he called around ten o'clock, I was in a mellow mood.

'How's the private eye doing?' he asked.

'No hits, no runs, no errors,' I said. 'At least I hope that last is correct. I saw Luther and Vanessa this evening.'

'Oh?' he said. 'That's interesting. I'd like your take on those two. And I've got a couple of goodies for you. Listen, I've finished up all the typing I had to do, and I'm on my way home to Queens. How's about I stop at your place – no more than half an hour, I swear – and we compare notes?'

'Sure,' I said, 'come ahead. I just had some of your wine so I owe you. Did you have dinner tonight?'

'Yeah, I ate.'

'What did you have?'

'A cheeseburger. At my desk. With a chocolate malt.'

I sighed. 'Al, that's no way to eat.'

'Tell me about it,' he said. 'See you in about fifteen minutes, Dunk.'

He looked wearier than ever, and accepted a glass of his red wine gratefully.

'You're working too hard,' I told him.

'Ahh,' he said, 'it comes with the territory. So how did you make out with Vanessa and Luther?'

I gave him a complete rundown. He listened intently, not interrupting. When I finished, he rose to refill his wineglass.

'That business about Ruby Querita being absent from the kitchen – that's pretty thin stuff, Dunk.'

'I know it is.'

'But I'll check it out. Ruby's brother, the guy in the clink on a drug rap – well, his lawyer is filing an appeal on the grounds of new evidence. Lawyers cost money. So maybe Ruby saw a chance of grabbing some big bucks. It doesn't listen – I don't think she's got the brains to pull it – but I'll give it a look-see. What did you think of Luther?'

'You said you thought he was in a financial bind, a potential bankrupt. Maybe. But I thought he's heading for an emotional crackup. Al, the guy is barely functioning.'

'Yeah,' he said, staring at me, 'you may be right. And Vanessa?'

'Were you attracted to her?' I asked him.

'Of course I was,' he said gruffly. 'I told you she came on to me. And even if she hadn't, I'd have been jolted. She's a lot of woman.'

'She is that,' I agreed. 'But there's more there than meets the eye. She wants to have lunch with me. She says she likes me.'

'Don't tell me she's coming on to *you*?'

'No, nothing like that. I think she just wants to know what's going on. She's figuring on becoming bosom buddies, excuse the expression, so she can pump me. Which makes me wonder why. Al, you said you had things to report.'

He loosened his tie, slumped deeper into the couch.

'A few things,' he said. 'The FBI came in on this. It's a local crime so they've got no jurisdiction. But anytime there's a heist like this – big cash or art work or, say, something small or valuable – they figure there's a good chance of it having been hustled across the state line for fencing, so they're interested. They weren't heavy about it – just wanted to know what was going on, and would I keep them informed, and did I need any help – ya-ta-ta-ta. The usual bullshit. No problem. Then we got in touch with Interpol. They're ready to cooperate – which will add a little muscle to those letters Finkus, Holding is sending out. That's Jack Smack's insurance company. Did you know they're contacting coin dealers all over the world?'

I nodded.

'Sure you did,' he said without rancor. 'And I suppose you know they got a letter from the crook, or someone who says he is, asking if they'd be interested in a buy-back?'

I nodded again.

'Well, they signaled yeah, they'd be interested, and today they got a second letter. The guy wants two hundred grand for the Demaretion.'

I looked at him, shocked. 'Al, how do you know all this? Don't tell me that Jack told you.'

He tried to laugh. 'That guy wouldn't give me the time of day. No, he didn't tell me. But I have a contact at Finkus, Holding. One hand washes the other.'

'Two hundred thousand?' I said, still astonished. 'Isn't that a lot for a thief to ask from the insurance company?'

'A lot?' he said. 'It's ridiculous!'

'What do you think Finkus, Holding, will do?'

'Try to bargain him down. They might spring for a hundred Gs – but I doubt it. They'll wait until the crook realizes he's got no other option except to take the coin to a fence and hope he can get ten percent. Then he'll settle. I still say it isn't a professional goniff. It's someone in the family.'

'Yes,' I said, 'I think you're right. Al, I could scramble you some eggs if you're hungry.'

'No,' he said, face creasing into that warm smile. 'Thanks, Dunk, but I'll skip. But I'll have a little more wine if you don't mind.'

'Help yourself. It's yours.'

I watched him as he sat brooding on the couch. Such a big, tired, *solid* man. Like Luther Havistock, he needed maintenance and wasn't getting it. I had never felt in a more comforting mood.

'Al,' I said, 'the last time you were here I said something about your staying the night in my bed – if you made the pitch. You said that when I decided, you wanted to be the first to know. All right, you are. Stay the night?'

He smiled wanly. 'You're a sweetheart, you are. I'd love to, Dunk. But I'm beat, I need a hot shower, and more than anything else I need sleep. I wouldn't be any good for you.'

'Let me be the judge of that,' I said. 'Go take your shower.'

Bodies are nice. I know that probably sounds inane, but it's true. Bodies are warm and smooth and slide on each other. I'm not talking about sex; I mean holding and hugging and saying silly things. You take your clothes off and you start giggling, don't you? Well, I do. Maybe not laughing out loud but feeling like it.

Al was wrong; he was *very* good for me. There's a lot to be said for snuggling. Closeness. That was what I had been starved for. He was no Adonis, but I was no Venus. If he had a layer of suet over hard muscles (those cheeseburgers and chocolate malts!), I was all twigs and splinters, being stretched out and bony.

Maybe it was our physical disparateness that put us in such a good mood. There was nothing heavy about what we did; it was just cuddling and kissing and touching. I think he was as hungry for it as I was. The intimacy. It doesn't always have to be sweat and shouts. It can be smiling affection.

We did some frivolous things, I suppose, but at the time they seemed important to me, and I think they were important to him. But there were no fervid avowals of passion – nothing like that. I suppose you'll think it was just a casual one-night stand, but it wasn't. It was *significant*.

I touched a reddish scar on his ribs. 'What's that?' I asked.

'A guy shot me.'

'Did it hurt?'

'No,' he said, 'it felt good.'

He kissed my hipbones, which have a nasty habit of poking up the skin. Then he kissed my stomach, which is flat and hard as a board.

'Pregnant,' he said. 'Definitely pregnant.'

'Bite your tongue,' I said.

'No,' he said. 'Yours.'

And he did.

That's the way it went. Just a man and a woman who had found a temporary cure for loneliness. I thought he'd conk out first, but I fell asleep before he did. I half-awoke once during the night to find I was all entwined about him, spoon fashion. I groaned with contentment, and pulled his warm, heavy body closer.

In the morning, fully awake, I discovered he had been up, dressed, and was gone. On my bedside table was a sheet torn from his notebook. It read: 'I love you, Dunk.'

That troubled me.

13

NEXT STOP: Wimpsville . . . or so I thought.

It was Saturday, and I called Roberta and Ross Minchen, hoping to make an appointment to see them that afternoon. I expected grumbles and hostility, but Roberta couldn't have been more agreeable.

'Of course we'll see you,' she said. 'Mother told me you had been hired, and Ross and I think it's a marvelous idea. We do hope you can get this mess cleared up as soon as possible. But I'm afraid seeing you this afternoon is out of the question; we're in the middle of preparing for a little party we're having tonight. Listen, I have a fabulous idea! Our guests won't be arriving until eight-thirty or nine – around there. Why don't you come over, say, an hour earlier or so, and we'll have a nice chat. Then you stay on for the party. I think you'll like our friends.'

'That's very kind of you, Mrs Minchen, but—'

'Roberta.'

'Roberta. But I wouldn't want to intrude.'

'Nonsense! You won't be intruding at all. Please say you'll come early and stay for our little gala. Who knows – you may meet a fascinating man!'

Her effusiveness was hard to resist, but I was doubtful about spending an entire evening at the Home of the Wimps. But then I reckoned I could stay for one drink, and if it was too much of a drag, make a hasty exit, pleading a fierce migraine, the unexpected onset of menarche, or *something*.

'All right, Roberta,' I said, 'I'll be there. Thank you. Is it a dress-up party?'

'*Au contraire,*' she said gaily. 'Very informal. Wear whatever you like. I just know everyone's going to *love* you!'

Then she giggled inexplicably. That giggle should have warned me that everything wasn't quite right at the House of Minchen – but how was I to know? How could anyone have known?

They lived in a lumpy apartment house on East 80th Street that was almost back-to-back with the Havistocks' building on 79th. It even had a similar lobby, with ancient attendant, frowsty odor, and walls of marble that might have been salvaged from Pompeii.

Even more startling was that the Minchens, a young couple, had apparently decided to make their apartment a smaller replica of the Havistocks'. Or perhaps they had furnished it totally with hand-me-downs. But there were the same brown velvet chairs and couches, stifling drapes, and suffocating bric-à-brac, whatnots, and a number of succulent plants that needed dusting.

But the most surprising thing, and quite out of character in that necropolis, was the largest television set I had ever seen – really an enormous screen. And atop cabinets on both sides, two videocassette recorders, and a portable video camera with power pack attached. Curious.

Roberta and Ross met me at the door, the soul of affability. They were both dressed informally: he in sport jacket, slacks, open-necked shirt, and loafers; she in a flowered print jumpsuit, zippered down the front, which, considering her dumpling body, gave her the look of a female Winston Churchill – or maybe an oversized Kewpie doll.

They were not the most attractive people I had ever met – he *would* crack his knuckles, and apparently they never called each other anything but 'dear' or 'darling' – but they were hospitable enough, got me seated in one of those hot, overstuffed armchairs, and insisted I have something to drink. I settled for a glass of chilled white wine. I thought they were both drinking watered vodka. Later I discovered it was neat 94-proof gin.

As usual, I started out playing humble, explaining that while I had no desire to pry into their private lives, solving the puzzle of the missing Demaretion did, of necessity, demand the answers to some personal questions.

'For instance,' I said, addressing Ross Minchen, 'I don't even know what your occupation is. Are you in textiles – like your father-in-law and brother-in-law?'

'Oh, no,' he said quickly, 'nothing like that. I'm vice president of the Digman-Findle Corporation. We do plastic extrusions.'

I didn't want to reveal my ignorance by asking him what the hell *that was.*

96

'He practically runs the company,' his wife said brightly. 'Don't you, dear?'

'Well, not quite, darling,' he said modestly, patting his long, thinning locks to make certain they were concealing his baldness.

I didn't have the chutzpah to ask him what his income was, but I figured the vice president of *anything* was doing okay dollarwise. Besides, everyone had said that at one time Vanessa had come on to Ross. Would a luxury-loving lady like that have cut her eyes at a guy who was destitute? Doubtful.

So I got down to the nitty-gritty, taking them over the events of that morning and early afternoon when the Demaretion disappeared. They said what everyone else had told me: there were a lot of people there, all mingling and moving about, and it was difficult, if not impossible, to say where any one individual was at any particular time.

I asked them the same question I had asked Vanessa and Luther Havistock: Did either of them notice anything unusual or unexpected that morning? They looked at each other, then shook their heads; no, they had not.

I had a sinking feeling that as a detective, I was a washout. It wasn't so much that people were lying to me, but that I was asking the wrong questions.

'Look,' I said desperately, 'I hope you understand that whatever you tell me will be held in strictest confidence. Neither of you will be quoted as the source of anything you might say. Now, with that in mind, I should tell you that Detective Al Georgio of the New York Police Department, and John Smack, investigator for Grandby's insurance company, both think a member of your family was involved in the theft of the Demaretion. If what they believe is true – and I emphasize that *if* – who in the family do you think might possibly be guilty?'

Again they stared at each other: he so pale, solemn, with the intent frown of a pallbearer; she with that blinking, rabbity look, eyes popping, lips pouting.

'Orson Vanwinkle,' Ross Minchen said finally. 'He's capable of it. The man is a rotter.'

Rotter? When was the last time you heard someone use that word? But I didn't laugh.

'It was Natalie, darling,' Roberta Minchen said to her husband. 'Definitely Natalie.' Then she turned to me, incisors gleaming. 'I hate to throw suspicion on my own sister, but let's face it, she's a disgrace. Those so-called friends of hers . . . I happen to know she's into the drug scene. Hopheads are always in need of money, aren't they?'

I was saved from answering by the front door chimes. The Minchens leaped to their feet.

'Our guests!' Ross cried.

'You'll just *love* these people,' Roberta assured me. 'They're so different.'

Within the next thirty minutes, four married couples arrived, all about the Minchens' age. I was introduced to everyone, and to this day cannot remember a single name – which is all right with me.

You would think, wouldn't you, that in any gathering of five couples there would be at least *one* lovely woman and *one* handsome man? I'm not saying strangers should be immediately judged by their physical attractiveness – God knows I'm no beauty – but let's face it, isn't comeliness the first thing that makes us think someone may be worth knowing when we meet them for the first time?

Not that all the Minchens' friends were ugly; they were not. But the men seemed shaped like milk bottles – remember how they looked? – and the women appeared to be down comforters tied in the middle. The men were balding, with a shocking assortment of smutchy complexions, tics, and scraggly mustaches. The women wore too much makeup, inexpertly applied, and instead of laughing, most of them whinnied.

I was ready to get out of there as soon as decently possible, but then I decided to stay awhile. It wasn't their sparkling personalities – they had none at all – it was their conversation. It was in a kind of inside code they all understood, but which was pure Lower Slobbovian to me. It went something like this:

'Wait'll you see what *we* brought!'

'Ours is better!'

'Harry says it's the best yet!'

'It's got to win an Academy Award!'

'Martha tells me I have a knack for it!'

'Three on one – come on, that's a little much!'

While this chatter continued, all with exclamation marks, the host and hostess ladled out the drinks. I had one more glass of white wine and nursed it, but the others guzzled like there was no tomorrow. One geezer who was trying to grow a beard and wasn't succeeding latched onto me and gave me a total examination, head to foot.

'Oh, my,' he said, showing tarnished teeth. 'I hope you're going to join our group. We need a wild card!'

What the hell?

This went on for almost an hour, and everyone was into their second or third round of booze, when Ross Minchen shouted, 'Showtime!' And immediately several others echoed, 'Showtime! Showtime!'

We all got seated, me included, facing the huge TV screen. Lights were dimmed, and Ross fussed with one of the VCRs, sliding in a cassette. By this time I realized I wasn't going to see *The Sound of Music* or *Gone With the Wind*. I didn't.

It was porn all right, the hardest of hard-core. But if that wasn't numbing enough, the performers were Roberta and Ross Minchen and their happy little band of flakes. The color was great, the sound was professional, and there they all were on the silver screen doing things which never occurred to me that people could do or wanted to do.

I mean, I've read Havelock Ellis and Krafft-Ebing, and in a bemused kind of way I can understand why someone might have a mad passion for an oak tree or go around sniffing an old piece of leather, but this stuff was *gross*. They were such *ordinary* people – business and professional men, career women and housewives – and really, seeing them naked, doing those things, wasn't exciting at all. It was scary and it was sad.

When they started the second cassette, I decided I better get out of there before viewing ended and new filming began. I thought I was leaving unobtrusively, they all had their eyes glued to the screen and were busy with muttered comments and nervous laughter. But Roberta caught up with me at the door and clamped a tight hand on my arm.

'I know this is all new to you,' she whispered, 'but you'll be back, you'll be back!'

I gave her a weak smile and edged out the door.

'It was Natalie,' she called after me. 'She's *obscene!*'

I got home as quickly as I could, stripped and showered. Soaped a long time and stood under a hard spray, washing it all away. I didn't let myself think of what I had seen. I kept repeating nursery rhymes: 'Mary, Mary, quite contrary . . .'

But later, in my shabby flannel bathrobe, sipping a vodka from Jack Smack's bottle, I *had* to think about it and ponder the vagaries of human beings. All of us. It was very unsettling. Foundations seemed to be cracking, and I had to remember one-on-one basketball in a Des Moines driveway to keep my mind from whirling off into the wild blue yonder.

I had no idea what effect the Minchens' aberrant behavior had on the disappearance of the Demaretion – if it had any effect at all. It was just another revelation of a family that was coming to look like a collection of misfits, totally unlike the personae they presented to the world.

Are we all like that? Ordinary and presentable, even wimpish, in public, and then, in private, something different and perhaps monstrous? Was I like that?

I think that was what depressed me most about the evening. Those stupid porn films were funny, when I thought about them, but the worst thing was that they made me doubt myself, and what I might be capable of. Just seeing those unhappy people in frantic action brought me down to their level.

14

I SUPPOSE I should have immediately told Al Georgio and Jack Smack about the Minchens and their coven of wife-swappers, but I just couldn't do it. I think I was too ashamed to relate what I had seen, not knowing how to describe it in polite terms. Also, at the time I didn't see what possible connection it might have with the stealing of the Demaretion.

So I didn't call either of them, and hoped to spend a quiet Sunday at home, cozying up with a five-pound *New York Times* and enjoying a breakfast treat of cream cheese, lox, and onion on a bagel. Then I intended to do some *very* deep thinking about the Havistocks, try to sort out my impressions, and see if I could devise a theory on who broke the Eighth Commandment and copped the coin.

But it was not to be the leisurely day I had planned.

First, Al Georgio phoned. He was on his way to pick up his daughter, Sally, and they were going to spend the day in Central Park, then take in a movie, and go to a new West Side restaurant that was reputed to have the best barbecued ribs in town. Would I like to come along, spend the day with them?

'Al,' I said, 'when was the last time you saw your daughter?'

'About a month ago,' he admitted.

'Then she wants to spend the day with *you*. The two of you – alone. She'd resent me, and quite rightly. Maybe some other time, Al; I'd love to meet her. But I have a feeling that today she'd like to have you for herself, and I'd just spoil things.'

He sighed. 'You may be right. I know she's all excited about today.'

'Of course she is. You haven't seen her in a month, and she was beginning to wonder if her father had deserted her. Now the two of you go out and have a wonderful day.'

'Okay,' he said, 'we will. Thanks, Dunk.'

I hoped that would be the last interruption of my Sunday tranquillity, but it was not to be. The phone rang again. This time – surprise! – it was Archibald Havistock.

'Miss Bateson,' he said in his diapason, 'I would like to have a brief private meeting with you, and this would be an ideal time. Mrs Havistock and the Minchens have gone to church, and Ruby Querita doesn't work on Sunday. May I impose on you and ask you to come over now? It shouldn't take long. Would that be an inconvenience?'

'Of course not, Mr Havistock. I'll be there as soon as possible.'

'Take a cab,' he said.

What else? He was paying expenses.

He met me at the apartment door himself and conducted me into the den-library where I sat across from his swivel chair at that enormous partners' desk. He excused himself, disappeared, and came back a few moments later with a silver tray laden with coffee pot, paper-thin china cups and saucers, silver spoons, pink linen napkins, creamer, sugar, a bowl of butter balls, a plate of warm miniature croissants, and a pot of Dundee's orange marmalade.

'Beautiful,' I said, eyeing that attractive brunch and forgetting my lost bagel. 'I won't have to eat another thing all day.'

That distant, somewhat chilly smile appeared again as he poured me a cup of steaming black coffee. 'Help yourself,' he urged. 'The croissants are from a new patisserie on Lexington Avenue. I think they're quite good.'

It was before noon on a Sunday morning, but he was dressed for a board of directors' meeting – or maybe a Congressional hearing. I think he was the most impeccably groomed man I had ever met. I mean he *glistened* – from his silvered hair to his polished wingtips. I wondered if he had his shoelaces ironed.

'I'm not going to ask you for a progress report,' he said, and I had the odd notion that he could shatter a champagne glass with that voice if he let it out at full power. 'I realize you have only started your investigation. But there are two things I wanted you to be aware of. First of all, it was my wife's suggestion that you be employed as our private investigator. Initially, I was opposed, feeling it best to leave the solution of the theft to professional detectives. Your knowledge of ancient Greek coins didn't seem to me a sufficient reason.'

'I can understand your feeling that way, Mr Havistock. They've certainly had more experience in detection.'

102

'But then, when I learned that members of my family were under suspicion, I changed my mind. I find it most distressing, Miss Bateson, that any of my children, their spouses, or our employees might be guilty of stealing the Demaretion. So I acceded to my wife's wishes, in hopes that you might be able to reassure us that no Havistock could or would do such a thing.'

'I told you, sir,' I said, 'I can't give you any guarantee on that.'

He waved my demurrer away. 'I understand that. I also appreciate your agreeing to come to me first with the name of the culprit, if it proves to be a family member, before going to the authorities. The second thing I wished to discuss with you is this: Orson Vanwinkle has informed me that you asked him questions about my signet ring. Was he correct?'

Now that was a shocker. I could have sworn that Horsy was so smashed he would never remember any of our conversation. I thoughtfully buttered and marmaladed another of those delicious croissants.

'Mr Vanwinkle is correct,' I acknowledged. 'I did ask about your ring.'

He nodded, regarding me gravely. 'I wondered about your interest, and then I realized . . . Whoever substituted the sealed empty case for the one containing the Demaretion must have had access to my signet ring since it was used to imprint the wax seal. Am I right?'

It was my turn to nod. Besides, I couldn't speak; my mouth was full.

He clapped his hands together with mild delight, and this time his smile had real warmth. 'Very, very clever of you, Miss Bateson. And those so-called professional detectives still haven't grasped the significance of the ring. My wife is right; we did well to employ you. You are a very intelligent, perceptive young lady, and I now have high hopes that you may succeed if Georgio and Smack fail. My only objection is that you did not come to me directly with your questions about my signet ring instead of asking Mr Vanwinkle.'

I dabbed at my lips with a pink linen napkin, so starched it could have been balanced on its edge. 'I didn't want to bother you, Mr Havistock.'

'No,' he said, shaking his great, leonine head, 'I will not accept that. When my wife and I asked you to investigate members of our

103

family, we were quite willing that we – my wife and I – should be questioned as well as the others. I want to make that perfectly clear to you: Mrs Havistock and I expect no preferential treatment whatsoever.'

'All right,' I said, pouring him and myself more coffee, 'I'll go along with that, and I'm happy to hear you say it. Now, about the signet ring . . . Is there one – or more?'

'Only one, to my knowledge.'

'Do you wear it?'

'Very infrequently. But I value it – a gift from my wife.'

'Where do you keep it?'

'Sometimes here,' he said, pulling open a small drawer at the side of his desk. 'Sometimes in my jewelry case in the bedroom. That's where it is at present.'

'So anyone in the household might have borrowed it temporarily?'

He sighed. 'I'm afraid so. I use it rarely – to seal documents and things of that sort. It's never locked up or hidden. Yes, anyone who knew of its existence would have easy access to it.'

I gave him a wan smile. 'Just as they had easy access to the two unused display cases in your bedroom closet.'

'Yes. That, too. I can't tell you how painful I find all this, Miss Bateson, but the more I learn about the crime, the more I tend to agree with Georgio and Smack: a family member was involved. It is not a pleasant prospect to contemplate.'

'You want the Demaretion back, don't you?' I asked.

He looked at me in astonishment. 'Of course. It is a glorious work of art.'

'I agree. I don't want it to disappear into some private collection where it'll never be seen again.'

'You think that's what will happen?'

'Unless we find it first. Mr Havistock, how would you characterize your relations with your family? Intimate? Close? Distant? Cold?'

He looked at me queerly, those azure eyes glittering. 'I have tried to be a good paterfamilias, and I would be the first to say I haven't always succeeded. My own father was a stern, despotic man, and I suspect I learned too much from him. Times change, and I should have changed with them, but I wouldn't or couldn't. More harshness, more discipline, was not the answer. I should have been more sympathetic, more understanding when the children were young. It was my failure. It was my fault.'

104

Suddenly he was no longer the complete, self-assured man but, by admitting guilt and weakness, someone much more human and likeable.

'I have no children,' I said, 'so I'm not qualified to give advice. But the time comes, I suppose, when you have to kick them out of the nest and hope they can fly.'

'Yes,' he said sadly, 'that time comes. Most of mine seem to have dropped – like stones.'

'I think you're exaggerating,' I told him boldly. 'They may not have come up to your expectations, but they are living their own lives. You must allow them to make their own mistakes. How else can they learn?'

He didn't answer, but I had the feeling that he was aware of the frailties of all his children – and his nephew as well – and spent too much time brooding on what he might have done differently to ensure their success and happiness.

I cabbed home from that meeting with a lot to ponder. But I resolutely finished the Sunday *Times*, wishing I had accepted Al's invitation to spend the day with him and his daughter. Then I did some laundry, slurped a blueberry yogurt, and prepared to spend the evening watching TV, with maybe a brief trip out into the living world to have a hamburger or a slice of anchovy pizza.

But I canceled all those noble plans and did something exceedingly foolish. I phoned Jack Smack, really hoping he wouldn't be in. But he was.

'Hey, Dunk!' he said, sounding genuinely glad to hear from me. 'How're you doing?'

'All right. I'm not interrupting, am I?'

'Hell, no. I'm just sitting here counting the walls.'

I wanted him to know this was a professional call – nothing personal. 'Something came up on the Demaretion case, and I thought you'd be interested.'

'Oh?' he said. 'Maybe we shouldn't talk about it on the phone. Listen, Dunk, have you had dinner yet?'

'Not yet,' I said, hating myself.

'There's a new place over on the West Side that's supposed to have the best barbecued ribs in town. Want to try it?'

'No, no,' I said hastily. 'Pork makes me break out in splotches.'

'Okay,' he said equably, 'then how about this scenario: I'll run out and pick up a couple of strip steaks and Idaho potatoes. I've

105

got the makings for a green salad. Meanwhile you cab down here – I'll pay the freight. I'm in a loft in SoHo. We'll have dinner, talk about the Demaretion, and after that, we'll let nature take its course.'

I didn't like that last; it scared me.

'All right,' I said faintly.

His loft looked like a factory: High Tech with everything in metal and Lucite. But he had a fully equipped kitchen – the largest compartment in the place. (The bathroom was the only enclosed room.) The bed, I noticed nervously, seemed to be double futons on the floor. Soft, plump, and lascivious.

He had a microwave, and fifteen minutes after I arrived he served up a yummy meal on a table of milk glass supported on black steel sawhorses. He also provided a bottle of super Cabernet. This lad knew how to live. Sour cream and chives with the potatoes, of course. He didn't miss a trick.

While we gobbled our food, I told him about the signet ring, and what Vanwinkle and Archibald Havistock had to say about it.

He stopped eating long enough to slap a palm onto the tabletop. 'God *damn* it!' he said wrathfully. 'I missed that, and I'll bet Al Georgio did, too.' Then he looked at me admiringly. 'Dunk, that was good thinking. You've got a talent for investigation.'

'Well . . . maybe. But it doesn't amount to anything. I mean, anyone in the family could have used that ring.'

'I know,' he said, 'but I should have seen it. I'm supposed to be the professional. Anything else?'

'No,' I said, deciding not to tell him about the Minchens' hobby. 'Nothing.'

'Well . . .' he said, working on his salad. (Too much salt in that salad.) 'We got another letter from our anonymous crook. The guy wants two hundred grand for the Demaretion. No way!'

'What will you do now, Jack?'

'Haggle.'

'How will you do that? By letter? Phone calls?'

'This guy is very clever. He sends us print-free letters from different zones in Manhattan. Practically impossible to trace. We reply by coded Death Notices in the *Times*. I know it all sounds like cloak-and-dagger stuff, but it works. In case you're interested, we're going to offer him twenty-five thousand.'

'You think he'll accept?'

'No,' Jack said, 'I don't think he will. He's got us by the short hairs, and he knows it. We'll probably settle for fifty Gs – around there. Meanwhile I'll keep gnawing at it. I may catch up with him before the payoff. Well . . . enough about business. I have some chocolate tofutti in the fridge. Interested?'

'Thanks,' I said, 'but not really.'

'Me neither. But I also have some Rémy Napoléon – and that I *am* interested in.'

'Jack, do you eat like this every day?'

'Of course not,' he said. 'I'd be a balloon if I did. I usually thaw something frozen. One of those complete gourmet dinners that tastes like glue. But once or twice a week I like to cook.'

'For yourself?' I asked.

'Sometimes,' he said, giving me that wisenheimer grin that implied sexual goings-on and probably didn't mean a damned thing – I told myself.

We collapsed on those yielding futons and sipped our cognacs from small jelly jars.

'I have Tiffany snifters,' he said, 'but occasionally I like to use these, to remind me where I came from.'

'And where was that?'

'Poverty,' he said, laughing shortly. 'I've made it, Dunk – so far – but I want to keep remembering the time when a peanut butter sandwich was a treat.'

I had absolutely no idea if he was telling the truth or putting me on. I did know the man was a consummate actor. He told amusing stories in a dozen dialects. His movements could be as graceful as a ballet dancer's steps or so gauche that they broke me up. He seemed driven to entertain, and I must say he succeeded. I never enjoyed myself as much. Couldn't stop giggling.

'You know,' he said, taking the empty jelly jar from my fingers and putting it aside, 'a friend of mine – a great cocksman – once told me that the best way to seduce a woman is to make her laugh. Do you think that's true?'

I considered. 'It's a start,' I said.

The problem was that when we were naked, flouncing around on those pads, he was still the entertainer. I didn't want to think of how many women he had been with to learn all the things he knew. He certainly educated *me*. He was such an expert – but somehow divorced, not really involved. Like an actor who has played the same role too many times.

All those reflections came later. At the time, I was whirled away,

107

brain detonated, unable to concentrate on anything but his physical beauty and skill and what he was doing to me. I was one long, throbbing nerve end, and he knew how to tickle it. What a craftsman he was! I loved him. I hated him.

He drove me home in his Jaguar.

15

I was beginning to learn how detectives worked. You couldn't sit at home or in your office and wait for people to come in and tell you things; you had to have the gall to go after them, pry, ask embarrassing questions, nag them, and generally make a nuisance of yourself.

I could do all that. Not only was I being paid for it (plus expenses), but I really loved the Demaretion and resented its theft. Also, someone had made a fool out of me – getting me to sign a receipt for an empty display case – so I had a personal interest in this affair. Revenge!

I retained that dauntless mood while I phoned Mrs Mabel Havistock on Monday morning, asking if I might see her as soon as possible. If she was surprised or discomfited, her voice didn't reveal it. She said she'd see me at precisely two o'clock that afternoon – in royal tones suggesting that I was being granted an audience with the queen. I thanked her meekly. So much for fearlessness.

My bravura mood got another jolt when the mail was delivered a little after noon. Three catalogues, bills from New York Telephone and Con Edison, and a plain white envelope. Just a typed Mary Lou Bateson on the front, with my address. No hint of the sender.

Inside, a single sheet of white paper. Typed in the middle in capital letters: LAY OFF – OR ELSE. No signature.

Very melodramatic, and very scary. My first reaction was an instant resolve to take the first plane back to Des Moines and spend the rest of my life practicing dunk shots in the driveway.

Second reaction: fury. What son of a bitch was trying to frighten me off the Demaretion case? How dare he! Third reaction: Call the police, which I did. It took me almost a half-hour to locate Detective Al Georgio. I told him about the anonymous threat.

'I'll be damned,' he said slowly. 'Plain white paper?'

'Yes.'

'The whole thing typed?'

'Yes.'

'You handled it?'

'Of course I handled it. How else could I read it? I tore open the envelope, took out the sheet of paper, unfolded it, and read it. How could I do that without handling it?'

'All right, all right,' he said soothingly, 'don't get your balls in an uproar. I'll pick it up and have it dusted. And you know what we'll get? Zip, zero, and zilch. Sounds to me like the kind of letters Finkus, Holding, has been getting: plain paper, no prints, typed on an Olympia standard. Well, we'll see . . . You know what this means, don't you, Dunk? You're getting close.'

'Close to *what*?' I wailed. 'Al, I haven't found out a damned thing.'

'What have you been doing? Who have you talked to?'

Then, because I had already told Jack Smack and was trying very hard not to favor either of them, I told Al about the signet ring and Vanwinkle's and Archibald Havistock's answers to my questions. His reaction was the same as Jack's.

'Jesus Christ!' he said disgustedly. 'I'm a dolt. I should have picked up on that. Nice work, Dunk. But they both said everyone in the family had access to the ring?'

'That's right.'

'Well, it's hard to believe the ring business was enough to trigger your black-spot letter. It must be something else.'

He paused and for a moment I was tempted to tell him how Roberta and Ross Minchen got their jollies. Then I decided that since it had nothing to do with the Demaretion heist, Al had no need to know.

'What are you doing today?' he asked me.

'Seeing Mrs Havistock in about an hour. I want to talk to everyone who was in the apartment on that morning.'

'That sounds sensible. And safe enough.'

'After I talk to her, it'll only leave Ruby Querita. I'll get to her next.'

He was silent. Then:

'Dunk, watch your back. Don't press too hard. I don't like that letter you got. It scares me.'

'Well, it sure scares the hell out of *me*.'

'Want to move into a hotel? Change your phone number? I can't provide 'round-the-clock protection; you know that.'

'No, I'll go along just the way I've been doing. Maybe I've heard something that threatens the crook – but what it could be, I have no idea. Al, how was your day with your daughter?'

'Wonderful,' he said. 'Just perfect. I told her about you. She said she'd like to meet you.'

'That's sweet. And I'd like to meet her. Next time you see her – okay?'

'You better believe it. And Dunk, do be careful.'

'I intend to be.'

'You've got my home phone number and where I can be reached during the day. Don't be bashful; call me anytime.'

'Thanks, Al,' I said gratefully. 'I'm hoping I won't get myself in a crisis situation, but if I do, it's nice to know you're there.'

'I'm here,' he said.

What a splendid June day it was! Rare sky, beamy sun, kissing breeze. Manhattan isn't all graffiti and dog droppings, you know. Sometimes the light and the shining towers can make you weep with pleasure. It was like that when I started out early and strode across Central Park to the East Side. I didn't even look behind me. Nothing could frighten me on a day like that.

Except possibly the matriarch of the Havistock clan. If Mrs Mabel didn't have bones in her corset, she sat as if she had: stiffly erect, spine straight. I wondered how long it had been since she had allowed that spine to touch the back of a chair. All in all, a very stern, domineering matron, and to avoid being completely intimidated, I had to keep reminding myself that this ogress had been the one who suggested my employment as the Havistocks' private investigator.

I had been admitted to the apartment by Ruby Querita, who gave me a small smile, signifying, I supposed, that she now recognized me as a friend of the family. But halfway down that gloomy corridor, Orson Vanwinkle brushed her aside and took over as usher.

'Hi, doll,' he said with his lupine grin. He also stroked my cheek, and I knew blossoms would never bloom there again. 'Madame Defarge is waiting for you,' he said, jerking a thumb toward the living room. 'Going to have a nice chin-chin?'

I nodded.

'About what?'

'About who stole the Demaretion,' I said, looking at him directly.

'Oh, that old thing,' he said, not at all disconcerted. 'Just a hunk of

111

metal as far as I'm concerned. The insurance company will pay off; you'll see.' Then he leaned closer and lowered his voice. 'When are you and I going to have another scene?'

'Scene?'

'You know – fun and games.'

I swear the man was certifiable. But that didn't make him any less dangerous. I walked away from him and entered the living room where I found her majesty sitting bolt upright on one of those loathsome brown velvet couches. She graciously beckoned me to sit beside her. She was wearing a lavender scent – what else? I would have bet her dresser drawers were packed with sachets.

'I don't like your hair,' she said, staring. 'You really must do something with it.'

'I know,' I said miserably. 'I intend to have it styled one of these days.'

'Do,' she said. 'I can give you the name of a good man. Now then, what did you wish to speak to me about?'

Not exactly a propitious beginning, but I plunged right in, explaining that I was interviewing everyone who was present in the apartment on the morning the Demaretion was taken.

'I have already related my activities on that morning to Detective Georgio. You were present. I answered all his questions.'

'*His* questions, ma'am. Mine are of a more personal nature.'

She looked at me coldly. 'Such as?'

'Detective Georgio and insurance investigator John Smack are convinced that a member of your family took part in the theft. Both are experienced men and would not make such an accusation lightly. Would you care to name one or more family members you think might possibly be involved?'

She made a sudden, distraught movement of one hand: a wild, jerky wave. 'I will not point the finger of suspicion at anyone. Certainly none of my kin.'

'As you wish, Mrs Havistock. But you have employed me to discover the truth, and your refusal to cooperate, no matter how well-intentioned, just makes my job more difficult. All right, let's skip family members and talk about employees. How long has Ruby Querita worked for you?'

'Almost ten years now.'

'You trust her?'

'Absolutely.'

'I understand her brother is in prison.'

112

'That has nothing to do with Ruby. I have complete confidence in her.'

'She works six days a week?'

'Five, plus a half-day on Saturday.'

'She cooks and cleans.'

'Cooks mostly, and does some light housework. Twice a week a man comes in from a commercial service to dust and vacuum. And once a month we have a crew from the same service to give the apartment a good going-over, including washing the windows and scrubbing down the bathrooms.'

'Were any of these commercial cleaners here on the morning the Demaretion was taken?'

'No, they were not.'

'But they were aware of your husband's coin collection?'

'I'm sure they were. It was on open display in his library. I spoke to him several times about that, asking him to put the coins in a bank vault, but he would not.'

'Numismatists are like that, ma'am,' I said softly. 'They like to have their collections readily available where they can see them, examine them, enjoy them. Whose idea was it to sell your husband's collection?'

'His. And I agreed. We are presently engaged in revising our estate planning, and rather than attempt to break up the collection amongst our heirs, with so many coins to each beneficiary, it seemed simpler to sell the collection and add the proceeds to the assets of the estate.'

'Then I gather your husband is no longer an active collector.'

'That is correct. I think he made his last purchase about five years ago. And since then he has sold off a number of items. At one time I think he had more than six hundred coins.'

'Oh?' I said, surprised. 'I wasn't aware of that.'

'I fail to see what these questions about my husband's collection have to do with the disappearance of the Demaretion.'

'Probably nothing,' I admitted. 'But I'm trying to learn as much as I can, in hopes that something small will lead to something bigger, then to something larger yet, and eventually we'll get to the truth of the matter. Mrs Havistock, I respect your decision not to single out a member of your family as a possible suspect, but I wish you would reconsider your decision. It might speed things up considerably if you'd be willing to give me a hint – no matter how tiny. I assure you I won't treat it as proof of guilt, or even as an accusation. It will simply

113

be a lead that will enable me to make a more thorough and efficient investigation. Won't you name *someone* you think might have been involved?'

I was watching her closely. As I made my plea, her heavy features began to sag. It was like putting a wax mask too close to a flame. But in this case it was flesh that was melting, all her features softening and flowing downward. It was a dreadful thing to see because it left her with nothing but sadness and tragedy, eyes dulled, resolve gone, strength fled.

'No,' she said in a low voice, 'I will name no one.'

So that was that.

I was in the outside hallway, waiting for the elevator. It arrived, and who should pop out but Natalie Havistock, frenetic as ever. She looked like she was dressed for a masquerade. The item I remember best was a mess jacket of soiled white canvas emblazoned with military shoulder patches.

'Hey, Dunk!' she said. 'Getting much these days?'

Then she embraced me and lurched up to kiss me on the lips – which I could have done without.

'What'cha been doing in the morgue?' she asked, and I had to laugh; she was so right.

'Talking to your mother, Nettie.'

'Mommy dearest? She's been in the doldrums lately. Something's been eating her, and I can guarantee it ain't a man. Listen, hon, would you like to go to a party tonight?'

'A party?' I said, startled. 'What kind?'

'A party-party. A bash. An orgy. Down in the East Village. Hundreds of people. Plenty of booze and grass. Maybe a line of coke if you know the right people. How about it?'

'Will your boyfriend be there?'

'Akbar El Raschid? That's what he calls himself. His real name is Sam Jefferson. You've heard about him, have you? Hell, yes, he'll be there. If you don't like the scene, you can split. Okay?'

I agreed. She opened her bulging shoulder bag and took out a gold ballpoint pen and pigskin notebook. I wondered what store she had honored with her light-fingered presence. She scribbled the address, tore the sheet away, and tucked it into the pocket of my suede jacket.

'Try to make it,' she urged. 'You'll have a ball.'

'What time does it start?'

'It'll open up around nine, but these things don't get moving until midnight. Wear your chastity belt.'

114

'Thanks a lot,' I said. 'You're really making it sound attractive.'

'Nah,' she said, laughing. 'You won't have to put out. Unless you want to. Listen, Dunk, you got a couple of extra bucks I could borrow?'

I thought swiftly. 'I've got a five you can have.'

'Five is alive!' she cried. 'But twenty is plenty! Pay you back one of these days. Remind me.'

So I handed over a five-dollar bill, figuring I could always fiddle my expense account and get it back from her father. Then she dashed into the apartment, and I waited patiently for the next elevator.

What do you wear to a party-party, a bash, an orgy in the East Village? Not basic black with pearls, that's for sure. Besides, I didn't own basic black and pearls. So I settled for jeans and a long-sleeved white 'bullfighter's shirt.' It had a ruffled front and was cut low enough to show cleavage – if I'd had any. And my suede jacket, of course.

I had no idea how to get to that address by bus or subway, so I cabbed down. After all it *was* part of my investigation; I wanted to get a line on Nettie's boyfriend. So it was a legitimate business expense – right?

The cabby wasn't happy about taking me to that neighborhood. 'Your life insurance paid up?' he asked.

Actually when he dropped me and I looked around, the street didn't seem menacing at all. Maybe not as clean as West 83rd, but there were no corpses in the gutter, and there were even two scraggly ginkgo trees struggling to survive.

The party wasn't hard to find. It was only a little after ten o'clock, but the decibel count was soaring. They were playing a Pink Floyd tape – I think it was 'The Dark Side of the Moon' –and the volume was turn up high enough to loosen your fillings.

There weren't 'hundreds of people' there, but maybe they'd arrive by midnight when 'things got moving.' But the top-floor apartment – half-attic and half-loft – was crowded enough. Thirty or forty people, I reckoned, of three colors, five races, and four sexes. It was a sort of zonked-out United Nations.

Nettie hadn't exaggerated about the booze and grass available: plenty of both. Plus platters of brownies. But fearing those might be laced with hash, or something stronger, I passed. No one paid any attention to me, which was okay. I poured myself a little vodka in a plastic cup – no ice available – and surreptitiously turned down the

115

volume on the cassette player. No one objected. As a matter of fact, I don't think anyone noticed. Maybe they were all tone-deaf.

I searched through the mob for Natalie but couldn't spot her. I did see a tall, lanky black propped against a wall, regarding the scene with amused contempt. He was wearing a red beret and had a single gold earring. Had to be Akbar El Raschid, né Sam Jefferson. Handsome lad with a little spiky Vandyke. I went up to him.

'I think we have a mutual acquaintance,' I said.

'Allah?' he said, looking at me lazily. Then he straightened away from the wall and inspected me. 'Hey, Stretch, you're a long one. Groupie for the Globe Trotters?'

'Not quite,' I said. 'The Celtics.'

He snapped his fingers. 'Got'cha,' he said. 'You're Dunk – right? Nat Baby told me about you. She says you're a foxy lady. Pleased to meet you, sweet mama.'

'Did you steal the Demaretion?' I asked him.

If he was shocked or insulted, he didn't reveal it. 'Who, what, where?' he said. 'Oh, you mean that coin Nat Baby's papa lost. Nah, I didn't lift it. It was a *coin*. If I was to decide on a life of crime, coins would have no interest for me whatsoever. I'd go for the green. Worth more and easier to carry. Coins too heavy. You know us coons – we're lazy, sweet mama.'

'This coin is worth a lot of loot.'

'So?' he said. 'You know how many bills you can pack in a little bitty suit satchel? Hey, how come you leaning on me? We just met, didn't we? Who you – Missy Sherlock Holmes?'

'I'm sorry,' I said. 'I apologize. But I'm getting paid to investigate the robbery. I'm asking everyone.'

'Say no more. But look at me; I'm pure as the driven snow – right?'

His smile was hard to resist. He brought me another vodka, offered me a drag on the cigarette he was smoking – which I declined – and began a fascinating commentary on the people roiling about us.

'Look at them,' he said. 'They got to be first of the first. New fads, new fashions, new restaurants, new music. The Trendies, I call them. They can't stand to be second. Pick it up, try it out, drop it down, go on to something newer. Like pickled kiwi fruit maybe, or steaks grilled over dried cow flops. You dig? They run and run and run. What's new? What's the latest? Well, patricide is in. Oh, yeah? Well, then I got to kill my daddy. Next year it's matricide. There goes Mommy. No verities – that's their problem.'

'Where did you graduate from?' I demanded.

He stared at me a long moment. 'I got an MBA from Wharton,' he said. 'You going to hold that against me?'

'No, but why don't you *use* it?'

'I'd rather steal, sweet mama,' he said, flashing the whitest choppers I've ever seen.

He was slender, loose, with a disjointed way of moving – like a marionette with slack strings. He seemed to be two men: flashy Harlem stud and sharp intellectual observer. I didn't know how seriously to take him. His talk could have been all taunts. Or maybe a mask for his despair. A complex character.

Then Natalie Havistock came rushing up and grabbed his arm – a proprietress.

'Hi, Dunk,' she said. 'Glad you could make it. This guy giving you his nigger jive? The Wharton MBA and all that? Bullshit! He's nothing but a field hand. Load that barge. Tote that bale.'

He showed his teeth again, and cupped one of her heavy breasts. 'Nah, honey mine,' he said. 'No jive. Dunk here asked me if I pinched your daddy's coin, and I admitted, yeah I did it. You and me, working together.'

'Don't listen to him,' Nettie advised. 'He's flying tonight.'

He was flying? *I* was flying! You could get a rush just by breathing that choky air. My brain was dancing a gavotte – and not just from the pot fumes. I couldn't decide how much Akbar El Raschid was putting me on. I thought, despite his indolent manner, he had a razor brain. What Netty called his nigger jive could have been an act, a devious way of concealing his guilt. I just didn't know.

As Nettie had predicted, by midnight the party was whirling, with new recruits arriving every minute. Someone turned up the volume on the cassette player, and my eardrums began to throb. A few people tried to dance, but most of the guests just stood swaying like zombies, smoking or drinking or both, looking about and grinning vacuously.

I circulated and talked to a few people. One was 'into' primal scream, one was 'into' Icelandic poetry, and one was 'into' high colonics. With luck, I'd never see any of them again.

It really wasn't my kind of a do. Some of those guests were so *young*. When I was their age, I went to parties where we played Post Office and Spin the Bottle. So I decided to take off. I still hadn't met the host or hostess, and knew that trying to make a polite farewell in that mob was useless.

117

I looked around for Natalie and finally spotted her in a corner, pressed up against Akbar El Raschid, gripping him by the lapels of his camouflaged field jacket. It was obvious she was angry about something. I could see she was yelling at him, leaning up to put her face close to his. She appeared furious, but he just looked down at her with his loopy smile.

It took me forever to find a taxi, and I wasn't overjoyed at roaming those mostly deserted streets at that hour. But I finally took a chance on a rusted gypsy cab and arrived home safely, so thankful that I overtipped the driver and said, 'Have a nice day.' At two in the morning!

When I unlocked the door, my phone was ringing, and I dashed for it.

'Hello?' I said breathlessly.

'Dunk?' Al Georgio said. 'Jesus, where the hell have you been? I was ready to call out the Marines. After that letter you got . . .'

'It was sweet of you to be concerned,' I said. 'I'm all right, Al. I went down to a party in the East Village to meet Natalie Havistock's boyfriend.'

'The stud? Have a good time?'

'Not really.'

'Learn anything?'

'First he said he had nothing to do with stealing the Demaretion. Then he said that he and Nettie did it together. I don't know what to believe.'

'Yeah, the guy's a flake.'

'When I left, they were having a big fat argument. I don't know about what. Probably doesn't mean a thing.'

'Probably not.'

'Al, did you know the Havistocks have commercial cleaners? A man comes in twice a week to vacuum, and once a month a whole crew gives the place a complete going-over.'

'Yes, I knew that.'

'Did you check them out?'

'Of course I checked them out. The second day I was on the case. What do you think – I walk around with my thumb up my – sure, I checked them out. Their alibis stand up.'

'Just asking,' I said humbly.

'That's okay, Dunk; ask anything you like. Now let me get some sleep.'

'Al, thank you again for checking on me.'

'You're welcome,' he said gruffly.

I showered and shampooed to get the smoke fumes out of my hair. After I used my dryer, conditioner, and comb, I took a good look in the mirror. Mrs Havistock had been right; I had to *do* something with it.

I fell into bed, thinking I'd be asleep instantly. But I wasn't. I kept flopping from side to side. Somehow I was convinced that I had heard something important that day, something significant. But what it was I could not recall. Finally I drifted into troubled slumber. I may have snored – I've been told I do that occasionally – but no man was there to give me an elbow in the ribs.

16

'Now YOU must call me Vanessa,' she said in the kindliest way imaginable, touching the back of my hand with her bloody talons, 'and I shall call you Dunk. Isn't that your nickname?'

I nodded, doing my best to smile.

She turned slightly and raised one finger. Immediately a waiter was at her shoulder, bending over deferentially – and also copping a peek down her bodice. She had that effect on every man within a fifty-foot radius: heads turned, chairs scraped and, I suppose, testosterone flowed.

'I shall have,' she said precisely, 'a very, *very* dry martini, straight up with a single olive. Dunk?'

'A glass of white wine, please.'

'Nonsense,' she said firmly. 'No one drinks white wine anymore. And a kir royale,' she said to the waiter. He nodded, grinning like an idiot, and scurried away. 'You'll love it,' she assured me. 'Champagne and cassis.' She looked around. 'Isn't this a *fun* place?' she said.

I agreed it was, indeed, a fun place.

What it was, actually, was a fake Tudor pub on Third Avenue near 62nd Street. Beamed ceiling, plastered walls, pseudo-Tiffany lamps, everything burnished wood, gleaming brass, and red velvet. A stage set, with the menu written with chalk on a posted blackboard. Mostly steaks, chops, and things like broiled kidneys and sweetbreads. The prices were horrendous.

We were two of five women in the crowded joint. All the other customers were male, three-piece-suited money types who kept looking up from their mixed grills to take another long stare at Vanessa Havistock. When two men were lunching together, I figured one of them had to say, 'We'll flip for them, Charlie. Loser gets the beanpole.'

That morning phone call had been a surprise. I thought Vanessa was just being polite when she had asked, 'Can we have lunch?' But no, there she was with an invitation to join her at the 'fun place' on Third Avenue. I accepted promptly. I wore an old droopy shirt-waist, knowing there was no way I was ever going to outdress *her*.

It took me awhile to understand why she had selected that pub. Then I realized it was practically a men's locker room, with hearty guffaws, slapped backs, and vile cigars. Our Vanessa wanted to be where the boys were. That was okay; every grown woman should have a hobby, and she just *reveled* in the attention she attracted.

She ordered for both of us – naturally; she wouldn't trust me to know what I wanted. So we had cold sliced beefsteak, very rare, with a salad of arugola and watercress.

'Lots of protein,' she said, patting my hand. What a *physical* woman she was. 'Very good in the sex department. By the way,' she added, 'how *is* your sex department?'

'Fabulous,' I said boldly.

'Glad to hear it,' she said, knowing I was lying in my teeth.

The kir royale was super, and so were those slices of cold beef, so rare that I wondered if they had even warmed the cow. But Vanessa soon made it clear that this wasn't to be a purely social occasion.

'Tell me,' she said casually, drizzling some olive oil over her salad, 'how is your investigation coming along?'

'All right. I've talked to a lot of people.'

'Oh?' she said, knifing her steak into smaller slabs. 'Who?'

'Just about everyone. You and your husband, of course. Mr and Mrs Archibald Havistock. Roberta and Ross Minchen. Orson Vanwinkle. Natalie and her boyfriend.'

'Oh, my,' she said, 'you have been getting around.'

I was fascinated by the way she ate. Those sharp white teeth tore into meat, greens, and a crusty baguette with ferocious joy. Something primitive in the way she consumed food, and I thought my initial reaction had been on target: she really had a lot of animality.

'About Ross Minchen . . .' she said, busy with her lunch and not looking at me. 'Don't you think he's . . . well, a wee bit *odd*?'

'Odd?' I said. 'What do you mean?'

'Oh . . .' she said vaguely, 'sometimes he does strange things.'

I could have sworn right then that she knew about the Minchens' videocassettes, but I never mentioned them. 'What kind of strange things, Vanessa?'

121

'Well . . . for one thing, he likes to compose pornographic haiku – those three-line Japanese poems.'

'Ross Minchen can write Japanese?'

'Oh, no,' she said, laughing merrily. 'He writes them in English. Some of them are quite amusing. Like dirty limericks, you know – but different.'

Weirder and weirder.

She ordered espresso for us and consulted the posted blackboard for desserts available. We agreed that everything offered sounded sinfully fattening, so we skipped. She took a pack of Kent III from her bag and held it out to me.

'No, thank you,' I said. 'I don't smoke.'

'Smart you,' she said. 'I'm hooked.' She extracted a cigarette, and instantly that infatuated waiter was at her side, snapping a lighter.

'Thank you,' she said.

'My pleasure, madam,' he murmured, and moved regretfully away.

'Isn't he sweet?' she said, in the tones she might have used to comment, 'What a nice fox terrier.' Then, smoking and sipping her coffee, she asked me my personal reactions to everyone in the Havistock family.

'I'm always curious to know what people think, meeting us for the first time,' she said, an expert at the Wry Pout.

I knew she was pumping me, ever so tenderly, to learn what I knew about the theft of the Demaretion. I should have told her that what I had learned could have been engraved on the head of a pin.

I told her only what I was certain she already knew. I was determinedly discreet, and she listened without displaying any reaction until we got onto the subject of Orson Vanwinkle. Then her dark eyes glittered, she raised a hand to brush one of those wings of raven hair away from her face, and her expression became absolutely feral.

'Orson Vanwinkle is a vile, vile man,' she said, very intensely. 'And if I were you, I'd have nothing to do with him.'

'I do have to question him,' I said mildly.

'I suppose so, but never, *ever* trust him. He's alienated everyone he's known. Went through a dozen jobs before Archibald took pity on him and hired him as a secretary. What a mistake that was! The man's a creep. Ugh!' she added, shaking her shoulders with disgust.

She signaled for the bill, and when it arrived, she took a credit card from her brocaded handbag. 'Isn't plastic wonderful!' she said, and I agreed it was wonderful. I thanked her for a delightful lunch, and she said we must do it again soon.

On our way out, the headwaiter, who apparently was an old

122

friend, greeted her effusively. He thanked her for her patronage, and said he hoped to see her again soon. Then he kissed her fingers. I could swear he passed a small, folded piece of paper into her palm, but on the sidewalk she fumbled in her purse to make certain she had her credit card, the little paper disappeared, and I wondered if I had imagined the whole thing.

'Got to leave you here, Dunk,' she said. 'My dentist is waiting. Nothing serious – just cleaning and a checkup, but I've put it off long enough.'

'Thank you again for the lunch, Vanessa. I enjoyed it.'

'We *did* have a good time, didn't we?' she said, and leaned up to kiss my cheek. 'Ta-ta,' she said.

I started south, figuring I might stop at Bloomingdale's to browse. I walked about twenty or thirty feet, then turned to look back. Vanessa was still standing in front of the restaurant, and when she saw me looking, we both waved. Then I continued south.

At 61st Street, I turned again and looked back. The sidewalk was crowded, but I thought I saw her walking rapidly north on the avenue. I reversed course and went after her. My legs are long, and I can move when I want to. I followed her up to East 65th Street.

It was the first time in my life I had ever 'shadowed' anyone, but I had read enough detective mysteries to know the rudiments. Don't get too close. Don't fall too far behind. Use the show windows of stores as mirrors. If necessary, cross the street and tail from the other side. Try to be as nondescript as possible – a little difficult for a skinny six-two female with a mop of wild hair.

But she never looked back, so I figured I was a success. She crossed the avenue, walked quickly toward Second, and entered a brownstone in the middle of the block. Then I crossed the street and inspected the residence from the other side. No dentist's sign. No brass plaques at all. Nothing to indicate it was anything but private apartments. Vanessa Havistock was nowhere to be seen.

I walked to Second Avenue, crossed the street again, and returned west. Taking a deep breath, I ducked into the vestibule of the building she had entered. Took a quick look at the names listed on the bellplate. No dentists. But there was one L. Wolfgang. That could have been Lenore Wolfgang, Archibald Havistock's chunky attorney.

I started out for Bloomies again, wondering if L. Wolfgang was the name on the slip of paper the headwaiter had handed her, wondering

123

if L. Wolfgang was someone else, wondering if she had gone into one of the other apartments in the brownstone to spend a few innocent minutes with a friend before seeing her dentist.

I didn't buy anything at Bloomingdale's, but I did pick up a steno's spiral notebook at a nearby stationery store. Then I went home and spent the rest of the afternoon writing down everything I knew about the disappearance of the Demaretion. It was time, I thought, to get things organized and make certain I had a record of events, conversations, and impressions before I forgot them.

It took longer than I expected it would – there was so *much*! I kept going back again and again to add recalled details. Finally, early in the evening, I read over what I had written and was reasonably certain I had included everything. But it didn't tell me a damned thing. I wondered how detectives like Al Georgio and Jack Smack could endure all those uncertainties and loose ends. I know they maddened me.

I poured myself a glass of red wine from Al's bottomless jug and put it on the floor alongside the couch. Then I lay down. That couch was only five feet long, so my bony ankles and feet hung over one end. I sipped slowly. Went over everything in my mind and couldn't see any pattern at all. I hadn't a clue.

Except that I had heard something of significance that hadn't registered. I hit my forehead with the heel of my hand, trying to jar my brain into awareness. It didn't work. I finished the wine and set the glass carefully aside so I wouldn't step on it when I got up. Then I napped. On the couch. I admit it.

I was awakened about eight o'clock by the ringing of a bell. I started up dazedly, thought it was the phone, then realized it was the front door. I padded over in my bare feet and stared out the peephole. One advantage of living on the ground floor was that I could see who was ringing my bell in the vestibule. Al Georgio. I buzzed him in.

'Disturbing you?' he asked.

'You woke me up,' I said. 'I was napping – can you believe it? At this hour?'

'I wish I was.'

'Tough day?'

'The usual.'

'Have you eaten?'

'Oh, sure. I had something.'

'Don't tell me,' I said. 'A cheeseburger and a chocolate malt.'

'Not tonight,' he said with that boyish smile. 'We sent out for Chink. Everything in cardboard containers. Delicious.'

'I can imagine. Al, there's about enough of your wine left for a glass for each of us. How about it?'

'Sure,' he said, 'let's kill it.'

He sat on the couch, rubbing his forehead wearily. 'I've really got nothing to tell you, Dunk. It's all bits and pieces. But I wanted to stop by to see if you're okay.'

'I'm fine.'

'No more threatening letters?'

'Nope. For which I am thankful.'

'I'll take the one you got along with me. Like I told you, we'll probably get nothing from it, but you never know. What have you been up to?'

'Had lunch today with Vanessa Havistock.'

'Did you? Get anything?'

'Only that she doesn't like Orson Vanwinkle,' I said, deciding not to tell him about that brownstone on East 65th Street. 'But then, no one does.'

'Yeah,' he said, 'the guy's not exactly Mr Clean. He's got a sheet – did you know that?'

'A sheet?'

'Criminal record. Minor stuff mostly. Traffic violations. Complaints by neighbors about excessive noise. A charge of public drunkenness. A couple of suits for bad debts that he eventually settled. The heaviest is a rape charge that was dropped. He probably paid off. A nasty son of a bitch.'

'He certainly sounds like it,' I said slowly.

'But all that stuff dates from more than five years ago,' Al said. 'Since then he's apparently cleaned up his act.'

'Since he went to work for Archibald Havistock.'

'Yeah,' Al said, staring at me, 'I had the same idea. I guess he's making a nice buck now, and Archibald told him to shape up or ship out.'

I shook my head. 'A leopard can't change its spots,' I said.

'And a bird in the hand is worth two in the bush,' Al said. 'How *are* you, Dunk? I've missed you.'

'That's nice. And I've missed you, Al.'

'This lousy job,' he said, groaning. 'I never have time to do what I want to do.'

'Like what?'

125

'Live a little. See you. See my daughter. Enjoy.'

'Al, do you think this Demaretion thing will ever get cleared up?'

He shrugged. 'It's getting colder and colder. We can spend just so much time on it, then it goes into the file. It'll still be open, but with new stuff coming along every day, we've got to ration—'

But just then my doorbell rang again.

'Oh, God,' I said, 'now who can that be?'

'Jack Smack,' Al said with a rueful smile.

He was right.

The greeting between the two men was cool.

'Hey, there,' Smack said.

'How you doing?' Georgio said.

And that was that. No shaking of hands. A kind of wary, glowering hostility. They both sat on the couch. I brought Jack a glass of his vodka. If Al was surprised that I knew what Jack drank, he didn't show it.

'How's it going, Dunk?' Smack asked.

'I'm surviving.'

'She got a threatening letter,' Georgio said. 'From the description, it sounds like it's from the same slug your company has been dealing with. Could we take a look at it, Dunk, please?'

I brought out the letter. The two detectives moved closer together on the couch and examined the sheet of paper, holding it lightly by the corners.

'It's the same,' Smack said. 'I'd swear to it. Same paper, same typewriter, and the *o*'s are filled in, just like on the letters we got.'

Georgio folded it up, put it back in the envelope, and slid it into his jacket pocket. 'I'll have our lab guys give it a look,' he said. 'But I don't think they'll find any more than you got, Jack.'

'They won't,' Smack said. 'We put some good people on it.' He looked at me thoughtfully. 'You know what this letter means, don't you, Dunk? A member of the Havistock family has to be involved. Who else would know you've been hired and are going around asking questions? Not an outside crook.'

'I'll buy that,' Al said. He turned to the other man. 'Trade-off time?' he suggested.

'Sure,' Jack said. 'What have you got?'

'Financial stuff.'

'Okay. You go first.'

'Archibald Havistock is worth about six mil. But a lot of it is in raw land, and mostly in his wife's name. He's not exactly in what they call a liquid condition. Not hurting, mind you, but not sleeping on a bed of greenbacks either.'

'Maybe that's why he decided to sell off his collection,' I said.

'Wouldn't be a bit surprised,' Smack said. 'Well, son Luther *is* hurting. He's in hock up to his pipik. The apartment, the car, the summer home – all on high-interest loans. And his out-of-pocket expenses must be brutal.'

'Like Vanessa's jewelry,' I said.

'Right. I think Luther is on the ropes. He's making about sixty-five thousand a year in salary and probably spending twice that. Maybe Daddy is helping him out, but I doubt it.'

'What about the Minchens?' I asked.

'They're in good shape dollarwise,' Al Georgio said. 'In addition to his salary, Ross is drawing against a trust fund. Not a big one but tidy. Enough to pay the rent every month. From what I hear, he's a tight man with a buck.'

'Heard the same thing,' Jack Smack said, nodding, 'and I can't figure it. He's got a nice bank balance, but for the past two years or so he's been making some hefty cash withdrawals and no investments to show for it. Five and ten Gs at a time.'

Georgio looked up sharply. 'Regularly? On a monthly basis?'

'No,' Jack said, 'four or five times a year. But it could still be blackmail. As far as I can find out, he doesn't play the horses or keep a cupcake on the side.'

Maybe, I thought morosely, Ross Minchen was spending it all on porn videotapes.

'We were talking about Orson Vanwinkle before you came in,' Georgio said. 'Now there's a case. Five years ago he was in brokesville, but now he's living the life of Riley.'

'Right,' Smack said. 'And there isn't even any Mrs Riley. I don't know where he's getting the loot, but he seems to be floating through life.'

'Maybe Mr Havistock is paying him a good salary,' I said.

Jack shook his head. 'I couldn't find out how much he's making, but it couldn't be enough to pay for Vanwinkle's toys. If his salary covers his brandy bills, it would surprise me. Did you get any skinny on the younger daughter?' he asked Georgio. 'The born-again hippie?'

'She draws a sweet allowance,' Al said. 'A trust fund when she marries – if ever. I think most of her allowance goes to that spade

127

lover of hers, and the other crazies she runs around with. She's supporting the whole kooky cell.'

Then we were all silent, looking at each other, then looking down at our drinks. I had a panicky moment when I wondered if the two men were trying to outlast each other, waiting for the rival to leave. If that were true, the three of us might be sitting there, wordless, when the sun rose over Brooklyn.

'Well,' I said brightly, 'if financial need was the motive for swiping the Demaretion, then Luther Havistock seems to be the best bet. Am I right?'

The two detectives nodded, not too confidently.

'It makes sense logically,' Georgio said, 'but I just can't buy it. Even assuming he could have made the switch when Archibald was in the living room, I still don't think he's got the balls for it.'

'I agree,' Smack said, 'but his wife has. Two desperate people. They could have been working together. She pushed him into it. That woman would steal the torch from the Statue of Liberty if she could figure a way to carry it.'

Silence again. I looked at them, sitting side by side on the couch. Al so heavy, solid, and dependable. Jack the tap dancer, slender, carefree, and oh so elegant. If I had my druthers – which? I honestly didn't know.

'Well . . .' Georgio said, sighing and heaving himself to his feet. 'I've got to be going.'

Smack finished his drink hastily. 'Me, too,' he said, rising. 'It's been a long day.'

I watched with dismay as both of them moved to the door. *Both* of them! I wanted to knock their heads together. But instead I kissed their cheeks and smiled sweetly when they thanked me for the drinks. Then I locked, bolted, and chained the door. The idiots!

I washed the glasses, emptied the ashtrays, and went in to shower. I washed my damned hair furiously, then tried to do something with it. As Al would have said, zip, zero, and zilch. I put on my pajamas and there I was – alone in bed again. It was getting tiresome.

128

17

THE NEXT day was a roller coaster. It started up, then swooped into the pits, and ended on the heights again. A little shattering, but it wasn't dull.

For breakfast, I had cranberry juice, an English muffin with blackberry preserve, and decaf coffee while I plowed through the morning *Times*. Then I went back to my steno notebook and entered everything I had heard the previous evening from Al Georgio and Jack Smack on the financial status of the Havistocks. I was convinced if I was organized, efficient, eventually my detailed notes on the crime would reveal the solution. Ho-ho.

The first phone call of the day came from Hobart Juliana – which pleased me mightily. Not only because I wanted to keep our friendship intact, but also because he had some good news to pass along. We chatted awhile about what was going on in his life, in my life, and life in general, and then he sprang a surprise.

'Dunk,' he said, 'I heard some office gossip this morning on very good authority. It concerns you, so I thought you should know.'

'What? What?'

'Well, apparently, from what I heard, the police detective and the insurance detective, both of them, came in to talk to god and Felicia Dodat. They swore there's absolutely no way you could have been involved in the disappearance of the Demaretion, and they said you should get your job back again, and it was cruel and unusual punishment to keep you on unpaid leave of absence.'

It's possible that tears came to my eyes. 'That was sweet of them, Hobie,' I said.

'Yes,' he went on, 'and the powers that be said they'd discuss it with that old fart attorney, Lemuel Whattsworth, before they decided

129

what to do. Anyway, Dunk dear, I wanted you to know that you have some clout on your side.'

'Thank you, Hobie,' I said, all choked up. 'You're a darling to tell me about it. As soon as I get out from under, I'm going to call you for lunch. Okay?'

'You better,' he said. 'I miss you, Dunk.'

Hobie missed me. Al Georgio missed me. That was comforting. I really wasn't alone. But what about Jack Smack – my one-night stand? He hadn't said he missed me. But that bastard probably didn't miss anyone.

I reflected on what I had just heard. I thought I knew why Georgio and Smack were trying to get my job back for me. After that stupid letter I received, they were concerned for my safety. So they figured if they got me reinstated at Grandby's, I'd give up my investigative work for the Havistocks and be out of the line of fire.

It *was* sweet of them, and I appreciated it. In fact, their kindness made me feel guilty about not telling them both about Vanessa's visit to the East 65th Street brownstone and the Minchens' porn parties. But I salved my conscience by deciding that they probably knew about that already.

I thought I understood their motives, but I wasn't certain I understood my own. If their plea to Grandby & Sons succeeded and I was put back on salary, would I give up my investigation of the Demaretion theft?

Never!

And why not?

Because I wouldn't be completely cleared until the real thief was caught. The moment I thought that, I realized how silly it was – pure rationalization.

The real reason I didn't want to give up the search for the Demaretion was because it was challenging, exciting, and I enjoyed it. It made me come face-to-face with how empty my life had been before this whole thing started.

Also, the investigation had enabled me to meet two interesting men who seemed to be attracted to me. As they say in New York, that ain't chopped liver!

I called the Havistock apartment, hoping to speak to the madame. I wanted to go over to East 79th Street and talk to Ruby Querita, but thought it politic to ask Mrs Havistock's permission first. But Ruby herself answered the phone and told me the lady of the house wasn't in. Neither was Mr Havistock. Neither was Orson Vanwinkle nor

130

Natalie. So, remembering I had carte blanche from my employers to talk to anyone and everyone, I told Ruby I'd be right over to ask her some questions. And hung up before she could object.

She greeted me at the door pleasantly enough and led me into a kitchen that looked big enough to service a cruise ship. We sat at an enameled table, and Ruby busied herself peeling fresh garlic cloves while we talked. That garlic odor was something. We had a neighbor in Des Moines who ate them raw, washed down with slivovitz. He was a friend, but not a *close* friend.

Ruby's dourness seemed to have lightened up since I first met her, and now she was almost companionable. I will not say she was ugly, but she was excessively plain – with a discernible mustache that didn't help things. I felt sorry for her. She looked like a woman who had worked hard all her life, knew nothing but the miseries, and didn't expect things to change much until she was put to rest.

I went into my spiel and took her through the events of that fateful morning. She answered all my questions readily enough. Yes, the caterer's men had brought the food for the birthday party, then left. The Minchens arrived. Natalie was there. Then Vanessa and Luther Havistock came in. Everyone was assembled.

People wandered in and out of her kitchen, mixing drinks, sampling tidbits. Ruby was aware of my arrival. And then the guards from the armored van were brought into the apartment by Orson Vanwinkle. She seemed to know everything that went on that morning.

'You were in the kitchen, here, all the time?' I asked.

She thought a moment. 'No,' she said finally. 'Not all the time. A man comes with flowers – for the lady – I let him in. Then, also, I was in the living room. Also, I went to a back storage closet for a punch bowl and glasses. I was in and out.'

It all added up to a big fat nothing. I had to keep reminding myself that she could be lying. It was difficult to believe.

'I understand your brother is in prison,' I said softly.

She shrugged, concentrating on the garlic cloves, gently peeling away the silk with a little paring knife. 'The devil's got him,' she said quietly.

'The devil?' I asked.

She looked up at me, and suddenly those dulled eyes blazed. 'He has forsaken our Saviour,' she said with great intensity. 'He must pay for his sins.'

131

I took a deep breath. 'I understand his case is being appealed. Are you helping him out, Ruby?'

She shook her head. ' "Vengeance is mine, saith the Lord." '

'Ruby,' I said, hunching toward her over the table, 'who do you think stole the coin?'

'That I do not know,' she said, looking down at what her fingers were doing, 'but it is God's punishment on this house.'

I was shocked. 'Why should God want to punish the Havistocks?'

She stopped her work, raised her head, glared at me. 'Because of their sins! They have sinned in the eyes of God Almighty, and they must suffer for their transgressions. Did they think their crimes would go unseen? Oh, no! Bitter is the fruit thereof. The first shall be last, and the last shall be first. A camel through the eye of a needle . . . Bring the innocent unto me. And what shall it profit a man? Blood of the lamb. Be sure your sins will find you out. Set thine house in order. Whoever perishes, being innocent? Blessed are all they that put their trust in Him. The Lord is my strength and my shield.'

She finally ran down, and I rose hastily, thanked her for her cooperation, and practically ran out of there. I was really shook.

I walked home, and all along East 79th Street I looked up at the glittering windows of those big apartment houses and wondered what was going on inside. Suddenly they no longer seemed bastions of solidity, respectability, or even of rationality. They were just stone and steel façades, shining in the June sunlight. And within – darkness.

I was still gloomy when I arrived home and had to force myself to make notes on the interrogation of Ruby Querita. It was all religious gibberish, I acknowledged, but might there not be a germ of truth there? Ruby had been with the family a long time. She was in a position to know what was going on. So why her outburst? What were the awful sins of the Havistocks?

This was the kind of stuff I wouldn't dare repeat to Al Georgio or Jack Smack. They'd tell me Ruby was a nut, and I was even nuttier to take her seriously. But that was masculine logic at work again. Sometimes you sense things, you *feel* things, and I felt Ruby Querita wasn't entirely irrational; she knew something.

When I'm in an antsy mood like that, I have to eat, so I opened the refrigerator door and examined the possibilities. Depressing. I settled for a poor little potato that had already been baked and was now all shriveled. I heated it up and opened a can of brisling sardines. (Do you know what sardines cost these days!) I washed that gourmet lunch down with a can of diet cola. I really know how to live.

I spent the afternoon doing chores: took in some dry cleaning, picked up a pair of shoes with new lifts, bought some frozen dinners – Lean Cuisine and Stouffer's – a loaf of French bread, treated myself to a jug of Gallo Hearty Burgundy and, throwing caution to the winds, purchased a Sara Lee cheesecake with chocolate bits. Enjoy a little, I told myself – remembering that depressing lunch.

I was stowing away my vittles when the phone rang – and the day's roller coaster took its downward swoop. It was Al Georgio.

'You sitting?' he demanded.

'No,' I said, 'I'm standing up.'

'Then hang on to something. I'm on East Eighty-fifth Street. The body of Orson Vanwinkle was found a couple of hours ago. The guy's stone cold dead in the market. Murdered. Shot to death.'

Silence.

'Dunk?' he said anxiously. 'You there?'

'I'm here,' I said faintly.

'I heard about it by accident. A buddy who knows I'm working the Demaretion heist got it on the squawker and alerted me. The homicide guys took over; I'm just hanging around the edges.'

'Al, what happened?'

'Dunk, it's only two hours old; no one knows much. No signs of forced entry. Apparently shot twice in the head with a small-caliber weapon. That's all we've got so far.'

'Al,' I said desperately, 'you think this has something to do with the Demaretion?'

'You want me to guess? All right, I'll guess. Yes, it's got something to do with the theft.'

'Al, will you call me back if you learn anything more? Better yet, can you come over when you're finished? I've got some frozen dinners and wine. We can eat, and you can tell me all about it.'

'It may be late.'

'I don't care how late it is. *Please*, Al.'

'Okay,' he said. 'Meanwhile, watch yourself, Dunk. Looks like the guy who wrote you that swell letter wasn't kidding. Be careful.'

'I will be,' I assured him, and when he hung up, I went around to check the locks on my windows and doors, still stunned from what I had heard. Orson Vanwinkle dead? Murdered? I didn't like the man, but no one deserves *that*.

I was so confused. Al said he thought it was connected to the

133

Demaretion robbery, and I thought so, too. But how? I frantically consulted my notebook, looking for the magic clue. Found nothing, of course. So I popped two Anacin. I suddenly had a headache that just wouldn't end.

Al called again shortly after eight o'clock and said he was on his way, but he didn't show up until a little after nine. He was in a furious mood.

'Son of a *bitch*!' he said angrily, flopping on the couch. 'This really screws things up.'

'I don't suppose you've eaten today,' I said. 'Have you?'

'What? No, I haven't.'

'Have a glass of wine and try to unwind. I'll put some food on. Your choice is meatball stew or vegetable lasagna. Which will it be?'

'I'll go for the stew.'

'Good for you. Only three hundred calories. But we'll have Sara Lee cheesecake for dessert.'

'So who's counting calories? God *damn* it! I can't figure it. Why Orson Vanwinkle? Why him?'

By the time I put things in the oven, poured us glasses of wine, and went back into the living room, he had calmed down a little, but was still brooding.

'Tell me about it,' I said. 'What happened?'

He sighed. 'We haven't got a hell of a lot. Vanwinkle had a cleaning woman who came in twice a week. She had a key to his apartment. The super of the building let her in the front door. She found the body and called nine-eleven. No signs of forced entry. So he let in someone he knew – right? Almost two grand in cash in his bedside table, so it wasn't a ripoff. Nothing else missing, as far as we can tell. He was shot twice in the back of the skull. Small caliber. Maybe a twenty-two. The ME guesses he died around midnight last night. Around there. We'll have to wait for the autopsy to be sure.'

I took a deep breath, feeling a wee bit queasy. 'Al, where do you go from here?'

'Not me. I'm not handling it, thank God. The homicide guys will try to trace his movements after he left the Havistocks' apartment yesterday afternoon. Around four-thirty. They've got a lot of work. They found his little black book. Plenty of names, addresses, and phone numbers. Mostly women. You're in it.'

'*Me?!*'

'That's right,' he said, smiling bleakly. 'The guy was either a Casanova or thought he was.'

'Al, I swear I—'

He held up a palm. 'Hey, Dunk, I'm not accusing you of anything. I think you've got more sense than to play around with a creep like that. But you're in his book, so you can expect a visit from the homicide dicks.'

'What should I tell them?'

'The truth. No more, no less. Actually, he had a kind of steady girlfriend. A frizzy blonde who looks like a nineteen-twenties type. A real boop-boop-a-doop girl. A flapper. Not a brain in her head, but apparently they've been making nice-nice for almost five years. I think he's laying a lot of loot on her.'

'Where was she last night when he was killed?'

Georgio looked at me admiringly. 'You're really learning the drill, aren't you? She says she was visiting a sick aunt in Riverdale. They're checking it out.'

I glanced at my Snoopy watch. 'Our dinners should be thawed by now. Hungry?'

'Famished,' he said.

We ate at my dinky dinner table, about as large as a bandanna. I had the vegetable lasagna, and Al had the meatball stew. Thank God for that loaf of French bread; he demolished it. But while we ate and drank, we couldn't stop talking about Orson Vanwinkle's murder.

'Who do you think hated him enough to do it?' Al asked me.

'Probably everyone,' I said. 'Natalie didn't like him. Vanessa called him a vile man. And then there's Ruby Querita . . .'

I decided to tell him about my conversation with her early that morning. He listened intently, and he didn't seem to think me nutty to believe there might be something in what she said.

'These religious fanatics . . .' he said, 'you've *got* to take them seriously. They'll massacre and say God told them to do it. Like Natalie's boyfriend, that born-again Muslim . . . Who knows what's going on in his tiny, tiny mind? But my big problem is that the homicide guys are going to be tramping all over my investigation of the Demaretion heist.'

'You still think the two are connected – the theft of the coin and Vanwinkle's murder?'

'Oh, hell yes,' he said, sitting back, dunking a crust of bread in his red wine, then munching on it – I never saw anyone do that before. 'I think it's all one case. But I don't like the idea of being pushed aside by the homicide squad. God damn it, it's *my* baby.'

'Of course it is.'

'All I can do is trade with them,' he said thoughtfully. 'One for one. If they're willing to cooperate, I'll cooperate.' He looked at me with a bleak smile. 'Interoffice politics,' he said, 'but that's the way things work. We're all trying to protect our backs and claim credit due.'

'That's understandable,' I said. 'It was the same way at Grandby's. And talking about that, thank you for making a pitch to get my job back. You and Jack Smack.'

'Oh, you heard about that, did you? Well, we figured that after you got that threatening letter, it might be smart to try to get you out of the target area. Now, with Vanwinkle scragged, I think it's more important than ever. Dunk, give it up, will you?'

'No,' I said instantly. 'The Havistocks are paying me to do a job, and I mean to do it.'

He stared at me. 'You might get your ass shot off,' he said. 'You know that, don't you?'

'Not me,' I said. 'Not enough ass to aim at.'

He laughed at that. 'You're always putting yourself down. You happen to have an elegant ass.'

'I think,' I said, 'this would be a perfect time to have the cheesecake.'

I didn't ask him if he'd like to stay the night, and he didn't ask if he could. It was just generally understood.

He insisted he smelled like a goat and *had* to shower. So I gave him a fresh towel and let him go ahead while I cleaned up and washed the few dishes we had used. I took the wine jug and our glasses into the bedroom, turned down the lights, undressed, and slid between the cool sheets. It was delightful and frightening at the same time – if you know what I mean.

He wasn't half as expert as Jack Smack, but twice as sincere. I didn't have to wonder if he was putting on an act, or think of how many women he had been with to learn the things he knew. Al didn't know all that much. But he was tender and solicitous, and there was a kind of brutal power there that Jack could never have. All I can say is that we had us a time. A good time.

Later, sitting up in bed, both of us sipping wine, he said, 'We just sinned. I'm Catholic – did you know that?'

'Going to confess what we did?'

'Nah,' he said, laughing. 'Why should I get a poor priest all stirred up? It'll be our secret. I guess I'm not a very good Catholic.'

136

'I was raised a Methodist,' I told him, 'but after I came to New York I got out of the habit. I haven't been to church in I forget how long.'

He patted the mattress. 'This is as good a church as any, Dunk.'

'I agree.'

'After I got divorced,' he said, 'I played around some. Not a lot, but enough. Mostly one-night stands. Fun and games. Not very satisfying.'

'No,' I said, 'it isn't.'

'I like being with you, Dunk. I mean *really* like it. Not just the sex – though that was great. I mean talking and laughing. Being together. We can keep on doing it, can't we?'

'I'm counting on it.'

'You have no special guy?'

'No,' I said, 'no one special.'

'Well, I have no right to ask you to devote your entire life to me. That's too heavy. But I just wanted you to know that while I'm seeing you, I'm not going to do any tomcatting around. I guess I really am a one-woman man. I'm not telling you that to get you to change your way of living. Nothing like that. I just wanted you to know how I feel.'

I turned to kiss his wine-sweet lips. 'You're a dear man, Al, and I love being with you. But I can't make any promises I won't keep.'

'I know that,' he said, 'and I'm not asking for any promises – except that you'll keep seeing me. For a while.'

'*That* I can promise,' I assured him. Then, because he was being so loving, I said, 'Al there's something I have to tell you.'

'Hey, listen,' he said, 'you don't *have* to tell me anything.'

'It's about the Demaretion. That case means a lot to you, doesn't it?'

'Oh, hell yes. A big theft. Important people. Lots of publicity. It would look good in my jacket if I broke it. Maybe a promotion. Especially now that Vanwinkle's murder is involved.'

I sighed. 'Then I think I better tell you . . .'

I described my evening with Roberta and Ross Minchen, their party, guests, and the torrid videocassettes. Then I told him about my lunch with Vanessa Havistock, and how she claimed an appointment with her dentist, but then had scurried to a brownstone on East 65th Street where there was an apartment in the name of L. Wolfgang.

'Maybe Lenore Wolfgang,' I said. 'Archibald Havistock's

137

attorney. You met her at their place. Al, I don't know what all this means – if it means anything.'

He had listened closely, never interrupting, and when I finished, he didn't say something stupid, like, 'Why didn't you tell me this before?' Instead, he said, 'You're becoming one hell of a snoop, Dunk.'

Then he said the porn party at the Minchens was interesting, but not something he really wanted to get involved with.

'Pornography in the privacy of your own home is in a kind of gray area,' he said. 'We'd never get a conviction unless they're peddling the stuff, which I doubt. Still, it's good to know. I might be able to use it as a club one of these days. About Vanessa and the brownstone – now that *is* interesting. You didn't happen to get the number of the building, did you?'

'I'm afraid not,' I said, ashamed. 'I'm not such a supersleuth after all.'

'That's okay,' he said. 'You're super in other ways. More important ways. Maybe in the next day or so you'll take a ride with me and point out the building. Okay? Then I'll find out if L. Wolfgang really is Havistock's attorney, and how long she's lived there, and what her connection is with Vanessa, and so forth and so on. It's a brand-new lead, and a good one. Thank you, Dunk.'

'You'll let me work with you on this?' I asked anxiously.

'You better believe it,' he said, turning to take me into his arms. 'I'm not going to let you go now.'

He was capable and I was eager, so we had an encore. Later we slept like babies. Well . . . maybe not *exactly* like babies. I heartily approve of twosies in one bed. I just hope I didn't snore.

138

18

THE NEXT morning – Al gone before I awoke – I looked in the mirror and decided that loving is good for the complexion. I don't mean I was radiant or anything like that, but I really did think that some tiny lines and wrinkles that had been worrying me had disappeared. Do you think sex is a kind of vanishing cream?

I had my usual skimpy breakfast and read every word in the *Times* about the murder of Orson Vanwinkle. It was a small front-page story with runover, and it didn't tell me any more than I already knew. Still, seeing it all in cold print was a shocker, and I remembered that poor idiot asking, 'Was it as good for you as it was for me?'

Just as Al Georgio had warned, homicide detectives came knocking at my door. Two of them, one skinny, one fat – like Laurel and Hardy. I answered all their questions as honestly as I could, but to tell you the truth, they didn't seem too interested. They were going through the routine, but I got the feeling I had already been eliminated as a possible suspect. For which I was thankful.

While they were in my apartment (I gave them coffee), Jack Smack phoned, but I told him I was busy and would call him back. After the detectives left, I called Jack, but *his* line was busy. I finally got through to him a little after noon.

'What do you think?' he asked. 'About Vanwinkle getting chilled. It ties with the Demaretion – right?'

'I don't know for sure,' I said, 'but I guess it does. You think so?'

'Absolutely,' he said. 'No doubt about it. Why else would anyone knock off a nothing like that?'

I was determined to play no favorites, and whatever I had told Al Georgio I wanted Jack to know. I swear that at that point in time – where did I learn that phrase! – I had no preference.

'Jack,' I said, 'I have some things to tell you. Shall I give it to you now, over the phone, or . . . ?'

'No,' he said promptly, 'not on the phone. Let me look at my pad . . . How's about dinner late tonight?'

'No,' I said, just as promptly. I wasn't about to become a shuttle-cock – you should excuse the expression. 'I'm busy tonight.'

'All right,' he said equably. 'Then how's about the Sacred Cow for cocktails? Around five o'clock. It's on West Seventy-second, not too far from where you live.'

'Why there?'

'I like the place,' he said. 'Meet you there at five.'

He hung up. I stared at the phone. He said and I did. I wasn't certain I liked that.

But other things happened that afternoon. I got a call from Enoch Wottle – dear old Enoch – and he didn't even reverse the charges.

'Dunk, love,' he said, 'how *are* you?'

'Oh, Enoch, I don't know how I am.'

'I can understand,' he said. 'I read in the paper and heard on the TV. Orson Vanwinkle is murdered, who was personal secretary to Archibald Havistock, who owned the Demaretion that was stolen. I don't like that.'

'I don't like it either, Enoch.'

'Please, Dunk,' he said, 'don't get involved.'

'Enoch, I *am* involved. I can't get out of it now.'

He blew out his breath. 'What a mess,' he said. 'Well, maybe what I have heard will help. This morning – it is still morning out here – no more than an hour ago – I got a phone call from an old friend in Rotterdam. We have done business together, and I trust him. He is one of the dealers I contacted when you asked me to see what I could find out about a Demaretion being offered for sale. This Rotterdam man said he had a call from a dealer in Beirut. I have heard of this Beirut goniff. Very, very shady. He buys from grave robbers. His coins have no provenance at all. But he does very well selling to private collectors. Anyway, according to my Rotterdam friend, this Beirut man asked if he'd be interested in a Demaretion in Extremely Fine condition.'

'Wow,' I said.

'Yes, that was my reaction. How often does a Demaretion come on the market? Of course it could always be a new discovery, a piece found in a hoard in that part of the world. But the coincidence is too much. A Demaretion disappears in New York, and a Demaretion shows up in Beirut. Fascinating – no?'

'Fascinating, yes,' I said. 'Enoch, I hate to ask you for more favors

– you've been so kind to me – but could you follow up on this? Try to find out if the Beirut dealer actually has the coin.'

'I will do my best,' he said. 'Dunk, I must tell you I am enjoying this. It is very, uh, romantic. But please, I beg you, do not put yourself in danger. The people mixed up in this are not nice.'

'I know that, Enoch,' I said, 'and I promise not to do anything foolish.'

'Good,' he said. 'I love you, and I miss you.'

Another man who missed me! It made my day. After I got off the line with Enoch, I did something I should have done before: I looked up L. Wolfgang on East 65th Street in the Manhattan telephone directory. No such animal. But there were two listings for Lenore Wolfgang, a residence on East 91st Street, and a business address on lower Fifth Avenue.

Just to make sure, I called Information and asked for the number of L. Wolfgang on East 65th Street. The operator told me sorry, it was an unlisted number. So that was that. Maybe Al Georgio could find out.

I entered what Enoch Wottle had told me about the Beirut dealer and the business about L. Wolfgang's unlisted number in my notebook. Then I sat back and stared at what I had written. Nothing. None of it came together. I didn't even have a crazy idea.

I was only a few minutes late getting to the Sacred Cow on West 72nd Street, but Jack Smack was already at the bar, working on a double vodka. Handsomest man in the place, without a doubt. He gave me a big *abrazo*, a kiss on the cheek, and held my hand. So maybe it wasn't just a one-night stand after all.

I ordered a white wine, despite Vanessa Havistock telling me it was unchic. Then I started babbling. I told Jack about Ruby Querita's religious mania and about Vanessa's visit to that East 65th Street brownstone with an apartment occupied by L. Wolfgang.

When I finished, Jack looked at me and shook his head in wonder. 'You're a dynamite lady,' he said. 'Did you tell Al Georgio all this?'

I nodded.

'Fair enough,' he said. 'I already knew about Ruby's craziness, but what do you think the business about Vanessa means?'

'I have no idea. Absolutely none.'

'I guess Al is going to check into that Sixty-fifth Street building.'

'I imagine he will.'

'Oh, he will,' Smack assured me. 'He's very thorough. A real professional.'

141

'Jack,' I said, 'did your company get another letter from the crook?'

'No,' he said, 'and that's what worries us. We should have had a reply by now to the notice we put in the paper. Maybe the guy who's writing us really does have the coin, but isn't satisfied with our offer and doesn't want to haggle. Maybe he's trying to peddle it somewhere else.'

'Beirut,' I said.

'What?'

'Beirut,' I repeated, and then told him about Enoch Wottle and his call to me that afternoon. Jack listened carefully, frowning.

'It just doesn't *sound* right,' he said. 'It's like two different guys are trying to sell the same merchandise. I mean, we were dealing with a man in New York – right? We could have come to terms; he had to know that. But no, he suddenly offers the Demaretion to a back-alley dealer in Lebanon. It doesn't make sense, Dunk.'

'I agree; it doesn't.'

He looked at me with a queer expression, then suddenly snapped his fingers. 'Unless,' he said, 'unless . . .'

'Unless what?'

'When did your friend in Arizona hear from his pal in Rotterdam?'

'This morning. An hour before he phoned me.'

'And when did the Rotterdam man get the call from the Beirut dealer?'

'Enoch didn't say, but I had the feeling it was very recently, and he called Enoch immediately.'

'Yeah,' Jack said, looking at me with a twisted grin, 'I'll bet it was recently. I'll bet it was after Orson Vanwinkle got dusted.'

'What does that mean?'

'How does this scenario sound: Orson Vanwinkle cops the coin. He's been the guy dealing with us, and he's the guy who sent you the drop-dead letter. But then Orson gets killed. Now someone else has the coin. And he's dealing with Beirut. Does that listen?'

'Button, button,' I recited, 'who's got the button?'

'Something like that. What do you think?'

'It could have happened like that,' I said, 'except there's no way Orson could have switched display case thirteen.'

'Sure there is,' Jack argued. 'Archibald was out of the library for a few minutes when Vanwinkle brought in the armored car guards. Orson could have made the switch right then.'

'Maybe,' I acknowledged, 'but how could Orson have known

that Mr Havistock would be absent? That's where it falls apart, Jack.'

'Shit,' he said disgustedly, 'you're right. Well, back to the old drawing board. Let's have one more drink, Dunk, and then I've got to run.'

'Heavy date tonight?' I said casually, hating myself for asking it.

'Not so heavy,' he said. 'Dolly LeBaron – Vanwinkle's sleep-in girlfriend. She's got herself an agent, and she's trying to sell her story to the tabloids. Her life with the murdered socialite – complete with intimate photos. Hot stuff. Isn't that beautiful?'

'Beautiful,' I said. 'Al called her a boop-boop-a-doop girl.'

'Al's right,' he said. 'She looks like she's ready to break into a Charleston at any minute.'

I got home, alone, about an hour later. Depressed. I told myself I was not, absolutely *not* jealous of Dolly LeBaron because Jack Smack was taking her to dinner. After all, hadn't he asked me first? Still . . .

I wasn't hungry – too many salted peanuts at the Sacred Cow – so I went back to my spiral notebook, rereading everything I had written and trying to make some sense out of it. Hopeless. Then I started thinking about Jack Smack's theory: two thieves involved. One steals the Demaretion and starts dealing with the insurance company. Then someone else gets possession of the coin and calls a disreputable Lebanese coin dealer for quick cash.

It sounded right, except that I still didn't think Orson Vanwinkle was the original crook. My mind was boggled. I was saved from complete mental collapse by a brief phone call from Al Georgio.

'Just got a minute,' he said, 'but I wanted you to know that last night was the best thing that's happened to me in God knows how long, and I thank you.'

'Al,' I said, 'you don't have to—'

'Got to run,' he said. 'We're all jammed up here. Now they say Vanwinkle's apartment was tossed.'

'Tossed?'

'Searched. Very cleverly done. But someone was looking for something.'

'The Demaretion?'

'Could be.'

'Al, there's something I've got to tell you. This morning I got a call from—'

'Phone you early tomorrow,' he said, and hung up.

So there I was, bereft again. I thought of people I might call and yell, 'Help!' But I got over that mood soon enough – I'm really an up person – and spent the rest of the evening just schlumpfing around, which is what I call doing unnecessary chores to keep busy, like changing the bedding, wiping out the ashtrays, and taking up the hem on a denim shirt. Swell stuff like that.

But I was thinking!

Mostly about Al's news that Vanwinkle's apartment had been tossed. That tied in with Jack Smack's theory that two thieves had been involved. Orson had been the first. Then someone had searched for and perhaps found the Demaretion.

Someone who was the second thief, and someone who was a murderer.

19

AL GEORGIO was true to his word and called me early in the morning
– so early that I was still asleep.

'Oh, God,' he said when he heard my grumpy voice, 'I woke you
up, didn't I?'

'That's okay.'

'Sorry, Dunk. Want me to call you back?'

'No, no. I'm wide awake now.'

'How many hours did you sleep?'

'About seven.'

'You're lucky,' he said. 'I got three. I'm running on black coffee
and bennies. Listen, Dunk, I'm going to be tied up all day, but
there's a favor I'd like to ask.'

'Shoot.'

'Never say that to a cop. I'm not going to be able to drive you
to East Sixty-fifth Street to get the number of that brownstone
Vanessa Havistock went into – the one with the apartment rented by
L. Wolfgang. Do you think you could get over there today, get the
number, and give me a call? Leave a message if I'm not in. After I
have the number of the building I'll be able to start checking records:
who owns it, who leases the apartments, and all that jazz. Will you
do it?'

'Of course, Al. I should have gotten the number when I was there.
It was stupid of me to forget.'

'Stupid you ain't. Dunk, last night you said you had something to
tell me.'

So once again I related the story of Enoch Wottle's telephone call
from Arizona, the friend in Rotterdam, and the Beirut coin dealer
who was trying to hawk a Demaretion.

'I'll be damned,' Al said when I had finished. 'This thing is getting
as fucked-up as a Chinese fire drill – please excuse the language.'

145

'I've heard worse,' I said.

'Did you tell Jack Smack about this Enoch Wottle's call?'

'Yes, I did.'

'What was his reaction?'

I told him about Jack's theory of there being two thieves – Orson Vanwinkle stealing the coin originally, then a second person getting possession of it and trying to peddle it in Beirut.

'The only trouble with it,' I said, 'is that I can't see how Orson could have switched display cases.'

'I agree,' Al said.

'But you did tell me his apartment had been searched.'

'Looks like it, but there's no guarantee someone was hunting for the Demaretion. But they were looking for *something*. I told you there was about two thousand in cash in his bedside table, and that apparently wasn't touched.'

'How did you find out the apartment had been searched?'

'Vanwinkle's little blonde flapper told us. She slept over, usually on weekends, and knew where everything was kept. She swears the place was tossed.'

'Al, I'd like to talk to her. Do you think I could?'

'Why not? She's not under arrest or being held as a material witness. Hell yes, talk to her; maybe you can get something that we missed. Give her a call. Her name's Dolly LeBaron, and she's in the book. Lives on East Sixty-sixth Street.'

'East Sixty-*sixth*?'

'That's right. Just around the block from L. Wolfgang's brownstone. Isn't that interesting?'

'Yes,' I said slowly, 'interesting. Coincidence?'

'In my business,' he said, 'you learn not to believe in coincidences. See what you can find out, Dunk. Talk to you later.'

He had a habit of hanging up abruptly without saying goodbye. But that was all right. At least he didn't say, 'Have a nice day.'

I showered, shaved my legs, dressed, and went out to buy the *Times* and a croissant. It was about 10:30 when I called Dolly LeBaron. Her 'Hello?' was high-pitched and breathy, a little girl's voice.

I stated my name and explained that I was a friend of the Havistock family, had met Orson Vanwinkle several times, and wanted to express my condolences to her on his untimely demise.

'Wasn't it awful?' she said. 'Absolutely the worst thing that's ever happened to me.'

And to Orson, I thought.

'Miss LeBaron,' I said, 'I've been hired by the Havistock family to investigate the theft of a valuable coin that disappeared from their apartment. I thought it just possible that Orson might have mentioned it to you, and I was hoping we could talk.'

'About what?' she said.

Not too swift, this one.

'About the disappearance of the coin,' I said patiently. 'Could you give me a few minutes today? I promise it won't take long.'

'Gee, I don't know,' she said doubtfully. 'My agent told me not to talk to anyone.'

'This isn't a newspaper interview or anything like that, Miss LeBaron. Completely confidential.'

'I'm going to have my picture taken at noon,' she said, then giggled. 'In a bikini. It's going to be on the front page of something.'

'Isn't that nice,' I said.

'The red, I think,' she said thoughtfully. 'The knitted one.'

I wasn't certain she had both oars in the water.

'How about three o'clock?' I urged. 'I can come over to your place. It won't take long.'

'Well . . . I suppose it'll be all right. What did you say your name was?' She had a slight lisp.

I repeated it.

'My name is Dolly LeBaron,' she said primly.

'I know,' I said. 'See you at three o'clock.'

Whew!

That gave me some hours to kill and, on the spur of the moment, I decided to call Hobart Juliana at Grandby & Sons and see if I could take him to lunch. He was delighted, and we made plans to meet at 12:30 at the health food place around the corner from Grandby's.

'My treat,' I insisted. 'I'll talk to you about the Demaretion theft and bill Archibald Havistock for the lunch.'

'Okay,' he said cheerfully.

We had mushburgers, alfalfa salad, and carrot juice. It was all so awful, it *had* to be good for you. Hobie got me caught up on office gossip. He reported that god had hemorrhoids, and Felicia Dodat was wearing green polish on her fingernails. Also, Hobie had brought in a fine collection of Mark Twain letters to Grandby's for auction.

'Hobie, that's wonderful!' I told him. 'Congratulations. Have they replaced me yet?'

'Nope,' he said, shaking his head. 'I'm still all alone in our little cubbyhole. From what I hear, that asshole lawyer, Lemuel Whattsworth, told them not to reinstate you until the crook is caught and the fair name of Grandby and Sons is cleared. He said to hold your job in "abeyance" – you know the way he talks.'

'What are they doing about appraisals of coin collections?'

'Using independent dealers on a consulting basis. It's costing god a lot of money – which makes me happy. You know, Dunk, you and I should have been making another fifty a week.'

'At least,' I agreed. 'Hobie, when is the auction of the Havistock Collection scheduled?'

'It isn't. The sale has been put on indefinite "Hold." With all the litigation going on – everyone suing everyone else or threatening to – all the attorneys got together and decided to postpone the auction until things get straightened out. The coins will remain in Grandby's vault.'

'That's awful,' I said. 'I'll bet Archibald Havistock wasn't happy about it.'

'He wasn't. I understand he screamed bloody murder – and who can blame him? Now he hasn't got the coins and he hasn't got the money. But he really doesn't have a leg to stand on. You know the standard contract that Havistock signed. Grandby's can schedule the auction at their discretion provided it's held within twelve months after the delivery of the merchandise. Hey, Dunk, what do you think about Orson Vanwinkle's murder?'

'I don't know what to think about it.'

Hobie loves to gossip. He leaned across the table eagerly. 'Did you hear anything that wasn't printed in the papers?'

'A few little things,' I said cautiously. 'Nothing important.'

He inched closer. 'I can give you a charming tidbit,' he said, lowering his voice. 'Vanwinkle was a member of what we call Manhattan's gay community. Not an active member, just occasionally.'

'That's impossible!' I burst out.

Hobie sat back. 'Believe me, Dunk, I *know*.'

'But he had a sleep-in girlfriend!'

'So? A lot of guys swing both ways. From what I hear, Vanwinkle was a nasty piece of goods. But he spent money like there was no tomorrow, so he was tolerated.'

After I left Hobie, promising to keep in touch, I still had about an hour to spare before my appointment with Dolly LeBaron.

148

So I decided to walk over to her place, having a lot to think about. Also, I wanted to detour to get the number of that East 65th Street brownstone for Al Georgio.

I walked slowly because it was a steamy day. July was right around the corner and New York's joyous summer humidity was building up. The sky was smoky, pressing down, and the sun was all haze. I was happy I had left my suede jacket at home; it would have been too much.

I thought about my conversation with Hobart Juliana during that dreadful lunch. (No more carrot juice for me!) Curiously, I found that I wasn't disappointed or depressed to hear that I wasn't to be immediately reinstated, despite the pleas by Al Georgio and Jack Smack. Maybe I was having too much fun playing girl detective. And the fact that Grandby's hadn't hired a replacement was a faint reason to hope they were keeping my job open for me.

I was sorry that the Havistock Collection wasn't going to auction. I knew how disappointing that must be to Archibald, but I didn't attach any great significance to the postponement. Boy, was I ever wrong!

Much more interesting, I thought, was Hobie's revelation that Vanwinkle had been AC-DC. I had no idea what that meant to the twin investigations of his murder and the Demaretion robbery, but at least it was another clue to Orson's personality. I wondered if Al and Jack knew about it. And if they did – why hadn't they told me? Maybe they were trying to protect my tender sensibilities. It is to laugh!

I ambled along, trying not to raise a sweat, and noticed how the rhythm of the entire city had slowed. Not so many pedestrians rushing and shoving. Mostly they were sauntering, men carrying jackets over their arms. Even traffic seemed to be moving slower, and it might have been my imagination, but I thought taxi horns were muted and a dog day somnolence had descended on Manhattan.

I stopped first on East 65th Street and got the address of the L. Wolfgang brownstone. To make certain I wouldn't foul up my report to Al, I jotted the number in a little notebook I carried in my shoulder bag. Then I walked around the block to East 66th and found Dolly LeBaron's address. I stood on the sidewalk, staring up. This was no row house.

It was one of those high-rise glass and steel condominiums that were sprouting up all over Manhattan. This one soared forever, with a hard glitter, sharp edges, and the look of a Star Wars rocket ship about to blast off. The lobby was a clean subway station with palm trees, and the elevator was a sterile white cubicle that reminded me of a false molar. Sometimes I have weird reactions to my surroundings.

Dolly LeBaron lived on the 42nd floor – which would have been enough to give me a terminal attack of the jimjams. The hallway had all the charm of a hospital corridor, and even the apartment doors – plain, white, flat panels – looked like part of some gigantic maze. It really was a creepy place.

She opened the door herself.

'My name is Dolly LeBaron,' she said, smiling brightly. 'What's yours?'

'Mary Lou Bateson,' I said for the third time, reflecting that she wasn't so great in the attention span department – or any other department demanding mental effort.

My first impression was one of shock – at how short she was. Couldn't have been more than five-two, and she was wearing heels. Otherwise, she was much as Al and Jack had described her: a young, petite blonde with frizzy curls, plumpish figure, and skin seemingly so soft and yielding that you'd think a touch would cause a bruise.

What they hadn't mentioned, and which perhaps I imagined, was a look of sweet innocence. A little girl in a woman's body. She was wearing a sashed wrapper in a hellish Oriental print, and there was no doubt, from the occasional flash I got of calf, thigh, and arm, that her body was almost completely hairless. *She* didn't have to shave her legs.

She led me into a one-bedroom apartment that dazzled, and I remembered my father's comment when we had visited a similar place in Des Moines. 'Looks like a Persian *hoor*house,' he had said.

Such a profusion of velvets, soft pillows, swagged drapes, mirrors, porcelain animals, ornate screens, serigraphs of female nudes on the walls, Art Deco female nudes on the tables, a plushy carpet (stained), and a leather rhinoceros bearing a hammered brass tray on its back. What, no incense?

We sat on a couch as saggy as a hammock, and she looked about vaguely. Wondering, no doubt, where she was. Who I was. What day it was.

'Thank you for seeing me, Miss LeBaron,' I said. 'It was very kind of you.'

'Dolly,' she said. 'Everyone calls me Dolly. What do they call you?'

'Dunk,' I admitted.

'Dunk,' she repeated, and apparently it never occurred to her to question the derivation of that nickname. 'Okay, Dunk.'

'How did the pictures go?' I asked her. 'You in the red bikini.'

'Oh!' she said. 'That was fun. This photographer said I had a marvelous body. He called me a vest-pocket Venus. Wasn't that nice?'

'Very,' I said.

'He wanted to take some nudes to send to *Playboy* – test shots, you know – but my agent wanted to talk money first. Everything is money, isn't it?'

'It surely is,' I agreed.

Even sitting on that droopy couch I towered over her and had to look down to meet her eyes. She was so small, soft, and vulnerable. I don't know why, but I thought of her as a victim. She seemed so defenseless.

'About Orson Vanwinkle . . .' I reminded her. 'That's what I came to talk to you about.'

'Wasn't it awful?' she said, wide-eyed. 'Just awful.'

'It was, Dolly. How long had you known him?'

'Oh . . .' she said uncertainly, 'maybe five years. Maybe more.'

'Was he good to you?'

'He sure was,' she said. 'But he really was a crazy guy.'

'Crazy?'

'We had such crazy times together.'

'I can believe it.'

'I mean we were doing coke and *everything*.'

'Dolly, did you tell all this to the police?'

She tried to recall. 'I may have,' she said finally. 'I really don't remember. There were so many of them.'

'How did you and Orson meet?'

'It was at a party. I think. Or maybe at a bar.'

'What were you doing before you met him?'

'I wanted to be a disc jockey,' she said. 'A girl disc jockey. I thought that would be cute – don't you think so?'

'I certainly do.'

'I love music. All kinds. Would you like to hear something? I have this marvy collection of tapes.'

'Thank you,' I said, 'but not right now. Then you met Orson Vanwinkle. And . . .'

'He sort of took care of me.'

'Was he generous?'

'Oh, yes! Horsy bought me this apartment. And let me furnish it. Isn't it beautiful?'

'It's lovely,' I assured her.

'Yes,' she said, looking about, 'lovely. What do you think is going to happen to it now? I mean, it was in his name and all. He was paying the maintenance. Do you think he left it to me in his will?'

'I have no idea.'

'Well, who cares?' she said with a bubble of laughter. 'Now I'm beginning to make some money on my own. Maybe I can keep the apartment. Or meet someone . . .'

It was all so sad I wanted to weep.

'Dolly,' I said, 'do you have any idea of who might have wanted to kill him?'

'Oh, no,' she said instantly. 'He was such a sweet man. Crazy, but sweet.'

'Did you love him, Dolly?'

'Well . . .' she said, her eyes drifting away, 'we had this situation.' I heard a slight lisp again.

'Did he ever talk to you about the theft of a coin from his uncle's apartment?'

She frowned, trying to concentrate, and I found myself frowning in empathy.

'No,' she said finally, 'I don't remember anything like that.'

'But he always had plenty of money?'

'Plenty,' she said, laughing gaily. 'Last winter he bought me a ranch mink. And we were going away together.'

'Going away? On a vacation? A cruise?'

'No. Forever. We were going to live on a French river.'

'A French river? You don't mean the Riviera, do you?'

'Yes, that's right, the French Riviera. We were going there to live. He told me all about it. It's gorgeous, and you don't have to wear a bra on the beach.'

'When were you going?'

'Real soon. Like in a month or so.'

'That's a big move to make, Dolly.'

'Well, Horsy said he was coming into an inheritance from a rich relative. I wish I had one, don't you? A rich relative?'

'I surely do. When did Orson first suggest that the two of you move to the French Riviera?'

'Oh, I don't know,' she said, drifting again. 'Maybe a few weeks

152

ago. Listen, are you sure you don't want to hear some music? Horsy bought me a videocassette player. I've really got some groovy tapes.'

'Maybe some other time, Dolly,' I said, rising. 'Thank you so much for letting me barge in.'

She rose too, then unfastened her sash and spread the wrapper wide. She looked down at her naked body with what I can only describe as a puzzled look.

'You really think *Playboy* would be interested?' she asked.

I stared for a moment. 'I really think they would,' I told her.

'Maybe I should diet,' she said.

'No,' I said hastily, 'don't do that.'

She walked me to the door. What a pair we made! Female Mutt and Jeff.

'Come back soon,' she caroled, giving me a sappy smile.

The moment I got home, I went to one of my illustrated coin books – for reasons I'll never understand. I stared at the photo of the Demaretion. To most people it would simply be a flat, round piece of metal, a medium of exchange. Enoch Wottle had taught me what it really meant, what avid collectors saw in it.

You thought of how old it was, how it had been minted, and the uses to which it had been put: dowry, bribery, ransom, tribute, rent, wages, investment, and on and on. Then you dreamed of all the people, now dead and gone, who had handled it.

If only that single dekadrachm could have talked! What a tale of human bravery, frailty, conquest, and defeat. Why, that one coin could have meant success or failure, joy or despair. The same might hold true for a US dime. Take one out of your pocket right now, and let your fancies explode. Who owned it before you? What were their lives like? Was that lousy dime important to them? It might have meant the difference between life and death; it was possible.

And now here was the Demaretion, a piece of metal almost 2500 years old, affecting the lives of a disparate set of characters from would-be Bunny Dolly LeBaron to austere Archibald Havistock. There was magic in money, magic to move people, affect their lives and turn them in ways they had never planned.

I closed the coin book and sat staring at the ceiling. That talk with Dolly had really shaken me. First of all, her soft vulnerability, ignorant innocence, and unthinking trust were enough to make me rethink my own life – what I wanted and where I was going.

And also, what she had said gave me the glimmer of an idea so outrageous, so unbelievable, that I tried to put it out of my mind. But it wouldn't go, and I consulted my spiral notebook to prove it or refute it. I couldn't do either, so I finally solved all my problems: I took a nap.

I awoke, groggy, at about six o'clock, and switched on my air conditioner. It was an old, wheezy window unit, but it worked, thank God, and while it was reducing my apartment from sauna to livable, I went in to shower. Halfway through, the phone rang – doesn't it always? – and I dashed out. It was Jack Smack.

'Hi, Dunk,' he said cheerfully. 'What'cha doing?'

'Dripping,' I said. 'You got me out of the shower.'

'Sorry about that,' he said, not sounding sorry at all. 'How do you feel about chili?'

'Love it,' I said, remembering that tasteless mushburger at lunch.

'Good. There's a new Tex-Mex place on West Twenty-third. How's about meeting me there in, oh, about an hour? We'll do the whole bit: chili and rice with enchiladas, chopped onions and cheese, jalapeños, and a lot of cold Mexican beer. How does that grab you?'

'Ulcer time,' I said, 'but it sounds marvelous.'

He gave me the address, and I went back to finish my shower. I wondered how much I should tell him, and Al Georgio, about what I had learned that day from Hobart Juliana and Dolly LeBaron. I was beginning to consider holding out on them – only because I was certain they were holding out on me. If it was going to be a three-way competition, I wasn't about to give anything away. If they wanted to trade, fine. But they'd get nothing for nothing.

The Tex-Mex joint turned out to be crowded, hot, smoky, and aromatic. We had to wait at the bar for almost a half-hour, but when we were finally seated, it was worth it; the food was really super. Hot, but not too hot. I mean steam didn't come out your ears, but the back of your scalp began to sweat.

We dug into our platters (liberally sprinkled with red-pepper flakes), and Jack Smack wasted no time . . .

'So tell me,' he said, 'how are you doing on the Demaretion?'

'Okay,' I said cautiously. 'Nothing earth-shaking. I talked to Dolly LeBaron today.'

'Did you?' he said. 'Learn anything?'

'Not much. Is she my competition?' I don't know why I asked that. It just came out, and I was ashamed.

He looked at me, amused. 'No, Dunk, she's not your competition. No one is. Dolly is an airhead.'

154

Unexpectedly, I came to her defense. 'She's a sweet, dumb, innocent girl who has been exploited by men.'

'Hey,' he said, 'don't go feminist on me. Dolly happens to be an amateur hooker. She could be selling gloves at Macy's if she wanted to. But she goes through life depending on handouts from men. Maybe she'll marry one of them. I hope so. I hate to think of what'll happen to her when her bits and pieces begin to sag.'

He was right and I knew it, but I didn't want to hear it.

'I still say she's a victim,' I said.

'Dunk, we're all victims,' he said patiently. 'Did she tell you anything?'

'Only that Vanwinkle had been very generous. He bought that condo apartment for her.'

'That I knew,' he said. 'Where *was* the guy getting his bucks? His parents are dead. He inherited bubkes. But five years ago he started throwing money around like a drunken sailor. I'm still trying to figure out how he could have copped the Demaretion.'

'He couldn't,' I said.

Jack sighed. 'It's a puzzlement,' he admitted. 'Did Dolly say anything else?'

I figured it was trade-off time. 'Nothing important. What's happening on your end? Get any more letters from the New York crook?'

'Not a word. We put a man on that Beirut connection you told me about, but it's too soon to expect any results. Did you hear anything from Al Georgio about that East Sixty-fifth Street brownstone?'

He was pumping me, and I resented it.

'No,' I said, 'not a word.' Then I decided to throw him a curve ball that could only confuse him further. Why should I be the only one all bollixed up? 'By the way,' I said casually, 'did you know that Orson Vanwinkle was gay? Occasionally.'

He stared at me. 'You're kidding.'

'I'm not. I heard it from a very reliable source.'

'Jesus,' he said, and drank off half a glass of beer. 'That's another noodle in the soup. I swear to God I've never had a mishmash like this before. Dunk, have you got any ideas at all? No matter how nutty.'

'None whatsoever,' I said, lying, but looking at him steadily. 'It's as much a jumble to me as it is to you.'

'Yeah,' he said disgustedly. 'What the British call a balls-up. Let's have some sherbet or ice cream to cool our gullets.'

155

We came out of the restaurant into a night that still held the day's shimmering heat.

'I'm parked around the corner,' Jack said, leading the way.

He didn't walk; he danced along the street. Not actually, of course, but that's the impression he gave. Light-footed and light-hearted. Whenever I was with him, I had the feeling that he might just float up and away – he was that insubstantial.

When we arrived at his black Jag, he walked around it, inspecting wheels, glass, finish.

'Nothing missing,' he reported happily. 'No broken windows. No dents. No scratches. My lucky night.'

It wasn't mine. I guess I had visions of going back to his loft and having a giggle on those crazy futons on the floor. But it was not to be. He drove me directly to my apartment, thanked me for an enjoyable evening, and gave me a chaste kiss on the cheek.

A perfect gentleman. The bastard!

20

THE NEXT morning, awake but still lying in bed, listening to my air conditioner cough and sputter, I thought of the previous evening with Jack. My feelings about him were really ambivalent, no doubt about it.

He was a gorgeous man, physically, and on the futons he was a tiger. Charming, good sense of humor, intelligent, mercurial enough to be interesting, and he owned a Jaguar and knew how to make Beef Wellington: What more could a growing girl want?

Except that the guy was a lightweight, a real tap dancer. If he had any capacity for emotional commitment to anyone or anything, he had never revealed it to me. I don't mean that I prefer solemn men, but I do like a soupçon of seriousness now and then. Jack the Smack seemed to float through life, bobbing on the current. Everything was a joke, and laughter was the medicine that cured all.

Still, he was good company and gave my life a lift: I couldn't deny that. So when the bedside phone rang, I half-hoped it was him, calling to apologize for not taking advantage of my good nature the night before. But it was Al Georgio.

'Morning, Dunk,' he said. 'Didn't wake you up this time, did I?'

'Nah,' I said, 'I've been up for hours.' Slight exaggeration.

'You didn't call me, but I wondered if you had a chance to check the number of that East Sixty-fifth Street brownstone.'

'Sure I did,' I said, and gave him the address.

'Good,' he said. 'Thanks. Shouldn't take me long to check it out. I'll let you know if anything comes of it. We're still going around in circles on the Vanwinkle kill. The homicide guys visit you?'

'That they did. But I got the impression they were just going through the motions.'

'They were,' Al said. 'I told them you were clean.'

Then, because I had already told Jack Smack and didn't want to

157

favor either of them, I said, 'By the way, Al, in case you or the homicide men haven't discovered it yet, Orson Vanwinkle was gay.'

Silence.

'Al?' I said. 'Are you there?'

'I'm here. Where did you hear that?'

'From a reliable source. I guess he was bisexual.'

'I guess he was,' Al said, sighing. 'That opens a whole new can of worms. Thanks for the tip, Dunk; we'll work on it. Now I'll give you one you won't believe.'

'Try me,' I said. 'I'll believe anything.'

'Vanessa Havistock has a record. Before she married Luther, she was Vanessa Pembroke. Ain't that elegant? Actually, her real name is Pearl Measley, and she's from South Carolina – but that's neither here nor there. She's got a sheet in New York. Want to guess what she was arrested for?'

'Indecent exposure?'

He laughed. 'Close, but no cigar. It was loitering for the purpose of prostitution. No record of trial. Apparently she was charged and released. How do you like that?'

'Incredible.'

'Yeah, it's an eye-opener. Call you later.'

He hung up abruptly again, leaving me with another unconnected item to add to my spiral notebook. I wondered idly if a computer might be able to assimilate all this, hum for a few seconds, then spew out a beautifully logical solution to the whole puzzle. I doubted that could ever happen. Computers deal with facts. We – Al, Jack, and I – had to juggle tangled human emotions and passions. Which calls for instinct and judgment – does it not?'

I showered, dressed, and went out for the morning paper and a hot bagel with a shmear of cream cheese. By ten o'clock I had devoured both bagel and *Times*, and was pondering what I might do that day to give the Havistocks their money's worth of investigation. Then my doorbell rang. I looked through the peephole, and there was Dolly LeBaron standing in the vestibule. I couldn't have been more discombobulated if it had been Martha Washington.

She came in, smiling bravely, carrying a shoebox-sized package in a brown paper bag that had been wrapped with yards and yards of wide Scotch tape. She was wearing a simple Perry Ellis dress that I had seen advertised for about $400. It was a muted pink linen, and she looked absolutely smashing.

'Hi!' she said brightly.

158

'Hi,' I said. 'How did you find me?'

'Well, after you left, I wrote down your name. Mary Lou Bateson – right?'

'Right.'

'So then I looked you up in the telephone directory,' she said triumphantly.

'Good for you,' I said. 'Would you like a cup of coffee – or anything else?'

'Nothing, thank you,' she said formally. 'But I appreciate the offer.'

So we sat on the couch, side by side, looking at each other with glassy stares. She really was a cute little thing, all bouncy curves and wide-eyed innocence. I could understand Orson Vanwinkle's infatuation. This kid was a living toy, and I imagined if he suggested they swing naked from a chandelier, she'd giggle and say, 'Okay.'

'Listen,' she said suddenly, 'you're the best girlfriend I have.'

That came as something of a shock. I had only met her once before, for a limited time. To me, that didn't add up to intimacy. Again I reflected that her back burners were not fully operative.

'Dolly,' I said, as gently as I could, 'surely you know other women. I've only talked to you once.'

'No,' she said, 'you're the only one. Mostly I know men.'

'What about your family?'

'They're in Wichita,' she said. 'We send cards.'

That hurt because it reminded me that I hadn't written home in more than two weeks. I resolved the moment she left, I'd write a long, long letter to Mom and Dad in Des Moines, and mail it that very day.

'It's these phone calls, Dunk,' she said, little frown lines appearing between her plucked eyebrows.

'What phone calls?'

'I get them all the time. Some during the day. Some wake me up.'

'Man or woman?'

'Man.'

'A heavy breather – or does he say anything?'

'Sometimes he says things.'

'Sexual?'

'No. He wants to kill me. It's scary.'

Oh, my God,' I said, remembering my threatening letter. 'Did you call the phone company?'

'No.'

159

'The police?'

'No.'

'Why don't you change your number? Get an unlisted number.'

'It wouldn't do any good,' she said helplessly. 'He'd find me.'

Did she know who it was?

'Who?' I asked her. 'Who'd find you, Dolly?'

A very brief pause, then: 'I don't know.'

'I have a friend who's a detective in the New York Police Department. Would you like to tell him about it? He's very understanding. Maybe he could do something about it.'

'No,' she said, 'he couldn't help me. Because you're my very best girlfriend, I was hoping you'd do me a favor.'

'Of course,' I said. 'Whatever I can.'

She thrust that crudely wrapped package at me.

'It's some personal stuff,' she said. 'But it's valuable to me. I was wondering if you'd keep it. Just for a while.'

'Dolly,' I said, 'I hate to take the responsibility. Don't you have a safe deposit box?'

'What's that? Well, whatever it is, I don't have it. It's just for a little while. I may go away,' she added vaguely.

I didn't think she was on anything. I mean she wasn't doped up or anything like that. It was just that the things she said and did were slightly askew. Her gears weren't quite meshing.

'Can you hide it?' she pleaded.

I looked around my apartment hopelessly. 'Maybe I can put it on a top shelf in a closet or cupboard somewhere. Put things in front to cover it. That's the best I can do. But, Dolly, I really wish you wouldn't ask me to do this.'

'You're the only one I know,' she said. 'Please?'

I couldn't resist that. 'All right. Will you come and take it back as soon as you can?'

'Of course!' she cried. 'Just as soon as I can.'

'But what if you don't? How long should I wait?'

She thought about that a long time. I could almost see the wheels turning as she labored with the mental challenge.

'A month?' she suggested.

'You'll come back and get it within a month?'

She nodded briskly.

'And if you don't?' I asked. 'What do I do with it then?'

'Burn it,' she said promptly.

'Burn it?'

160

'Put it in the insinuator.' That's the way she pronounced it.

So if she didn't reclaim something valuable to her, something personal, I was to destroy it. Curiouser and curiouser.

She left that clunky package on the couch and stood up.

'I knew I could depend on you,' she said, taking a deep breath. 'I just knew it. You won't open it, will you?'

'Of course not,' I said, insulted.

'I knew you wouldn't.' She craned up to kiss my cheek. But she was so short, and I was so tall, that I had to bend down to take her peck. She smelled nicely of something sweet and fruity. A little girl's scent.

When she was gone, I came back into my living room to stare at that bundle and wonder what I was letting myself in for.

I picked it up and shook it gently. Naturally I suspected it might contain the Demaretion. But who would be simple enough to wrap a single coin in a shoebox? Not even someone as loopy as Dolly LeBaron.

Anyway, there was no rattle, no sound at all. Whatever was within the package was well-swaddled. I hefted it. Surprisingly light. How much did a bomb weigh? The moment I had that awful thought, I resolutely put it out of my mind. Sweet, sappy Dolly would never do anything like that. Would she? Unless she was just the messenger.

Other questions, other answers . . .

Should I open it?

Absolutely not. I gave her my word.

Should I tell Al Georgio and Jack Smack about it?

No.

Then what should I do with it?

Hide it – but only for the month she requested.

And then?

Burn it in the insinuator.

Carrying it rather gingerly, I wandered about my apartment looking for a good hiding place that thieves with limited time might have trouble finding. I finally settled on the top shelf of the metal cabinet in my kitchen, above the sink. I tucked it far in the back, behind packages of pancake mix and instant rice. Let the roaches have a field day on that Scotch tape.

I really did write that letter home – which made me feel virtuous. I stamped it and ran outside to drop it in the corner box. A droopy day with an army blanket over the city, rain threatening, and everyone frowning as they mooched along. I was depressed and, other than the weather, couldn't understand the reason.

161

Then I figured out it was that visit from Dolly LeBaron and the package she had left in my care. That was a downer – and I didn't understand why. But somehow it seemed as menacing as the creepy sky. I didn't like the idea of being trusted custodian of a parcel, contents unknown. It could be stolen goods, drugs, or anything else illegal. That made me a receiver, didn't it? I could hear myself stammering to a judge, 'Your Honor, I just didn't know what was in it.'

Before I got myself in a real snit, I decided to get out of the house and *do* something. What I planned was to go up to the American Numismatic Society and see if I could dig up any information on Archibald Havistock's collection of ancient Greek coins. Oh, I knew what was in the Havistock Collection, now languishing in the vault at Grandby & Sons. What I was interested in were the coins Archibald had sold off, according to wife Mabel, over the past five years.

So I shouldered my bag, locked up, and started out. I admit I wasn't as alert as I should have been. I wasn't 'living defensively,' which is what everyone says you must do in New York. Anyway, I didn't look ahead, and so I failed to see the three guys lurking in the areaway beyond the outer door. But they were obviously waiting for me.

The moment I was in the vestibule, caught between two doors, two of the thugs hustled in, and the third stood on guard with his back against the outer door. Here it is, I thought: my first mugging. Or worse. But it was not to be.

The two guys crowding into the vestibule with me were in their middle twenties, I guessed. Wearing punky outfits: running shoes, a lot of stone-washed denim and creaky black leather, studded bracelets, chain belts, sharks' teeth necklaces – the whole bit. I remember one of them had a gold tooth in front.

'Hi, there,' gold tooth said, grinning.

I thrust my shoulder bag at them. 'Take it,' I said. 'Just don't hurt me. Please.'

'Nah,' the other one said. He had a silly blond Stalin mustache. 'We don't want your gelt. Mary Lou Bateson – right?'

I nodded frantically, absolutely determined not to wet my pants.

'Got a message for you,' gold tooth said. 'You should stop asking questions. You dig?'

I kept nodding.

162

'You're making a lot of people uncomfortable,' mustache said. 'So just be nice and lay off. It's healthier that way. For you.'

Their voices were not particularly menacing. They spoke in quiet conversational tones. But what they were saying was all the more frightening for that. They talked like businessmen, professionals, offering terms on a sale or contract. I never doubted them for a moment.

'Listen,' I started, 'I don't—'

'No,' gold tooth said, 'you listen. Just walk away from it. The coin and everything and everyone connected with it. Give it up. It's got nothing to do with you – right?'

'We're being gentlemen, aren't we?' mustache added. 'Very polite. We haven't touched you, have we? So you take our advice, and that's the way it'll stay. You keep poking your nose into things that don't concern you, and we'll have to come back.'

'Then we might not be so polite,' gold tooth said. 'Then we might touch you. So-long, sweet mama.'

And they were gone, whisking through the outer door, joining their guard, the three of them walking rapidly away. I watched them go, trying to breathe and gradually becoming aware of my shaking knees and trembling hands.

I went back into my apartment and found a miniature bottle of cognac I had been saving for medicinal purposes. Now was the time. It took me almost a minute to get that damned screw top off, but I finally managed, and drained the brandy out of that little bottle in three gulps. Then, gasping, I staggered to the couch, collapsed, and waited for my hypertension to ease.

I went over that brief encounter and had no uncertainty whatsoever about their threats; they meant what they said. They had looked perfectly capable of any kind of violence: knifing, bombing, rape, murder – you name it. I had been lucky. Those messenger boys would obey any orders. 'You want us to toss acid in her face? Sure, boss.'

But I'm a stubborn dame, and as fear faded, my indignation grew. The bastards! Did they really think I'd cave in that easily? And what was the reason for the whole megillah? Whoever sent them must have felt threatened by my investigation. But *why*, for God's sake? I hadn't learned anything that threatened anyone.

Unless I had heard something important that I wasn't aware of.

I reviewed the melodramatic dialogue with the two amateur Scarfaces. 'Just walk away from it,' gold tooth had said. 'The coin and everything and everyone connected with it.' No clue there. His warning included all I had done and every person I had met since going to work for Grandby & Sons.

But then, just before they had scuttled out, gold tooth had said, 'So-long, sweet mama.'

And who had first called me that? Sam Jefferson, aka Akbar El Raschid, Natalie Havistock's misanthropic boyfriend. But what did I know about *him*?

I went into the kitchen to make a call. I was reaching for the phone when suddenly it rang. I jerked my hand away as if I had touched something hot. Has that ever happened to you? Then I took the phone off the hook. Slowly.

'Hello?' I said cautiously, remembering Dolly LeBaron's problems.

'Ms Bateson?'

'Yes.'

'This is Lenore Wolfgang's secretary. Ms Wolfgang would like to meet you this afternoon for a short time. Would that be convenient?'

'All right,' I said. 'When and where?'

'Here at our office. Three o'clock.'

'I'll be there,' I said.

'Please try to be prompt. Ms Wolfgang has a very tight schedule today.'

Screw you, ms, I thought, slamming down the phone.

So now I was being hassled by a lawyer's secretary, in addition to being muscled by goons in the vestibule of my home, getting a drop-dead letter in the mail, and being saddled with a mysterious package by the pea-brained mistress of a murdered bisexual lecher.

I think it was at that precise moment that, wrathful and tired of being pushed around, I decided no more Ms Nice. I wasn't going to pass along *any* information to Al Georgio or Jack Smack. Fine, upstanding lads, but they weren't the ones being leaned on, and I had enough chutzpah to think I could take care of myself, solve my own problems, and to hell with all men, friends and enemies alike.

So, of course, the next thing I did was to make a call to a man: Hobart Juliana at Grandby's, asking for a favor.

'Hobie,' I said, 'remember your telling me that Orson Vanwinkle had this, ah, certain predilection?'

'Predilection?' he said, giggling. 'What a sensitive way of putting it! Yes, I'd say he had a predilection.'

164

'Is there any way you can find out if he had someone special? A regular?'

Short pause, then: 'Is it important, Dunk?'

'It is to me.'

'Then I'll try, dear. No guarantees. I'll make some phone calls. Will you be in today?'

'I have to go out this afternoon, but if you learn anything – or nothing – will you call me tonight?'

'Of course. Either way.'

'You're a darling.'

'I agree,' he said. 'And let's never eat mushburgers again.'

'My sentiments exactly,' I said.

Then I went back to my spiral notebook, bringing it up-to-date with all the happenings of that crazy day. By the time I finished jotting my notes, it was too late for my planned trip to the American Numismatic Society. So I had an endive salad with watercress and cherry tomatoes, and then sallied forth to keep my appointment with attorney Lenore Wolfgang. God forbid I should be late; her secretary would have the fantods.

What a bummer of a day it was: a drizzle that was half steam and a breeze that smelled like it was coming from some giant exhaust pipe. I wore a plastic raincoat, which was like being swaddled in cotton batting. I finally got a cab going downtown on Broadway, and the driver was playing a Willie Nelson tape on his portable. That lifted my spirits a little – but not enough.

Lenore Wolfgang had her office in one of those hunks of masonry on Fifth Avenue just north of 42nd Street: a big, brutal building. When you looked up, you had the feeling it might topple onto you at any moment. I searched the lobby directory and eventually found her listing: Getzer, Stubbs & Wolfgang. I rode up to the 36th floor in a bronze elevator that had been sprayed with a piny deodorant that was supposed to make you think you were in the north woods. Fat chance.

I got in to see her right away, which was a surprise; I was certain she'd keep me waiting. She shook my hand with the grip of a wrestler, then got me seated in a leather club chair in front of her clumpy oak desk. She sat in a swivel chair and parked her heavy cordovan brogues atop the desk. She had a wad of chewing gum stuck to the sole of her left shoe, but I didn't mention it.

She was wearing a dark flannel suit, man-styled shirt with a wide ribbon tied in a bow at the neck. No jewelry. Minimal makeup. The

165

face was big, fleshy, and a little overpowering. A very strong, hard woman. As tall as I, but blockier. If I was a basketball player, she was a linebacker for the Steelers. And if she smoked cigars, I wouldn't have been a bit surprised.

'I understand the Havistocks have hired you to investigate the theft of the Demaretion,' she started.

I didn't know if that was a statement or a question, so I said nothing.

'I advised against it,' she said sternly, staring at me. 'I think criminal investigations are best left to the professionals, don't you?'

'In most cases,' I agreed. 'But in this one, the professionals seem to agree that a member of the family is involved. The Havistocks are aware of it, and I'm sure it's upset them. They wanted a personal representative looking into it.'

She stirred restlessly, recrossing her ankles and leaning forward to tug her flannel skirt over her lumpy knees.

'Well . . .' she said finally, 'I don't suppose it can do any great harm. Have you discovered anything?'

'No,' I said. 'Nothing important. And the murder of Orson Vanwinkle complicates matters.'

'How so?' she said sharply. 'You think he stole the coin?'

'It's possible.'

She shook her head. 'Can't see it,' she said. 'He was a vain, weak man with no self-discipline whatsoever. But I can't see him as a common thief. Defrauding old widows would be more his style.'

A rather harsh opinion, I thought, of a homicide victim. But then he couldn't sue for slander, could he?

'I would appreciate it,' she continued, 'if you would keep me informed on the progress of your investigation. Weekly reports, say.'

She was backed by a wall of thick law books. All the furniture in her office was massive. Colors were muted, brass shined, surfaces dusted. Everything bespoke the solidity and majesty of the law. But I was not about to let her muscle me. I had enough of that in the vestibule a few hours ago.

'I don't think that would be wise,' I said evenly. 'I was employed by the Havistocks. I promised them periodic progress reports. Whatever they wish to tell you is up to them.'

She took it well, merely nodding with no change of expression. 'My only reason for asking,' she said mildly, 'is that Archibald Havistock is my client, and naturally I want to protect his interests.'

'Naturally,' I said. 'How long has Mr Havistock been with you, Miss Wolfgang?'

'Oh,' she said, 'about five years now.' Then she looked at me strangely. 'Why do you ask that?'

I shrugged. 'No particular reason. Just an idle question.'

She frowned, took her feet off the desk, and stood up. I rose also, figuring this incomprehensible interview was at an end. But then she said something that gave me a clue to the reason she had called me in.

'By the way,' she said casually, 'in addition to my office here and my private apartment, a co-op, I also rent a small place on East Sixty-fifth Street for the convenience of out-of-town clients and visiting friends. This morning I received a call from the owner of the building saying he had been contacted by a detective from the New York Police Department who asked questions about the apartment, who leased it, who occupied it, and so forth. Do you know anything about that?'

When I played high school basketball, I had always been better on defense than offense.

'Not a thing,' I said. 'It's all news to me. But I suppose that since the murder of Vanwinkle they're investigating everyone who knew him.'

'Yes,' she said thoughtfully. 'I suppose they are. Thank you for coming in, Miss Bateson. I hope to see you again soon.'

I got that bone-crusher grip again. When I went down to the street, the drizzle was thickening, and there was no way I was going to get a cab on Fifth Avenue. So I plodded over to Eighth on 42nd Street – not exactly a scenic wonderland.

Traffic was murder, but on that slow ride home in a taxi that seemed to have been stripped of springs and shock absorbers, I had time to think about the interview with Lenore Wolfgang.

She was obviously worried about the brownstone apartment on East 65th. But her concern could be completely innocent. Who wants the cops coming around and asking questions? On the other hand, she had gone into unnecessary detail to explain why she leased living quarters in addition to her primary residence.

It was not until I was inside my own primary (and only) residence, the door locked, bolted, and chained, that I recalled another little goody from the conversation. I dug out my notebook to verify what I was thinking.

Wolfgang said that Archibald Havistock had been her client for

167

about five years. And Orson Vanwinkle had been Archibald's private secretary for about five years, during which he started throwing simoleons around like the money cow would never go dry. And Archibald had been selling off coins in his collection for about five years. Al Georgio had told me detectives don't believe in coincidences. So what cataclysmic event five years ago triggered all the activity?

I've mentioned that I had a wild idea of what had been and was going on, an outrageous notion I could hardly believe myself and which I certainly couldn't prove or even describe. But this latest intelligence from Lenore Wolfgang made the cheese more binding. Things were beginning to fit.

I have no clear recollection of what I did for the remainder of that miserable day. I know Hobie Juliana called and said he hadn't been able to discover anything specific about Orson Vanwinkle's gay contacts, but would keep trying. And both Al Georgio and Jack Smack called, just to say hello. They didn't tell me anything, and I didn't tell them anything. Still, it was nice of them to check to see if I was still alive.

By evening it was pouring outside, so I ate in. I forget what it was – nothing memorable. Probably scrambled eggs or Cup-a-Soup: something like that. I tried watching television, but before I knew it, I was flipping pages of my notebook again, the TV set still flickering while I tried to make sense of all those random scribbles.

I went to bed early, thanking God I was inside a locked, bolted, and chained cage. The animals were all outside, prowling. I fell asleep listening to the gush of rain. It was a dreamless sleep. Granted only to the innocent and pure of heart. That's me. Damn it.

21

THE NEXT morning my phone kept ringing off the hook. *Four* calls before ten o'clock: a new world's record – for me at least. I was dazzled by this unexpected popularity, remembering when I had gone a week or two without a single call, and then, when I did get one, it was some guy trying to sell me an encyclopedia of the mammals of North America.

The first came from Roberta Minchen, all gush and giggles. She thought it would be *fun* if we had lunch at the Russian Tea Room at 12:30, and could I possibly make it?

If this was going to be another attempt to recruit me into her cast of bare-ass TV stars, I wanted no part of it. But then I reflected a free lunch was not to be scorned, and what could happen over vodka and blintzes? Besides, maybe I could get something new out of her. So I accepted.

The second call was from Hobie Juliana.

'Got something for you, Dunk,' he said. 'I don't know how accurate it is, but I thought I'd pass it along anyway. The late, unlamented Orson Vanwinkle, while alive, was having a thing with a black stud, a guy who went by one of those crazy Arabian names.'

'Oh-oh,' I said.

'Something wrong?' he asked.

'Hobie, it couldn't have been Akbar El Raschid, could it?'

'That sounds like it. Wears a single gold earring.'

'And a red beret,' I said.

'My God, Dunk, do you know him?'

'I think I've met the gentleman. Hobie, I just can't believe it. Orson and Akbar have got to be the oddest of all odd couples.'

'Well, you never know,' he said judiciously. 'I told you Vanwinkle was throwing money around. That might have had something to do with it.'

169

'Probably,' I agreed. 'Thank you so much for your help, dear.'

'One of these days will you tell me what this is all about?'

'When I find out,' I promised, 'you'll be the first to know.'

After we hung up, I pondered the implications of what I had just heard. Could Vanwinkle have been financing Akbar's merry little band of would-be revolutionaries? And if so, was Natalie Havistock aware of her boyfriend's liaison with her cousin?

Every time I learned something new, instead of diminishing the puzzle, it added to it. The whole thing grew and grew, like a blob that might eventually take over the world. Sighing, I added this latest intelligence to my notebook, reflecting that if things continued the way they were going, I might have to start Volume II.

The third call was one I never expected to get – from Felicia Dodat at Grandby's. She was all chirpy charm, couldn't have been sweeter, and carried on like a maniac about how they all missed me and couldn't wait until I returned. Uh-huh.

In fact, she went on, she and Mr Grandby and attorney Lemuel Whattsworth thought it might be 'productive' if I stopped by that afternoon, just for an 'informal chat' to review my 'situation.'

And what situation is that? I wanted to ask – but didn't. I told her I had a lunch date and couldn't possibly meet her before three o'clock. She said that would be just fine, and she was looking forward to seeing me.

'Have you found a man yet, Dunk?' she asked, her snideness surfacing.

'Two of them,' I told her, and hung up.

I knew exactly why the powers that be at Grandby & Sons wanted to have an 'informal chat.' They knew I was working for the Havistocks and wanted to pump me, find out what I had discovered. After all, Grandby's was still on the hook for the Demaretion, and the insurance company was in no hurry to pay off. I didn't imagine that state of affairs was doing god's hemorrhoids any good.

The final call of the morning was from Vanessa Havistock with *another* luncheon invitation. If this kept up I'd need a social secretary.

'Oh, I'm so sorry,' I said, 'but I already have a date for lunch.'

'With a man, I hope,' she said lightly.

Then, like an idiot, I told her: 'No, as a matter of fact, it's with your sister-in-law, Roberta Minchen.'

'Why, that's wonderful,' she said immediately. 'I'll give Bobbi a call and ask if I can join you. You don't mind, do you?'

'Of course not.'

'Won't it be hilarious,' she said. 'We'll have a real hen party.'

I didn't know if she was being ironic or not. With her, it was hard to tell.

'Now then,' she continued, 'another thing . . . Luther and I are having a very informal buffet dinner next Tuesday night, and we'd like so much to have you. Do you think you can make it?'

I was tempted to say, 'Let me take a look at my appointment calendar.' But I didn't have the gall. 'Yes,' I said, 'I'd like that. Thank you very much.'

'Lots of yummy food,' she said. 'Plenty to drink, and the handsomest men in Manhattan. I think you'll have a ball.' She paused a moment, then: 'Listen, Dunk, I have a wonderful idea. I'm on my way to Vecchio's on Madison Avenue to buy some new rags for the party. Could you meet me there at, say, eleven o'clock, and we'll pick out something wicked and scrumptious for me. We'll leave in plenty of time for lunch. How does that sound?'

Why did I have the feeling I was being manipulated?

'Sounds fine,' I said faintly. 'I'm supposed to meet Roberta at the Russian Tea Room at twelve-thirty.'

'No problem,' she said. 'It won't take me that long to pick out something. And I'd really like to get your opinion. I trust your taste.'

Bull*shit*!

Vecchio's was the kind of place where they took a good look at you through the plate glass door before they unlocked and allowed you to enter and blow a wad. It was an Italian boutique, Milanese, and if you could find a blouse under $600 or a dress under $2,000, it had to be last year's styles.

The doorman probably would have taken one look at my denim sack and turned away in horror, but I had walked over through Central Park, and arrived just as Vanessa was climbing out of a cab with a flash of bare thigh. The guard took one look at *her* and practically tore the door off its hinges.

Inside, an Adonis in a black silk suit came running forward to smother her hands with kisses. 'Signora!' he kept crying. 'Signora!'

'Down, Carlo, down,' Vanessa said, laughing. Then she introduced me.

'Signorina,' he said, bowing. I didn't even get an exclamation point.

That was some lush joint. Polished marble floors, Corinthian columns, subdued lighting, and sinfully luxurious chairs and couches covered with lemony cowhide. Not a garment in sight. I

171

gathered you told them what you were interested in, and they whisked things out of an inner stockroom to display for the signora's pleasure.

'Something splashy, Carlo,' Vanessa said. 'For a party. You know what I like.'

'But of course,' he said, turned, and snapped his fingers at two assistants hovering nervously in the background. 'The red with sequins,' he ordered. 'The white Grecian drape. The fringed black.'

They scurried, and hustled back with the three gowns. I'd have given my eyeteeth to own any of them, but of course I could never have gotten into them. I would have looked like an elephant in rompers.

Carlo exhibited them with dramatic flair, caressing the fabrics with his fingertips, shaking the hangers so the dresses billowed and swayed.

'Amusing,' he said. 'No?'

'What do you think, Dunk?' Vanessa asked.

'I love them all,' I confessed.

'Mmm,' she said, inspecting the gowns critically. 'The drape is a little too full for me, and the sequined red is hookerish – don't you think?'

This from a woman with a record of loitering for the purpose of prostitution. It was to laugh.

She selected the fringed black: a short sheath with spaghetti straps, cut reasonably high in front and no back at all. Wear that thing backwards and you'd be in *biiig* trouble. The fringe hung in tiers, and moved, swayed, flipped as the wearer walked.

'Let's try it on,' Vanessa said, and I wanted to say, '*Both* of us?'

We went into a dressing room as elegantly appointed as a Roman vomitorium. All right, I'm exaggerating, but it *was* splendidly furnished, with more mirrors than a fun house. Vanessa began to undress, casually, which made me a little uneasy. Despite my basketball team experience, I've never been an uninhibited locker room type.

'Tell me,' she said, unbuttoning, unsnapping, unhooking, 'have you found out who ripped off the Demaretion?'

'No,' I said, 'I haven't.'

'Orson's murder really shook me,' she chattered on. 'I didn't like the man – I told you that – but even so, I was devastated by his death. Do they know who did it?'

'They're investigating.'

172

'Tell me about it,' she said bitterly. 'I had a two-hour session with the homicide detectives. My God, I hope they don't suspect *me*. I wouldn't hurt a fly.'

A zippered fly? I was tempted to ask.

By then she was stripped down to high-heeled shoes, little white bikini panties, and nothing else. I'm one long hunk of cartilage, but she had a body that just didn't stop. I mean, it *gleamed*. Perfectly proportioned with a narrow waist, flare of hips, a luscious tush, and a really exceptional pair of lungs. Incidentally, I didn't see that tattoo Orson Vanwinkle had mentioned.

She inspected her practically naked body in the three-way mirror, turning this way and that, lifting her arms.

'What do you think?' she said. 'Not so bad for an old dame – right? The thighs are still firm.'

'So is everything else,' I said.

She touched her breasts lightly, a brief caress. 'There's a little silicone in there,' she said, 'but that's just between us girls. Do you think Orson did it?'

'What?' I said, startled. 'Oh, you mean steal the Demaretion. No, I don't think he did it. He couldn't have.'

'Natalie then,' she said, her voice muffled as she pulled the fringed dress over her head. 'She's nutty enough. Or Ruby Querita. There's a freak for you.'

She was pointing fingers in all directions, and I wondered if she was just running off at the mouth or had good reasons for her suspicions. But maybe the theft of the Demaretion and Vanwinkle's murder were the most dramatic things that had happened in her life in a long time, and she was trying to keep the excitement alive. Good party talk.

She turned her back to me. 'Zip me up,' she ordered, and I did. Then we both inspected the result in the mirrors.

Some result! The dress looked like it had been painted on her, and the tiers of fringe made it sexier. I don't know why, but I thought of a striptease dancer with tassels on her pasties.

'What do you think?' Vanessa asked.

'Beautiful,' I said. 'But about an inch too long. They can take up the hem.'

She looked at me with astonishment. 'You're absolutely right,' she said. 'Will you call Carlo and the fitters, please.'

Within minutes, there were four people hovering around her, clucking and murmuring and rolling their eyes. The hem would be

173

shortened, certainly. 'And perhaps, signora,' Carlo said, 'if I may suggest it, the straps taken up. Not a lot – no! A trifle. To fit snugly. Ah, what a glory!'

After things had been chalked and pinned, Vanessa undressed, dressed, and we moved out into the main room. She didn't even flash a credit card.

'Bill me, Carlo,' she said gaily.

'But of course, signora,' he said, bending to nibble on her fingers again. I may have been imagining it, but I could have sworn he passed her a little folded slip of paper – just like the headwaiter at that Tudor pub on Third Avenue. Then he released her hand and shook mine. 'Signorina,' he said, really not interested.

I never did find out what that fringed black cost. Probably more than my entire savings account at Chemical Bank.

I was willing to admit that Vanessa Havistock had a lot of talents, and one of them was obviously the ability to get a cab. She had no sooner stepped off the curb and held up one finger languidly than a Checker pulled up with a screech of brakes. I wish I had that gift.

On our way to the Russian Tea Room, she suddenly said, "Are you a close friend of Roberta's?'

'Close?' I said, surprised. 'Hardly. I think I've seen her twice.'

'Be careful,' Vanessa said darkly. 'She's not exactly the Flying Nun, you know.'

Roberta Minchen was at a table, waiting for us. The Christmas decorations were still up, as always, in the back room. The place was already crowded, and the clack of conversation was rising.

'Look what I've got,' Roberta said, giggling and holding up a glass. 'Peppered vodka. It's delicious.'

She was wearing one of her high-collared, flowery chiffons, and I tried not to remember what she had looked like in that videocassette I had seen. Not Academy Award material – unless all those men would nominate her for Best Supporting Actress.

Vanessa had her very, *very* dry martini straight up with a single olive, please, and I asked for a vodka gimlet. Then, to keep things simple, we all ordered the same luncheon: avocado stuffed with crabmeat salad. Kiddo, I told myself, you're *living*.

It took about three seconds for the talk to get around to the Demaretion robbery and Orson Vanwinkle's murder. The Havistock women thought both events were connected.

'It stands to reason,' Roberta Minchen said, rabbity teeth gleaming. 'I mean we were all living such a nice, peaceful existence,

174

and then those two awful things happened, one right after the other. There must be a link between them.'

'I agree,' Vanessa said. 'And I still think Orson was involved in stealing the coin. He was such a creep.'

'Wasn't he?' Roberta said, blinking. 'I just never did understand why Daddy kept him on. Do you know, Vanessa?'

'Why, no,' she said tightly. 'How in hell would I know something like that?'

That was my first intimation that there was a tension between the two. Maybe not outright hostility, at the moment, but a kind of wariness. The sparring kept up after our luncheon plates were served.

'Even Mother didn't like him,' Roberta said. 'But he was Archibald's nephew, and I guess she didn't want to say anything. Did you know his girlfriend, Vanessa? Dolly LeBaron?'

'I met her once,' Vanessa said. 'Once was enough. You had them over to your place, didn't you?'

'We tried to be friends. Briefly. But they really weren't our kind of people.'

'Oh? I'd have thought you'd hit it off.'

I was silent, listening to this dueling with fascination.

'He just drank too much,' Roberta said. 'And she's a flibbertigibbet.'

'Do you really think so?' Vanessa said. 'As I said, I only met her once, but my impression was that behind the Marilyn Monroe exterior was a real barracuda.'

'It takes one to know one,' Roberta said, smiling sweetly.

Vanessa stared at her coldly, then turned to me. 'Have you met her, Dunk? Dolly LeBaron?'

'Yes, I've met her.'

'What was your take?'

'Not too bright.'

'Bright enough,' Vanessa said grimly, 'to latch on to Orson and take him for whatever she could get. That's where all his money went.'

We were silent then, digging into our avocados. But the truce didn't last long.

'How is Luther?' Roberta asked. 'The last time I saw him he looked so pale and thin.'

'Luther is fine,' Vanessa said.

'Is he still biting his fingernails?'

Vanessa glared at her. 'Is Ross still cracking his knuckles?'

175

I prepared to push back my chair if dishes started flying. But their jousting remained verbal.

'After all,' Roberta said, 'Luther *is* my brother, and I *am* interested in his welfare. You shouldn't let him drink so much.'

'Butt out,' Vanessa said, her face becoming almost ugly with anger. 'Just butt out. I don't tell you how to manage that nerd you're married to, do I? Advice from you I don't need.'

'Ladies,' I murmured, but it did no good.

'At least,' Roberta said, 'Ross is a good provider.'

'I won't ask what he provides,' Vanessa said nastily. 'After all, you're paying for the lunch, and I never insult the woman who pays the bill.'

'Or the man either,' Roberta said. 'You're always very sweet to the one who picks up the check.'

'What's that supposed to mean?' Vanessa demanded.

'If the shoe fits, wear it.'

Thank God the waitress arrived just then to remove our empty plates. I swear that if that snarling had gone on much longer, I'd have stood up and stalked out with as much dignity as I could muster. It was embarrassing. But the waitress saved the day, and we all ordered coffee, no desserts, in calm, controlled voices.

'Ruby Querita,' Vanessa said, looking at Roberta with no expression. 'What do you think?'

Roberta pouted her lips. 'Yes,' she said, 'I think it's very possible she took the coin. Her brother's in jail, you know. She needs money to get him out.'

They both turned to stare at me.

'And killed Orson Vanwinkle?' I said. 'Why would she do that?'

'Maybe he saw her do it,' Vanessa said. 'He was going to turn her in to the cops, so she shot him.'

'Yes,' Roberta said, nodding wisely, 'that makes sense.'

Again I had the feeling of being pushed in directions I didn't want to go.

'It doesn't make sense to me,' I said. 'Letters were written to the insurance company, offering to make a deal: the Demaretion returned for cash. I don't think Ruby would be capable of that.'

'Maybe she got someone to write the letters for her,' Vanessa said.

'Now you're reaching,' I told her. 'Ruby is very religious. She lives by the Ten Commandments. I really don't think she'd steal.'

'Then it was Natalie,' Roberta said firmly. 'She'd steal – as a kind of joke, you know. I hate to say it about my own sister, but she's capable.'

What a family!

I was never so glad in my life when that awful luncheon finally ended. I told them I had an appointment uptown, and left them together on the sidewalk as soon as I decently could, after thanking Roberta for her hospitality.

'We must do it again soon,' she said brightly.

In about 1998, I thought.

I walked away from them as fast as I could, not looking back. If they started pulling hair after I was gone, that was their problem. And if it came to a knockdown and dragout fight, I'd have bet on Vanessa; she was the ballsier of the two.

I had time to kill before my appointment at Grandby & Sons, so I sat for a while on a bench in Central Park. Then an ancient dodderer came along, dropped his newspaper in front of me, bent slowly to retrieve it, and tried to look up my skirt. Just an average day in the Big Apple. I rose hastily and strode over to Madison where the weirdos were younger and better dressed.

What a lunch that had been! But valuable, I thought. It gave me new insights into the stresses and pressures within the Havistock family. I didn't know what it all meant, but I never doubted for a moment that it was significant. If I could understand those enmities, I might be a lot farther along in finding out who copped the Demaretion and who knocked off Orson Vanwinkle.

Madison Avenue, from 57th Street northward, is really something: my favorite window-shopping tour. All the riches of the world: art galleries, boutiques, antique shops, jewelers, wine stores, swank hotels, and crazy little holes-in-the-wall where you could buy things like polo mallets, porcelain picture frames, and furniture made of Lucite. Bring money.

I still had a lot of Des Moines in me, and a street like this was an invitation to a world I'd never known. I couldn't help laughing, because I knew I'd never know it – but I could admire it. That didn't depress me. I was happy just to be able to goggle at all those baubles, dream, and go home to my Lean Cuisine. *Things* are nice, but they're not everything. Right?

I timed my stroll and got to Grandby & Sons a few minutes before three o'clock. If the meeting didn't take too long, I planned to stop in and give Hobie Juliana a big hug, in thanks for all his help.

We all met in Grandby's conference room, an austere chamber

that needed only candles and a casket on a trestle to pass as a funeral parlor. We sat at wide intervals around a polished table, and lawyer Lemuel Whattsworth, Mr Congeniality himself, opened the game.

'Miss Bateson,' he said, 'you have been employed by Archibald Havistock to investigate the theft of the Demaretion. Is that correct?'

I nodded.

'You realize, of course, that technically you are still employed by Grandby and Sons, on temporary leave of absence.'

'Technically,' I said. 'Meaning I'm not getting paid.'

'There is a conflict of interest involved here,' he said, sucking his teeth happily. 'It is quite possible that Grandby's and Archibald Havistock may, eventually, if this matter is not speedily and satisfactorily resolved, be in litigation re the loss of the Demaretion and recompense demanded for its reserve value as stated in the auction contract.'

'So?' I said.

'Surely you can see the awkward position into which you are placing your legitimate employer,' he droned on. 'I refer, of course, to Grandby and Sons. You have, in effect, become a hireling of a party who may very well become our adversary in a court of law.'

'Hireling?' I said. 'Watch your language, buster. All I'm trying to do is clear my name.'

Stanton Grandby, looking more like a plump penguin than ever, gave a little cough and tried to smile. He didn't succeed.

'What we'd really like to know,' he said, 'is whether or not you've made any progress in your investigation.'

'Not much,' I said casually, sitting back. Let them sweat.

'Dunk,' Felicia Dodat said, 'you have no suspect?' She really was wearing green nail polish.

'Oh, there are a lot of suspects,' I said. 'Too many. But if you're asking me if I know who stole the Demaretion, the answer is no, I don't.'

They looked at each other, then all three looked at me.

'But you feel you *are* making progress?' Stanton Grandby asked anxiously.

I considered that. 'Yes,' I said finally, 'I think I am. I've collected a lot of information. I agree with Detective Georgio and investigator Smack: the robbery was committed by a member of the Havistock family.'

'Ah-*ha*,' lawyer Whattsworth said with some satisfaction. 'You're sure of that?'

'No,' I said, 'I'm not sure of anything.'

His confidence evaporated. 'How long,' he asked in his papery voice, 'do you anticipate your investigation will continue?'

'As long as it takes,' I told him.

Again they exchanged glances. If a signal passed between them, I didn't see it.

'Under the circumstances,' the attorney said, 'it seems somewhat unfair to you that your income should derive solely from a party with whom Grandby's may very well find itself in an antagonistic position.'

After digging through that tortured syntax, I gathered he was saying that I wasn't making enough money.

'I agree,' I said.

'Therefore,' he continued, 'we suggest that you terminate your employment by Archibald Havistock. Your leave of absence will be ended, and you will be returned to a salaried position with Grandby and Sons. It will be understood that you shall be relieved of all your regular duties, allowing you to continue your investigation into the theft of the coin.'

'No,' I said promptly.

'No?' Stanton Grandby cried.

'No?' Felicia Dodat cried.

'No,' I repeated firmly. 'The Havistocks put me on salary after you people took me off. I promised them I'd do everything I could to solve the crime. I intend to keep that promise.'

'But didn't they demand certain conditions?' the attorney said slyly. 'That you weren't to investigate too closely members of the immediate family?'

'Absolutely not,' I said. 'I asked for a free hand, and I got it. The only condition to which I agreed was that, if a member of the family turned out to be the criminal, I would inform Mr Havistock before I told the authorities. I assumed the reason for that was so he could arrange legal representation for the accused family member before he or she was arrested and charged.'

'Yes,' Whattsworth said dryly, 'I would say that is a logical assumption. However, it is extraneous to the basic interests of Grandby and Sons. What I now propose is that you continue your employment by Archibald Havistock, if you insist, but at the same time you return to a salaried position with Grandby's. With the absolute understanding, of course, that we shall become privy to the results of your investigation at the same time you reveal those results

179

to Mr Havistock, and that you shall provide us with weekly written reports on your progress.'

'Verbal reports,' I said. 'Not written. And not weekly reports, but periodically – whenever I've got something to tell you.'

'Oh, Dunk,' Felicia Dodat said sorrowfully, 'you're being so difficult.'

'Am I?' I said. 'I thought I was being cooperative.'

The lawyer looked at god. 'Mr Grandby,' he said, 'are you willing to accept those terms?'

The penguin squirmed. Then he nodded. 'All right,' he said.

'Oh, Dunk,' Felicia caroled, 'it's so nice having you back with us again.'

I had two words for her, and they weren't Happy Birthday.

I stopped down to see Hobie Juliana and tell him the good news, but he was out of the office on an appraisal. So I left Grandby's and walked back home through Central Park, proud of the way I had handled that confrontation. I was now making *two* salaries with complete freedom to conduct the investigation any way I chose. A slam dunk!

I knew what Grandby's was after, of course, and why they had put me back on salary. If a member of Archibald Havistock's family was involved in the theft, they wanted to know about it as soon as possible. It would give them leverage in the anticipated lawsuit. Also, by paying me, they thought they were insuring against any possible cover-up on my part.

Not very complimentary to me, but understandable.

That night, mercifully free of phone calls – I had gibbered enough – I lay awake in bed a long time, thinking over the events and conversations of that day. But then I found I was not pondering the investigation so much as I was reflecting on myself, and what was happening to me.

I was changing, no doubt about it; I was aware of it. I won't say I was naïve prior to my involvement with the Havistock Collection, but I was inclined to accept people at their face value, believing what they told me. I suppose I had lived a sheltered existence; crime and homicidal violence were things I read about in newspapers and novels, or saw in movies and on television.

But during the past weeks I had become intimately acquainted with what I guess you could call the underbelly of life. People *did* lie. They were *not* what they seemed. And they were capable of acting irrationally, driven by passions they could not control.

180

And my experiences with Al Georgio and Jack Smack were added evidence of how often the heart and glands overruled the mind and good sense. I suppose I should have learned all that at an earlier age, but I hadn't. Finally, finally I was suffering a loss of ingenuousness, if not innocence.

I was becoming, I thought, wiser, more cynical, street-smart. So something had been lost and something had been gained. But if you asked me what the bottom line was, I couldn't have told you.

22

AFTER BREAKFAST the next morning, I devoted myself to 'choring,' which is what, in my Iowa home, we called those endless boring tasks that had to be done: putting out the garbage, dusting, changing the linen, washing the sinks, etc. When I was satisfied with the way my apartment looked (it could have been more sparkling, but I lacked the willpower to tackle the windows), I left the house to pick up some dry cleaning.

This time I was careful to inspect the vestibule and areaway before I ventured out. On my way to the dry cleaners, I passed a newsstand and thought I might buy a copy of *Vogue* to see what I should be wearing, wasn't, and never would. But all thoughts of fashion fled when I glimpsed the screaming headline of the *Post*.

HIPPY SOCIALITE TRIES SUICIDE. And there was a photograph of Natalie Havistock with a dopey grin, wearing a beaded headband and earrings that looked like they had been snipped from the lid of a sardine tin.

I bought a *Post* and read the story on the sidewalk, oblivious to the people brushing by. It said that Natalie Havistock, younger daughter of wealthy tycoon Archibald Havistock (has there ever been a *poor* tycoon, I wondered), had been found unconscious in her bedroom at her parents' home on East 79th Street, apparently after ingesting alcohol and drugs that had not yet been identified.

She had been rushed to Wilson Memorial Hospital, only three blocks away, where, after treatment, doctors had pronounced her condition 'stable.' Her parents stated that no note had been found, and could give no reason for their daughter's attempted suicide.

I trotted home, errands forgotten, and called the Havistock apartment. Busy signal. Waited a few minutes and called again. Still busy. Waited. Called. Busy. Finally, on the fourth try, I got through. Ruby Querita answered. I identified myself.

'How is Nettie?' I asked. 'Have you heard anything?'

'*Nada*,' she said dolefully. 'They all at the hospital. I don't know how things are.'

'All right,' I said. 'Thank you, Ruby. Maybe I'll go to the hospital myself and see what's happening.'

Her voice dropped to a whisper. 'I told you, didn't I? Sin and you must suffer. This family is marked. Didn't I tell you?'

'You told me, Ruby,' I said, and hung up.

My idea of a hospital is a big shiny place with wide corridors, white walls, and tiled floors. Everything spotless and gleaming. Forget it. Wilson Memorial looked like a crumbling castle right out of *Young Frankenstein*. Gloomy, gloomy, gloomy. With narrow hallways, walls painted a sick brown, and worn linoleumed floors. I learned later it was a sort of temporary refuge for the terminally ill. I could believe it. If they weren't terminal when they were admitted, that place would push them over the edge.

The nurse at the lobby desk gave me a sad smile. I told her I'd like to see Natalie Havistock.

'Are you a member of the immediate family?' she asked.

'No,' I said, 'I am not. Actually, I don't want to see Natalie, but I have an important message for her father, Mr Archibald Havistock. I understand he's here. As soon as I see him, I'll be on my way.'

The scam worked.

'Room four-twelve,' she said, handing me a pass. 'Please make your visit as brief as possible.'

'You better believe it,' I said. 'Hospitals depress me.'

'Me, too,' she said mournfully, which I thought was an odd thing for a nurse to say.

I found the dismal corridor outside room 412. I also found Ross Minchen sitting on a scarred wooden bench, cracking his knuckles like a maniac.

'Hello, Ross,' I said.

He looked up, and it took him a couple of beats to recognize me. 'Oh, hi,' he said, not rising. 'Dunk – right? How're you doing?'

'How is Nettie doing?'

'Okay, I guess. They pumped her out. They're releasing her at noon. Mabel and Archibald are in with her now. The cops took off.'

'I thought Roberta and Vanessa would be here.'

'They were,' he said, 'but they left. I think they had some shopping to do.'

'And Luther?' I said. 'Wasn't her brother here?'

'Luther? No, he didn't show up. I guess he's busy. I'm just waiting to drive them all back home. Then I've got to get to the office.'

'Sure you do,' I said, sitting down beside him. 'I'll bet your work is piling up.'

'It really is,' he said, nodding. 'Unless I'm there every day, you wouldn't believe how things pile up.'

Mr Wimp himself, with those scrawny locks of hair combed sideways across his balding skull. Hard to believe this guy was the producer of X-rated videocassettes. You'd have thought that knitting antimacassars was more in his line.

'Ross,' I said, 'have you any idea why Nettie would do such a thing?'

'Gee,' he said, 'I really don't. Of course, she runs with a wild gang. I mean, they're probably dropping dope and all that. I don't know what the world is coming to.'

I didn't either.

Then stupid me, I had to ask: 'Are you and Roberta going to Vanessa's party?' I heard myself saying it and could have chomped off my tongue.

'No,' he said. 'Is she having a party?'

'Probably not,' I said hastily. 'After this business with Natalie. It was a very vague thing. She'll probably call it off.'

'We don't see much of them,' he said, looking down at his big, spatulate hands. 'Vanessa and Roberta don't get along.'

'That's a shame,' I said. 'Families should stick together.'

'Yeah,' he said, 'that's what I think. We tried to get Vanessa and Luther to join our, ah, little circle, but they weren't interested. How about you?' he said, brightening. 'Have you thought about it?'

'Frequently,' I said.

'And?'

'Still thinking,' I told him.

'Nothing to it,' he said. 'It's fun – you'll see. We're having another do next Friday. Can you make it?'

'I'm not sure,' I said then, swiftly, 'Wasn't it awful about Orson Vanwinkle?'

He looked at me, unblinking. 'The man was a crud,' he said. 'I don't mean I wanted him dead, don't get me wrong, but I can't be a hypocrite either and pretend I'm all broken up at his passing. I figure he got what he deserved.'

'No one seems to have liked him,' I said. 'Except Dolly LeBaron.'

184

'Oh, *her*,' he said scornfully. 'As greedy as he was. They were two of a kind. Listen, about next Friday, why don't you—'

But I was saved from more excuses when Mabel and Archibald Havistock came out of room 412. I rose and went to them.

'How is she?' I said anxiously.

'Much better,' Mrs Havistock said. 'We're taking her home in an hour. Thank you for your concern and for coming by.'

'How did you hear about it?' Archibald asked.

I reckoned he might as well know. 'It's on the front page of today's *Post*,' I told him.

'Oh, yes,' he said bitterly, 'it would be.'

Ross Minchen was still seated on his wooden bench, playing a merry tune on his knuckles. I gently urged the Havistocks down the corridor, away from him. I moved them to the end of the hallway, to a window where we could look out at a shadowy airshaft.

They were two somber people, faces creased with sorrow. But they retained their dignity, both of them erect and steady. I admired their stalwartness. Both seemed capable of absorbing blows without flinching and without complaint. Well, I thought, they have each other, and that's how they survive.

'I promised you a progress report,' I said. 'If you feel this is a bad time for it, please tell me and we'll leave it for later.'

'No, no,' Archibald said. 'Let's have it now. What have you found out?'

'First,' I said, 'I must tell you that Grandby and Sons have put me back on the payroll, with the understanding that I can spend all my time investigating the robbery. If you object to that, if you feel there's a conflict of interest involved, I want you to know that I'll reject their offer and work only for you.'

He looked at me a long moment. 'Thank you,' he said finally. 'You are a very straightforward young woman. I like that. No, I see no reason why you should not be employed by Grandby's at the same time you're working for us. Actually, we all want the same thing, don't we? Have you discovered who stole the Demaretion?'

'No, I have not. But I do feel I am making progress. Orson Vanwinkle promised his girlfriend that they'd soon be leaving the country permanently to live on the French Riviera. That certainly sounds like he expected to come into a great deal of money shortly, and makes him the Number One suspect.'

Husband and wife exchanged glances, just the briefest of eye-flickers.

185

'But I don't believe it,' I went on. 'Mostly because I cannot possibly conceive how Orson could have switched display cases. It was a physical impossibility.'

'Perhaps he had accomplices,' Mabel Havistock said faintly.

'Who?' I demanded. 'The guards from the armored van? Ruby Querita? I don't think so. Mr Havistock, you were out of your library for perhaps two minutes. The switch had to be made then: a prepared empty display case, sealed with your signet ring, substituted for the case containing the Demaretion. It had to be done by someone in the family, someone present in the apartment for the birthday party.'

'Not Nettie?' Mr Havistock said, his magisterial features expressionless, ice-blue eyes revealing nothing. 'Don't tell me it was Nettie?'

I didn't answer his question, but asked one of my own: 'The *Post* story said Nettie didn't leave any note. Is that correct?'

Mabel nodded, eyes skimmed with grief. 'We can't understand it,' she said. 'She was always such a bright, cheerful child. Laughing and joking. Perhaps it was something we did. Or failed to do.'

I had been debating with myself whether or not to tell them. But now, seeing that imposing woman suffering from a guilt trip, I thought I would.

'There are some things you should know,' I said. 'What I'm going to tell you is rumor and supposition. Nothing is proven. Orson Vanwinkle was bisexual. He had many homosexual encounters. This comes from a reliable source. Nettie's boyfriend is a black. Are you aware of that?'

'We are,' Mr Havistock said stonily.

'Her boyfriend was also one of Orson's homosexual contacts,' I said. 'I wish I could have spared you this, but I don't want you to blame yourselves for a situation over which you had no control.'

They didn't crumple. If anything, they straightened, drew deep breaths. They seemed to have a source of stamina I wished I could have tapped.

'You're certain of this?' Archibald asked.

'Mr Havistock, I'm not certain of *anything*. I'm just reporting what I've heard. That's what you're paying me for. But I think what I've heard is true. And it might possibly explain Natalie's suicide attempt. She discovered her boyfriend's, uh, sexual proclivities, argued with him about it, and he refused to change the way he lives.'

'I don't understand,' Mabel said, completely flummoxed. 'Why would those two men have anything to do with each other? They belonged to different worlds.'

'Money,' I said promptly. 'I think Orson was paying Akbar El Raschid and, through him, financing that gang of kooks Akbar commands. Maybe it was just the excitement Orson liked. The threat of violence. Radical chic.'

Archibald Havistock thought about it a long time while we all stared out at that haunted airshaft. Then he turned to me.

'Possible,' he said. 'It's possible. Orson was what I'd call a flighty man. Not quite as steady as I would have liked. Are the police aware of what you've told us, Miss Bateson?'

'They're aware of Vanwinkle's sexual activities,' I said. 'Whether or not they know about his liaison with Nettie's boyfriend – that I don't know. They'll probably find out.'

He nodded. 'Do you have anything else to tell us?'

'No, sir, not at the moment. A lot of wild guesses, crazy ideas, rumors I've got to track down. But nothing that even resembles fact or evidence. Do you want me to continue my investigation?'

'Absolutely,' Mrs Havistock said. 'We want to know the truth. Don't we, Archibald?'

'Yes,' he said.

'All right,' I told them, 'I'll keep at it. Now I'd like to ask a favor of you.'

They waited.

'May I go in to see Natalie? Just for a few minutes?'

They looked at each other.

'You won't disturb her?' Mrs Havistock said. 'Ask questions?'

'Of course not. I do like her and I want her to know I care.'

'All right,' Archibald said. 'Just for a few minutes.'

I started away from them, then turned back. I addressed Mrs Havistock.

'Ma'am,' I said, 'the last time we spoke you mentioned that you and your husband are involved in estate planning.'

'Yes,' she said, 'that's correct.'

'Does that include the drawing up of new wills for both of you?'

'It does,' Mr Havistock said. 'Why do you ask?'

'I don't know exactly,' I said fretfully. 'Except money seems to be the thread that runs through everything: the stealing of the Demaretion and the murder of Orson Vanwinkle. Have the wills been completed?'

'No,' he said, 'they have not.'

187

I thought he was a little short with me, and I assumed he resented my intrusion into his private financial affairs. But I would not stop.

'Were members of your family aware that you were preparing new wills?'

'I assume they were,' he said. 'Don't you think so, Mabel?'

'I'm sure they were,' she said. 'We made no secret of it.'

'Thank you very much,' I said. 'I'll get back to you the moment I have anything important to report.'

23

Poor Natalie looked so weak and drawn, white as the sheets she was lying on. She held out a thin hand to me.

'I can't do anything right, can I?' she said.

'You're alive,' I said, kissing her cold fingertips. 'That's right. How are you, love?'

'Oh . . .' she said, 'I don't know. I'm not thinking straight.'

'You'll clear up,' I assured her. 'I just stopped in for a few minutes to say hello.'

'It was sweet of you,' she said. 'Did you find out who boosted the coin?'

'Not yet.'

'You will,' she said. 'You're a determined lady. The cops haven't found out who snuffed Orson, have they?'

I shook my head.

'Well, who cares,' she said. 'That little Barbie Doll of his – what's her name?'

'Dolly LeBaron.'

'Yeah, a real dolly. She'll find another bankroll, and in a year – a year? Hell, within a month – the world will be rolling along without him. That's what's going to happen to all of us, isn't it?'

'Nettie, don't talk like that. Your mother and father are outside. They're really shook. They love you and want you to have a happy life. You're important to them.'

'I guess,' she said, sighing. 'I've been a pain in the ass to them. Two different worlds – you know?'

'You made the front page of the *Post* today,' I told her.

'I did?' she said, brightening. 'Hot shit! Have you got it with you?'

'I have it at home,' I said. 'I'll save it for you if you can't get a copy. You're wearing a beaded headband and tin earrings.'

189

'Oh, that old shot,' she said. 'It was taken years ago at the Slipped Disco. I was stoned out of my skull.'

'You look like it,' I said, and we both laughed.

She reached for my hand again. 'Listen, Dunk, when I get back to the land of the living, can we see each other again?'

'Absolutely,' I said.

'Promise?'

'Of course. I'm counting on it. If you promise me something first.'

'What?'

'If you ever get in the mood to try something like that again, will you call me first?'

'Okay,' she said, 'I will.'

We linked our little fingers, shook, and both of us said, 'Pinkie square!'

I didn't know what it was – maybe the sultry July day or maybe that childish business of 'Pinkie square!' – but on the way home I had a sudden, irresistible urge to chaw on a frozen Milky Way. And I wasn't even pregnant! Anyway, I stopped off to buy three of the candy bars. I put them in the freezer and waited patiently. I remembered they've got to be so hard you think you'll break your teeth – but you never do. The joys of my youth!

I was entering all the happenings of the morning into my notebook when I received my first phone call of the day. I thought it might be Al or Jack, alerting me to Natalie's attempted suicide. But it was Enoch Wottle, calling from Arizona. I was delighted.

'Enoch, dear,' I said, 'I love to hear from you, but you've *got* to call collect. I don't want you spending your money on my business.'

'It's nothing,' he said blithely. 'I'm never going to outlive my bonds. Dunk, darling, how are you and what's happening?'

I gave him a précis of what had been going on, including my reinstatement at Grandby & Sons.

'Good,' he said firmly. 'They should be ashamed of themselves for putting you on leave of absence in the first place. Are you any closer to finding out who stole the Demaretion?'

'Closer,' I said, 'I think. But close doesn't help. I'm still not sure who did it, Enoch.'

'But you suspect?'

'I suspect, but it's so crazy I don't even want to talk about it.'

'All right,' he said equably, 'then I'll talk. I have something that might help. I checked with my friend in Rotterdam who, in turn, contacted that Beirut dealer. Dunk, from what everyone says – if

190

they're telling the truth – that Demaretion being offered for sale is absolutely authentic. Provenance will be supplied during serious negotiations. It sounds legitimate to me, Dunk. Not the source of the coin,' he added hastily. 'Not how the seller got hold of it. But the dekadrachm itself – that's not a fake. Does that help you?'

'I think so,' I said slowly. 'I'm not sure how it fits in, but everything helps. Thank you so much, Enoch. You've been a treasure.'

'Now then,' he said briskly, 'what's next?'

'What's next? Enoch, you've done enough for me. Spending your own money on phone calls and cables. I can't ask you to do anything more.'

'Ask!' he urged. 'Ask! Dunk, sweetheart, let me tell you something. My life is drawing to a close; I know it. But what am I supposed to do, just sit and *wait*? So what I do for you, I do for myself also. To keep busy, to be needed, wanted – that is something at my age.'

My eyes teared. 'All right, Enoch,' I said, 'you certainly can help. Who else has your knowledge and experience? Tell me: Why would a collector – not a speculator but a true collector – sell off part of his coin collection?'

He thought a moment. 'Financial need,' he suggested. 'That would probably be the first motive. Some investments go wrong, the stock market takes a nose dive, he needs ready cash. So he sells off some coins. That would be the first motive. Another would be that he wants to upgrade his collection. He sells off the lesser mintages, maybe some duplicates, so he can buy higher quality.'

'But the true collector who sells and doesn't buy, doesn't add, that's unusual, isn't it, Enoch?'

'I'd say so, unless he's in a real money bind.'

'Archibald Havistock has been selling for the past five years,' I told him. 'About a hundred items, maybe more. I'd like to find out how much he got for them. Not for individual coins, but the total. How do I do that? Go to the Society?'

'No,' he said immediately. 'Privileged information. They wouldn't know – and if they did, they'd never tell you. Do you know who he dealt with?'

'No, I don't. But he's a wealthy man, Enoch. Very upright, very honest. He wouldn't deal with shlockers.'

'That means there are maybe a half-dozen people in Manhattan he'd go to. I know them all. You want me to check?'

'Would you?'

'I would and I will. This gives me something to do. I feel important.'

'You *are* important, Enoch, and I love you.'

'Why aren't you fifty years older?' he said, groaning. 'We could make such beautiful music together.'

I laughed. 'Enoch,' I said, 'you're a dirty old man.'

'I was a dirty *young* man,' he said, 'and I haven't changed. Dunk, darling, as soon as I learn something, I'll get back to you. It may take some time.'

'I don't care how long it takes,' I said, 'but be sure and reverse the charges.'

'All right already,' he said, 'I'll reverse. Thank you, Dunk.'

After we hung up, I wiped my eyes. Sweet, sweet man. Thanking me. For what? I knew. I returned to my journal and continued entering all the latest intelligence I had garnered that day. Then I dashed to the refrigerator. The Milky Ways weren't yet hard enough, but I chewed on one with pleasure, remembering hot summer days in Des Moines when I was all legs and a stomach that could never be filled.

Would you believe I pigged down all three frozen Milky Ways that afternoon? I did, and I'm not ashamed of it. I should tell you that in spite of the Lean Cuisines I gobble, I'm blessed with a fantastic metabolism and can eat anything without putting on a pound. Sometimes I wish I could – in the right places.

Maybe all that sugar gave me energy, or maybe what I had heard that morning made me think I was making progress; whatever it was, I was in a charged mood and had no desire to spend the evening all by my lonesome. So I called Al Georgio.

And while I listened to his phone buzz, I wondered why I hadn't called Jack Smack. Did my choice indicate a preference – or was it just a chancy act with no significance whatsoever? I didn't know.

I had to wait almost three minutes before they located him and got him to the phone. He came on breathless and laughing.

'Hey there, Dunk,' he said. 'I was going to call you in a half-hour, I swear. How're you doing?'

'Surviving,' I said. 'How are *you* doing?'

'Surviving,' he said. 'I guess you heard about Natalie Havistock?'

'I read it in the *Post*. I went over to the hospital this morning and saw her.'

'You did? They wouldn't let me in. She say anything about why she tried to off herself?'

'She didn't say and I didn't ask. I was with her for only a few minutes, and it was just girl talk. Anything new on the Demaretion?'

'Nah,' he said disgustedly. 'A lot of little bits and pieces that don't come together. The same goes for the Vanwinkle kill. The homicide guys are still checking out all the names in his little black book. I passed along your tip that he was AC-DC, and they're working that angle. Nothing yet.'

'Listen, Al,' I said, suddenly bold, 'I'd like to take you to dinner tonight.'

'You would?' he said. 'That's the best offer I've had all year. What's the occasion?'

'I was put back on salary at Grandby's, and I'm still working for the Havistocks, so I want to celebrate. How about it?'

'Sounds great. But we'll go Dutch. Got any idea where you want to eat?'

'There's a new Chinese restaurant in the neighborhood I'd like to try. Over on Amsterdam. The menu in the window looks good. It's Szechwan. Too hot for you?'

'You kidding? I put Tabasco on my corn flakes. What are you giggling about? The joke wasn't that funny.'

'The name of the restaurant . . .' I said. 'It's called Hung Lo.'

'My kind of joint,' he said. 'Pick you up about eight?'

'Try to park if you can,' I said, 'and we'll walk over. It's only two blocks away.'

Hung Lo, although recently opened, looked like a million other Chinese restaurants in New York. But there were a lot of Orientals at the tables, which Al and I figured was a good sign. Also, the menu said you could have your food with or without monosodium glutamate, and you could designate mild, hot, or superhot.

'Let's go with hot,' I suggested. 'If it's not incendiary enough, we can always pepper it up. But if the superhot turns out to be too much, we're stuck with it.'

So that's what we did, ordering eggrolls and barbecued ribs as small appetizers, wonton soup, and deciding to share our main dishes, shrimp with peanuts, shredded pork with garlic sauce, and servings of white and fried rice.

'And beer instead of tea,' Al told the waiter. 'Cold, cold beer. Okay, Dunk?'

'Just right,' I said.

193

Maybe I was hungry despite those Milky Ways. I know Al seemed to be famished. We went through all that food like a plague of locusts. I had a bottle of Heineken, and Al had two. Then we had pistachio ice cream and opened our fortune cookies. Mine read: 'Your fondest wish will come true.' Al's was: 'The wise man wants for nothing.'

'The story of my life,' he said. 'That's what I'm getting – nothing.'

I excused myself, telling Al I wanted to find the ladies' room. But I grabbed our waiter, paid the bill, and tipped him. Then I went back to our table.

'All set?' Al said. 'I'll get the check.'

'I took care of it,' I said.

He looked at me, shaking his head. 'You're sneaky, you know that? I said we'd go Dutch.'

'That's what *you* said. I didn't agree.'

He laughed, took up my hand, kissed the palm. 'You're something, you are. The new woman.'

'Not so new,' I told him. 'A little worn around the edges.'

'You're worn?' he said. 'I'm frayed.'

We strolled slowly back to my place. He insisted on stopping off to buy a cold six-pack of Heineken. Which was all right with me. I could still feel the glow of the Szechwan cooking, and I was happy we hadn't ordered the superhot. My eyebrows would be charred.

We hadn't said a word about the Demaretion or the murder or Orson Vanwinkle all evening. I think we both wanted a brief respite from all that. So we chatted lazily about new movies, whether roast duck was better with mandarin oranges or black cherries, and the problems Al was having with his cleaning woman. She kept stealing his Future floor wax.

'I swear she's drinking the stuff,' he said.

When we got home, he asked if he could make himself comfortable, and I said sure, go ahead. He took off his jacket and eased out of his shoes. He was wearing a knitted sport shirt with no animal insignia, which gave him a plus in my book.

No way was he ever going to be an elegant, dapper dude. He just didn't have the body, and he just didn't care. But there was something comforting in his lumpiness. Winston Churchill wasn't Beau Brummell, and neither was Pope John XXIII. But both men made you feel good just to look at them, they were so *solid*. They knew life wasn't to be taken lightly. The same with Al Georgio.

194

'I got a Sunday coming up with my daughter,' he said. 'I'd like you to join us. Will you?'

'You sure it will be all right?'

'No, I'm not sure,' he said. 'But let's try it.'

'Okay.'

'You like the beach?'

'Love it, but I've got to be careful. I freckle, get red, and then I peel.'

'So you cover up,' he said, shrugging. 'Maybe we'll go to Jacob Riis. The water should be warm enough by now. Do you swim, Dunk?'

'Like a fish,' I told him. 'An eel.'

'You're always putting yourself down. Does it bother you that you're so tall and slender?'

We were both working on cold beers, drinking out of the bottle. I took a deep gulp before I answered.

'Thank you for saying slender instead of skinny. It doesn't *bother* me, but I know it's there. When I look in the mirror. The way people sometimes stare at me. Trying to buy clothes that fit. But I can handle it.'

'I figure you can handle just about anything,' he said. 'Fifteen years ago my waist size was thirty-two. Now it's forty. I've tried everything: diet, working out. Nothing helps. So I've learned to live with it. I know I'm a slob.'

'You're not a slob,' I said indignantly. 'Don't say that. You're just a very, uh, robust man.'

'That's me,' he said. 'Robust.'

He said it so wryly that we both laughed, and that made our physical shortcomings seem unimportant.

'What about you, Dunk?' he said, staring at me. 'What do you want? Marriage? The patter of tiny feet?'

'I don't know,' I said, looking down at my beer bottle. 'I really don't. I'm not sure I'm ready for all that yet. I want to *do* something first.'

'Seems to me you've done a great deal.'

'Not enough. Tonight my fortune cookie said my fondest wish will come true. Al, I don't even know what my fondest wish *is*. I'm just floating.'

'Nothing wrong with that. I'm the same way. Sooner or later things will point us in one direction or another. No use trying to force it.'

195

'That's the way I feel. Things will happen.'

'They always have,' he said. Then, suddenly: 'May I stay the night?'

I knew that if I had said no, he'd have said, 'All right.' But I said, 'Sure. I paid for dinner, didn't I?'

He cracked up. When he finally got his guffaws under control, he said, 'I love you, Dunk, I really do. You're a lot of woman.'

'You can handle it,' I told him.

'I'm going to give it the old college try,' he said.

He was ponderous in bed, almost solemn. It was obvious that sex was a serious thing to him. But it's nice to be with a man who doesn't think it's just recreation. Al thought it was important, and every kiss was a commitment.

Lord knows I wasn't an artful or practiced lover. Very little experience. So what Al brought to our coupling was new – for me. He was so – so *earnest*. Not clever but sincere. I'm not sure I'm telling this right, but he gave me more comfort than pleasure. Just snuggling in his strong arms gave me a feeling of relief and contentment.

As if I had come home.

24

I AWOKE the next morning and found Al had departed. He left a little note on my bedside table, a page torn from his pocket notebook: 'Thank you for dinner – and everything. Especially everything. Al.' Sweet man.

By the time I bathed (bumping my noggin on the shower head, as usual) and dressed, I realized I had an enormous appetite that a bagel and a cup of coffee would never appease. I mean I was *ravenous*. There was a down-home diner over on Columbus Avenue, a scuzzy place, that on a scale of 1 to 10 ranked 1 for cleanliness and ambience and 20 for their country breakfasts. I decided I was going to have grits and fried bologna – and if you haven't tried it, don't knock it.

I went through my new drill of checking the vestibule and areaway before I went out. All clear. But when I got to the corner, there was Sam Jefferson, also known as Akbar El Raschid, leaning negligently against the mailbox. He flashed his white teeth at me.

'Morning, sweet mama,' he said.

Then, when he saw my reaction – I didn't know whether to scream, run or both – he held up both hands, pink palms outward.

'Hey,' he said, 'look. No shiv, no gun, no brass knuckles. All I want is a few minutes of your valuable time.'

'I already spent a few minutes,' I told him. 'With two of your goons. The mustache and the gold tooth.'

'Yeah,' he said. 'I know. That was stupid, stupid, stupid, and I apologize. Okay?'

'I don't like getting hassled.'

'You know anyone who does? How about it – friends again?'

I considered a moment, then: 'What do you want to talk about?'

'Nettie,' he said. 'My main woman.'

'I'm on my way to breakfast,' I said. 'Grits and fried bologna. You want to come along?'

'Grits?' he said, his eyes glazing over. 'Haven't had them in five years. Oh, yeah, let's go. The treat's on me.'

In the greasy diner, sitting in a back booth, he looked around and then inspected the tattered menu.

'The cook has *got* to be a brother,' he said. 'Who else is going to offer ham hocks for breakfast? Sweet mama, if the food's as good as it sounds, I'm going to move right in. Let's go for broke.'

So we both had field hand breakfasts with the best hashbrowns I've ever tasted and chicory-laced coffee that made you sit up and take notice.

'About Nettie,' he said, digging into his grits, 'you hear what happened to her?'

I nodded.

'Silly, silly woman,' he said, groaning. 'She had no call to do that.'

'Apparently she thought she did. Your argument with her was about Orson Vanwinkle, wasn't it?'

'Oh, you know about that?' he said, not surprised. 'So do the cops. They been around asking questions. Yeah, our little altercation was about that honky flake. You know, some flakes are crazy and funny. He was crazy and not so funny. A miserable shit if the truth be known.'

'Then why did you have anything to do with him?'

He paused in his eating to stare up at me and rub a thumb and forefinger together. 'Mon-eee. The mon-eee, sweet mama. That guy leaked green. You think I'd have given him the time of day if it wasn't for the gelt? I got big plans, and big plans need venture capital. That schmuck came up with the funds.'

'And Nettie found out?'

'Yeah, she found out. She was the one who introduced us, but she didn't know he was a butterfly. She just thought he was a nutty drunk with an open wallet. Listen, Dunk, I want you to know – I didn't scrag him. And none of my lads did either.'

'I believe you.'

'Why should I want to knock off the golden goose? Someone else chilled him, and I really grieved. But only because the bank was closed. You dig? I'm telling you like it is.'

'I believe you,' I repeated.

'So . . .' he said, motioning the waitress over to refill our coffee cups, 'my big problem now is Nettie. She means a lot to me.'

'Does she?'

'I kid you not. I want to tell her how I feel, but I can't get through

198

to her. I call her private number, but someone else answers and won't put her on. They got her sewed up.'

'Do you blame them?'

'I guess not. I'm not the all-American boy they figured she'd grab. But, at the same time, look at it from my point of view. I really do have a thing for her and want to tell her so. That business with Vanwinkle was just that – business. All I want to do is say to her how I feel. Then, if she tells me to get lost, I'll get lost, and that'll be the end of that, I swear.'

'What do you want from me? What can I do?'

'Just call her. They'll let you talk to her. Tell her I'll be at the 787 number all afternoon. She knows what it is. If she wants to call me, that'd be great. If she doesn't, that's her decision, and I'll abide by it. Will you do that?'

I thought about it a moment. 'All right,' I said, 'I'll try. But she may not be in.'

'Keep trying,' he urged. 'I'll be at the 787 number afternoons for the next few days.'

I sat back, wiped my lips with a paper napkin, stifled a small belch. 'Tell me,' I said, 'where was Orson Vanwinkle getting all his money?'

'Beats the shit out of me,' he said. 'Nettie and I used to talk about it. I mean he was a secretary – right? But he had cash like you wouldn't believe. And he was laying off a lot of it on that Miss Cuddles of his. Maybe he was printing it in his bathroom – who knows? But he never had the shorts, I can tell you that.'

I looked at him. 'You didn't like the man, he disgusted you, but you went along for the money?'

He looked at me just as directly. 'That's right, sweet mama. If you believe in something strong enough, then nothing you have to do makes you turn back. You got a goal, and that's all that matters.'

'What's your goal?' I asked him.

'A small thing,' he said, flashing his teeth again. 'I just want to remake the world, that's all.'

'Lots of luck,' I said.

'You make your own luck,' he said. 'I learned that a long time ago. You'll call Nettie?'

'I'll try.'

'Good enough,' he said. 'I do thank you. Something else I've got to ask you: Are you tall or am I shrinking?'

I laughed. 'It's me,' I said. 'Turn you off?'

199

'*Au contraire*,' he said. 'If it wasn't for Nettie, I'd love to shinny up you. But things being what they are, that'll have to remain a wild fantasy.'

'You better believe it,' I told him.

When I got home, I called the Havistock apartment and asked to speak to Natalie. Ruby Querita answered the phone and said that her parents had taken Nettie to their family physician for a checkup; they would probably all be home in an hour or so. I asked her to tell Natalie I had phoned and to please call me back.

Then I settled down to read my morning *Times*. But I found my eyes rising from the paper to stare at the wall. What Akbar El Raschid had told me was pretty much what I had already figured, but where *was* Orson Vanwinkle's money coming from? My next step, I resolved, was to brace Archibald Havistock directly and ask him how much he was paying his private secretary. He might refuse to answer. But that in itself would be a kind of answer, wouldn't it?

Natalie did call back, almost two hours later, and said she was feeling a lot better, her mind had cleared, and she was determined to solve her problems one by one, instead of being overwhelmed by all of them at once.

'Good for you,' I said. 'That's the way to do it. Now I don't feel so guilty about giving you another problem.'

I told her about my breakfast with her boyfriend and what he had asked me to do.

'So,' I said, 'if you want to talk to him, he'll be at the 787 number this afternoon. It's up to you.'

'How did he look?' she said eagerly.

'He looked all right. The same way he looked when I met him at the party.'

'Isn't he the most beautiful man you've ever seen?' she said breathlessly.

'He's very handsome.'

'That crazy little beard of his,' she said. 'It drives me wild.'

I had the unsettling feeling that since the Demaretion had been stolen, I had wandered into never-never land.

So far, most of my detecting activities had been limited to asking people questions and trying to make sense out of what they told me. I figured that's the way most professional investigators worked. I mean, how many detectives go crawling across a rug on their hands and knees with a big magnifying glass looking for clues? Interrogation was the name of the game.

But my questioning of the principals involved had resulted in more puzzles than solutions. One of the things that still bugged me was that East 65th Street brownstone apartment. Lenore Wolfgang had given me a facile explanation of why she rented it. But it didn't account for Vanessa Havistock entering the building.

Apparently Al Georgio had accepted the attorney's story. At least he hadn't told me differently. But then there were a lot of things I hadn't told *him*. I decided I'd try to find out a little more about Wolfgang's pied-à-terre.

So I cabbed over to the East Side on a muggy July afternoon, the whole city one big sauna. But I was too busy concocting a scenario to be bothered by the heat. What I planned to do was locate the superintendent of the building, and charm, wheedle, or bribe him into telling me if anyone occupied Lenore Wolfgang's apartment on a regular basis. Then I intended to describe Vanessa Havistock and ask him if he had ever seen her on the premises.

Full of confidence, I strode fearlessly into the vestibule of the brownstone to check the number of the Wolfgang apartment. Instant shock. No Wolfgang listed. The space her name label had occupied was now just a little strip of bare brass. I stared at it, not believing.

It took me a few moments to recover. What *was* going on? To one side of the bell plate was a small sign: RING BASEMENT BELL FOR SUPER. I looked around; no basement bell. Then, getting my wits together, I went outside again and down three steps into the areaway. There I found the super's bell, pressed it, and improvised a fast new scam while I waited.

There were two doors, the outer a grille of forged iron in an attractive foliage pattern. It was locked. The inner door, a solid wood slab, was the one that was opened. The gorilla in a man's suit who stood there glared at me through the iron grille. He had the beginnings of a beard, but I didn't think it was deliberate; he had just neglected to shave – for almost three days.

'Good afternoon,' I said, smiling brightly. 'I heard there's an apartment available in this building.'

'You heard wrong,' he growled. 'Nothing available.'

He began to close his door.

'Wait a minute,' I cried desperately. 'Didn't Lenore Wolfgang move?'

'Yeah, she moved,' he acknowledged. 'But's it's been rented. Lady, we got fifty people on a waiting list. At least.'

I opened my shoulder bag, fished in my purse, pulled out a ten-dollar bill. I folded it lengthwise, poked it through the iron grille. He stared at it.

'What's that for?' he demanded. 'I can't get you on the waiting list. You got to go to the owner. His name and address are in the vestibule.' He pronounced it "vestabool."

I waggled the ten-dollar bill. 'I don't want to get on the list,' I said. 'I just want a little information.'

His hand struck like an adder, plucking the bill from my fingers. 'Yeah?' he said. 'What?'

'When did Lenore Wolfgang move?'

'Coupla days ago. The new tenant moves in tomorrow. That's it?'

'Not for ten bucks, that's not it,' I said indignantly. 'Did you ever see a woman use Wolfgang's apartment? Tall, full-bodied, long black hair, lots of makeup and jewelry.'

Something came into his eyes, a shifting of depth, a certain shrewd knowing. 'Yeah,' he said, 'I seen a woman like that. Plenty times. A real looker.'

'She used the Wolfgang apartment?'

He nodded.

'You ever see a man go up there when she was here?'

He stared at me. 'No,' he said, 'I never seen no man with her.'

He slammed the inner door. From which I concluded that someone had paid him more than I had. He was an honorable man – in his way.

I went home via bus, which was a mistake; it was a long, miserable, fume-choked trip. But I had a lot to think about. Vanessa *had* been using Wolfgang's place, as I originally suspected. And about a week after Al Georgio queried the building's owner, Lenore had given up her apartment – which, in Manhattan, is an act akin to hara-kiri.

The fact that Vanessa had been playing around came as no great surprise; I never figured her to be a one-man woman. And I couldn't see her having a lesbian relationship, especially with Lenore Wolfgang, who wore chewing gum on her shoe. No, Vanessa was having trysts with a man – or men – in that apartment. Was that where the money was coming from to pay for the jewelry, the summer home, that sumptuous Park Avenue apartment? Interesting idea: Vanessa reverting to loitering for the purpose of prostitution.

All this was supposition, of course – pure guesswork. But it did fit the facts, and the longer I considered it, the more logical it seemed.

There was only one thing wrong: I couldn't see where it had any connection with the disappearance of the Demaretion. I should have considered a little longer and thought a little harder.

No phone calls for the rest of the day – which made me irritable. I wanted Al Georgio and Jack Smack to volunteer vital information that would enable me to solve the mystery to the applause of all. I realized how unfair that was – I wasn't telling them what I had discovered – but still it rankled. I was an amateur sleuth, and they were experienced professionals. You'd think they'd drop a few crumbs my way, wouldn't you?

I got myself in such a tizzy thinking about it that it took two hours of knitting to calm me down. Then I could laugh at my anger and admit that I better plan on solving the puzzle by myself or never solve it at all. Al and Jack had their own jobs and responsibilities. And I was sure they wanted the glory of breaking the case as much as I did.

That night, my stupid air conditioner making a racket, I lay naked between the sheets, reading the latest how-to book on 'fulfilling your latent potential.' I kept flipping the pages, looking for the magic secret that would enable me to become successful, irresistible, and shorter. I didn't find it.

I was listening to WQXR on my bedside radio with half an ear. I decided that after the midnight news, I'd turn off the radio, switch off the light, and wait for sleep.

Later, I was to reflect that I had been present when the Demaretion disappeared, Al Georgio had telephoned to tell me of Vanwinkle's death, and I had read of Natalie's attempted suicide in the daily press. Now I was to learn of the latest tragedy from the radio while lying naked in bed reading a self-improvement book. If that's not running the gamut, I don't know what is.

It was just a brief mention; the news announcer made no big deal of it. He merely said that the body of a young woman, apparently strangled, had been found in an East 66th Street apartment. The victim had been identified as Dolly LeBaron. The police said the slain woman had reportedly been a close friend of Orson Vanwinkle, whose recent murder was still under investigation.

After the initial impact of those words, I found I was weeping. That poor, silly girl with her red bikini and doomed dreams. She had told me I was her closest girlfriend, which was ridiculous, but now, hearing of her violent death, I thought it just might have been true, and wept the harder.

I didn't even begin to wonder how her murder might impinge on the investigations of the Demaretion theft and/or the Vanwinkle homicide. Only one thing concerned me. I flung out of bed, dashed bareass through the apartment, turning on lights as I went.

In the kitchen, I opened the cabinet over the sink and probed in back with trembling fingers. I was searching for that package Dolly LeBaron had left in my care.

25

I READ the gory details in the morning papers. Dolly's body had been discovered by neighbors who noticed her door was ajar. She was lying on her back in the living room, wearing an opened Oriental happy coat, and nothing else. Police didn't believe she had been sexually assaulted, but awaited the autopsy for final determination.

That garish apartment was a shambles. Furniture had been overturned and slashed, closets and cupboards emptied, dresser drawers spilled, even the lid of the toilet tank removed. The killer had obviously been searching for something. (I could have told him where it was – in my kitchen.)

There was little data on Dolly's background, other than she was from Wichita and had come to New York to seek a career on the stage. There were some snide references to what had befallen her, including a mention that she was known as a 'party girl,' as if that was sufficient justification for what had been done to her.

The big angle in all the tabloid stories was her relationship with Orson Vanwinkle – both of them murdered within weeks. Dolly had been strangled and Orson shot, but the police were investigating the possibility that a single killer was responsible for both deaths. They had also found 'quantities' of marijuana and cocaine in Dolly's trashed apartment.

Her parents were flying in from Kansas to reclaim her body after the autopsy was completed.

I stared at the front-page photos of Dolly in her red bikini.

She would have liked that.

I hardly had time to breakfast, read the papers, and wonder what it all meant when I got a call from Al Georgio. He was very abrupt.

'I just talked to Jack Smack,' he said. 'He's not involved in the Vanwinkle and LeBaron kills, but he thinks they're connected to the coin robbery. I think so, too. Maybe it's time the three of us sat down together and compared notes. How about it?'

'Yes,' I said, 'that makes sense to me. Where do you want to meet?'

'How about your place? Have any objection?'

'Of course not. When?'

'Noon today. We'll bring something to eat and something to drink, so don't go to any trouble.'

What they brought were three quarter-pounders and three cheeseburgers from McDonald's, plus enough French fries to stuff a pillow. Also, a cold six-pack of Michelob Light. We sat around my cocktail table, munching and sipping while we talked.

'The ways things are going,' Al said, 'if we wait long enough, everyone connected with this case is going to get knocked off. Then all our worries will be over.'

'Al,' I said, 'was there anything about Dolly's murder that wasn't in the papers?'

'Not much, except there were no signs of forced entry. So she let in someone she knew.'

'Just like Vanwinkle,' Jack said, nodding. 'You're going on the theory that it's the same killer?'

'Seems likely,' Al said. 'Now we've got to go back and check everyone in Orson's little black book to find out where they were when Dolly was dumped.'

'Was anything stolen from her apartment?' I asked him.

'The place is such a mess it's hard to tell. It must have taken at least a half-hour to do that much damage. Can you imagine? The killer chills Dolly and then stays on the scene for thirty minutes or more, tearing up the joint. He must have been desperate.'

'You think he found what he was looking for?' Jack said.

'Who the hell knows,' Al said roughly.

'The Demaretion?' I suggested.

'Yeah,' Al said, 'it could have been that. Assuming Vanwinkle copped the coin. After he was snuffed, the killer searched his place and didn't find it. He figures Orson gave it to his girlfriend to hold for him. So the perp visits her place and goes through the whole drill again.'

'Perp?' I said.

'Perpetrator,' Al said. 'Jack, what's new on your end?'

'Not a whole hell of a lot. Our contact in Lebanon says, yeah, that Beirut coin dealer is trying to peddle a Demaretion. It seems to be the real thing. But our man wasn't able to find out who the principal is.'

'Thin stuff,' Al said. 'Dunk, you got anything?'

'Did you check out that East Sixty-fifth Street apartment?' I asked.

'I called the owner,' he said. 'Yes, it's rented by Lenore Wolfgang, Archibald Havistock's lawyer. She keeps it for friends and out-of-town clients. I haven't had time to dig any deeper than that.'

'I did,' I said. 'I went over there yesterday. Wolfgang gave up the apartment a few days ago. But while she had it, Vanessa Havistock used it frequently. The super wouldn't say if she was meeting a man there.'

The two men stared at me, then turned to stare at each other.

'Now what the hell does that mean?' Al said.

'Nothing,' Jack said. 'It's garbage. So Vanessa was playing around. Big deal. I can't see it affecting anything.'

That offended me. 'Wolfgang's apartment was right around the block from where Dolly LeBaron was murdered. What's that – a coincidence?'

Al finished a cheeseburger, sat back, and opened his second beer. 'All right,' he said, 'let's all blow a little smoke. Let's have some wild theories of what went down here. It doesn't have to be logical or touch all bases. Just a hazy idea of what happened. I'll start. I figure Orson engineered the Demaretion grab. He plans the whole thing, but someone else in the family makes the switch. My prime suspect is Luther Havistock, who's hurting for money. Then they argue about the split. Luther blows his cool and decides that since he actually lifted the Demaretion, he's entitled to a bigger share. So he scrags Orson and Dolly, looking for it. Now before you tear that story apart, let's have your own fairy tales. Jack, you go next.'

Jack hunched forward over the cocktail table, popping French fries like they were vitamin pills. And he was still working on a quarter-pounder.

'I'll go along with your idea that there were two crooks involved,' he said. 'First of all, we get these neatly typed letters offering to make a deal on the return of the coin. Then suddenly the letters stop, and we hear someone's working through a Beirut dealer. That adds up to two different guys – right? I agree that Orson was involved – he probably wrote the letters to us and that threatening letter to you, Dunk – but I don't think his partner was Luther Havistock; I think

207

it was the younger daughter, Natalie. And she was working for her screwball boyfriend, Sam Jefferson, who claims to be a born-again Muslim, Akbar El Raschid. Well, he may or may not be, but if he has Muslim contacts, what's a better place to peddle the coin than Lebanon. Doesn't that make sense?'

'I hadn't thought of that angle,' Al Georgio said. 'It's a possible. Dunk, let's have your daydream.'

I really didn't want to tell them about my crazy idea because I thought they'd laugh at me and treat my solution with amused contempt. It was such a fragile flower that I didn't want it trampled before it had a chance to bloom. Also, I wasn't so sure about it myself.

'I'll go along with the two thieves theory,' I said cautiously. 'Vanwinkle was involved, no doubt about it. But I can't see either Natalie or Luther Havistock being the partner in crime. Natalie would steal from Saks Fifth Avenue, but I can't believe she'd steal from her own father. Call it woman's intuition or whatever you like, but I just don't think she's guilty. As for Luther, yes, he's in hock and seems to be close to a crackup, but do you really believe he's capable of killing two people? And if he did, who the hell is trying to sell that coin through the Beirut dealer? If it really is Archibald's Demaretion, then what's the point of murdering Orson and Dolly and searching their apartments trying to find it? No, there's someone else involved, someone who actually has the coin right now.'

'Oh, my God,' Al said, groaning. 'Don't tell me you think there are *three* people involved.'

'I don't know,' I said desperately. 'I suppose it sounds silly, but you've got to admit the coin was offered by the Beirut dealer *before* Dolly was killed.'

We all sat there, staring gloomily at each other. Then we reached simultaneously for more food and beer and busied ourselves, ruminating.

'You know what I think?' I said finally, and the two detectives looked at me hopefully. 'I agree with both of you that the murders of Orson and Dolly are connected to the theft of the Demaretion. But analyze it. What, actually, *is* the connection? Because the robbery and the murders happened so close together, we assume they're linked. But when you look at it logically, the only connection is that all this is occurring in the same family. Archibald Havistock's favorite coin gets swiped. Then his private secretary, and the secretary's girlfriend, are killed. Let me ask both of you: Is there any real, hard evidence that Orson was actually involved in the theft?'

They thought awhile.

'No,' Al admitted, 'nothing I can take to the bank.'

'He just seemed the most likely suspect,' Jack Smack said. 'You think he *wasn't* involved, Dunk?'

'I didn't say that. But I'm not sure that stealing the coin was the reason for his murder. He led a wild life. Maybe there are other motives involved. I think we're all trying to neaten this thing up, trying to get the facts to fit our theories, and disregarding the facts that don't fit.'

'Thanks a lot,' Jack said. 'You're giving me a lot of confidence.'

'I don't know what you're getting at, Dunk,' Al said, frowning. 'Are you suggesting that the Vanwinkle and LeBaron homicides had nothing to do with the coin getting copped?'

'It's possible, isn't it? I guess I'm not explaining this very well, but it seems to me that there might be two crimes involved here. All right, Orson was the link between them. But isn't it conceivable that the killer searched his apartment, and Dolly's, for something other than the Demaretion?'

'For what?' Al demanded. 'Drugs? We found them in Dolly's place. Easy to find, but they hadn't been touched.'

'Money?' Jack suggested. 'Vanwinkle was supposed to be a heavy spender. Maybe we're trying to make something big out of what are really two run-of-the-mill burglary-homicides: a crook looking to make a cash score and panicking.'

'You don't really believe that, do you?' Al asked.

'No,' Jack said, 'I don't. The coin is mixed up in it. Somehow. Anyone got anything to add?'

We all stared at each other, expressionless and silent.

When I was a kid in Des Moines, after supper on Friday nights, my mother always went off to choir practice. Then my father, my three brothers, and I would sit around the kitchen table and play poker. We played for matches, and had a lot of fun.

I got to be a pretty fair poker player, mostly by learning to judge the strength of my father's and brothers' hands by their body language. When they were holding something good, they squirmed, blinked repeatedly, or maybe drummed their fingers. And when they were bluffing, their features froze; they thought they were giving nothing away.

209

Now, looking at Jack and Al, I had the feeling they were both bluffing. Not only were they not telling me all they knew, but they weren't telling each other either. That was all right; it saved me from having a guilt trip about what I was holding back.

'Well . . .' Al said, draining his beer, 'I guess we've gone as far as we can go. No hits, no runs, and God knows how many errors. Let us all pray for a lucky break.'

'Amen,' Jack said. 'If you look at this whole thing coldly, we're still on square one, aren't we?'

'I wouldn't say that,' I protested. 'It seems to me we've collected a lot of information.'

'Oh, yeah,' Al said, 'but what does it all *mean*? Thanks for the use of the hall, Dunk.'

He rose, Jack stood up, and the two of them moved toward the door. Al hung back a few steps and came close to me.

'Sunday?' he said in a low voice. 'With my daughter?'

I nodded.

'Call you,' he said.

Then they were gone, and I was left to clean up the mess from our lunch. But I really didn't mind. One quarter-pounder remained, and I wrapped it in aluminum foil and put it in the fridge. With a nice green salad, that would be my dinner.

I went back into the living room and took up my knitting while I did some heavy thinking.

Both detectives thought Orson Vanwinkle had been involved in the switch of the Demaretion display case. I did, too, but couldn't believe that was the reason for his murder, or Dolly's. Why search their apartments when the coin was being offered for sale in Beirut? What a puzzlement!

Jack Smack had come up with a fresh idea, suggesting that Akbar El Raschid was trying to peddle the coin in Lebanon because of his Muslim connections. A neat notion, but I didn't buy it. No logical objections – just the way I felt. Natalie and Akbar might be a couple of screwballs, but I didn't think they were capable of the clever theft of the coin, let alone two cold-blooded murders.

Luther? A maybe, but I doubted it, for the reasons I had given Al and Jack. I admit I was going by my visceral reactions, but what else could I do? I didn't have the resources of the NYPD or Jack's insurance company to provide research. So I was on my own.

Who else might have conspired with Orson? Vanessa? Very, very doubtful. They had said they hated each other, and I believed it. The Minchens? What motive could dear Roberta and Ross have for killing Orson and Dolly? What about Ruby Querita? Now there was a possibility. She was such a religious fanatic that she might slay and call it God's vengeance.

But finally, finally, I had to face the cause of all this maundering. I was trying to postpone thinking about my most important decision. What on earth was I going to do with that crudely wrapped package Dolly LeBaron had entrusted to me? Sighing, I considered the options.

1. She had said she would reclaim it within a month. She obviously wasn't going to do that.

2. She had also said that in the event she didn't come back for that dumb package, I was to destroy it. Burn it in the 'insinuator.'

3. And she made me promise not to open it.

My thinking about all this was wild and disconnected. I really should burn the damned thing. But what if she had left it to someone in her will? I had vowed not to open it, but what if it held clues to the identity of her killer? To whom did I owe primary responsibility? To poor, dead Dolly? Should I follow her instructions to the letter, as honor dictated, or disregard them in hopes the Scotch-taped brown bag contained the answers to all my problems? A dilemma.

In the end, I solved it by doing nothing. I left the package where it was, not even looking at it or touching it, and I decided not to mention it to Georgio or Smack just yet. In poker terms, I guess you could call it my ace in the hole.

I spent a gloomy evening. I've told you that generally I'm an up-person – look on the bright side, think positively, things will turn out for the best. But I was down that night. I guess the actuality of Dolly's death really hit me. I couldn't mourn for Orson, he was such a slime, but Dolly was different.

I know everyone thought her a chippy, and I suppose she was. But she was also young, pretty, and hopeful, and it was hard to believe she had done anything in her life to explain or justify what had happened to her.

It made me think deep, deep thoughts about my own life, my hopes and dreams, and how they might all be brought low. No one likes to reflect on death – right? I mean, in our minds we all know we're mortal. But we push that away and concentrate on popcorn and balloons. Our own dissolution is just too bleak to face.

211

I did something that night I hadn't done in years and years. I got down on my knees at bedside, pressed my hands together, bowed my head, and prayed for the immortal soul of Dolly LeBaron. I concluded by reciting the child's prayer that begins, 'Now I lay me down to sleep . . .'

26

THE RADDLED blue Plymouth was waiting for me when I popped out with my beach bag at eight o'clock on Sunday morning. Behind the wheel, Al Georgio in kelly green slacks and a sport shirt in a hellish plaid. In the back seat, daughter Sally, wearing jeans and a T-shirt, a blue ribbon tied about her long wheaten hair. A beauty!

'Hi!' she said when I climbed in front.

'Hi!' I said.

'Are you my daddy's girlfriend?' she asked.

'Nah,' I said, 'I'm just a stranger thumbing a lift.'

'Boy oh boy,' Al said, 'I can see this is going to be one great day.'

But on the trip out to Jacob Riis Park, it began to seem as if it might be exactly that – a great day.

I ignored Al and turned sideways in the passenger seat so I could talk to Sally. It wasn't difficult; she was a bright, voluble kid with opinions on everything.

'Why do you wear your hair like that?' she asked.

'Like what?' I said. 'I don't wear it like anything. That's my problem.'

She regarded me gravely, head tilted to one side. 'I think you should have it cut short,' she pronounced. 'Like a loose feather cut – you know?'

'Not a bad idea,' I acknowledged.

'Dad says to call you Dunk. Okay?'

'Sure,' I said, 'that's fine.'

'How tall are you, Dunk?'

'Six-two, give or take a little.'

'Are you a model?'

'I'm a model of something,' I said. 'I don't know what.'

'You're pretty enough to be a model.'

213

'And you're a sweetheart for saying it,' I told her. 'What's in the hamper?'

'Lunch,' she said. 'Fried chicken and potato salad. Father probably bought it all at some greasy spoon.'

'Hey, come on,' he said indignantly. 'I made the chicken myself, and the potato salad comes from a very high-class deli.'

'I was just kidding,' his daughter said. 'Also, some cheesecake, lemonade for me, and a bottle of wine for the old folks.'

'Keep it up, kiddo,' her father told her, 'and you're going to be walking to Jacob Riis.'

She giggled and threw herself back in the corner of the rear seat, hugging her knees.

'I'm wearing a bikini,' she said. 'What are you wearing?'

'A black maillot,' I told her. 'Norma Kamali.'

'Is that the one cut high on the legs and no back?'

'That's the one.'

'I love that suit,' Sally said dreamily. 'Maybe by next year I'll be big enough to wear it. If my old man will spring for it.'

'You keep talking like that,' Al said ferociously, 'and you're not going to make next year.'

She giggled again, and for the next hour she and I chattered about fashions, her schoolwork, boyfriends, rock groups, movie stars, television shows, and the pros and cons of washing your hair in beer. What a knowledgeable kid she was! And she wasn't shy about spouting off. Not in an obnoxious way, mind you, but firm and convinced. She really was a darling.

She was wearing makeup – not a lot, but some – which threw me a little. When I was her age, I'd have been kicked out of the house if I used perfumed soap. But the times, they are a'changing. And even without the lip gloss and a touch of eyeliner, she'd have been a beauty. She was going to break a lot of male hearts, and I was afraid she knew it.

'I think my father should get married,' she said to me. 'Don't you?'

'Will you cut it out, Sally?' Al said, laughing. 'You promised to behave.'

'I crossed my fingers behind my back,' she said. 'You didn't see me. Well, don't you think he should get married?'

'If he wants to,' I said.

She thought a moment, frowning. 'I think my mother might get married. She's got a boyfriend.'

'Do you like him?'

214

'He's okay, I guess. But he wears a toupee. That puts me off – you know?'

'Whee!' Al said, banging the steering wheel with his palms. 'It's Looney Tunes time, folks!'

We beat most of the heavy traffic and got out to Jacob Riis sooner than I expected. Al had a folding beach umbrella in the trunk, along with a big blanket and two beach chairs. He carried all that while I managed the wicker hamper. Sally scampered ahead of us. We set up about thirty feet from the shoreline, the sea reasonably calm and clear, sun shining, sky washed. A gorgeous day.

The moment we had the blanket spread, Sally kicked off her loafers, shucked T-shirt and jeans. Her little bikini was cute: a strawberry print with ruffles around the top and hips. What a bod the kid had! She was going to be a problem, but I didn't tell Al that.

She took off her hair ribbon and went running down to the water, blonde hair floating back in the breeze.

'No swimming till I get there,' Al yelled after her. Then he turned to me. 'She can dog-paddle,' he said, 'but still . . . I hope you don't mind her, Dunk. What she comes out with.'

'Mind her?' I said. 'I love her. She'll never need any assertiveness training.'

'That's for sure,' he said. 'She's so *bright*. Sometimes it scares me. Want to try the water or would you rather get some sun?'

'Swim first,' I said, 'then sun.'

I heeled off my sandals and struggled out of my denim tent. Al stared at me.

'I know,' I said. 'I look like a black Magic Marker.'

'You look beautiful,' he said, and I think he meant it. I made no reference to his salt-bleached khaki shorts that almost came to his knees.

Sally stayed close to shore, floating around, never getting over her depth. Al and I went out a way. He swam like the kind of man he was, with a heavy, ponderous overhand stroke, wallowing a bit, but making steady progress. He had thick, muscled shoulders and arms, and I figured he could get to Europe if he put his mind to it.

We had a good swim, my first of the summer, then turned around and came back in. Sally was already spread-eagled on the blanket, all oiled up. I dried off, then spread on my Number 15 sunscreen. Al had a swarthy skin; he could get a better tan walking a block down Broadway than I'd get all summer.

The two of us sat on beach chairs under the umbrella. Al opened the bottle of chilled rosé, and we each had a paper cup. Good stuff.

'The ocean was great,' I said. 'Just great. Nothing like that in Iowa.'

'Ever want to go back?' he asked me curiously.

'For a visit? Sure. But permanently? I don't think so. Not yet. How're you going to keep them down on the farm – and so forth and so on.'

'I really don't know a hell of a lot about you,' he said. 'I mean your background and all. Before you came to New York.'

'Ask away,' I said. 'If there's anything you want to know.'

'No,' he said, 'not really. But then you don't know a hell of a lot about me, do you?'

'Nope,' I said, 'and I'm not going to ask. If you want to tell me, you'll tell me.'

'You're so goddamned trusting,' he said. 'I could be Attila the Hun and you wouldn't know – or care.'

'Will the two of you please lower your voices,' Sally said severely from the blanket. 'I'm trying to take a nap and don't want to listen to your personal confessions.'

'That's a crock,' her father said, laughing. 'You're listening to every word and you love it.'

She giggled. 'You're awful,' she said. 'If you weren't my dad, I wouldn't put up with you.'

'You're stuck with me, babe,' he told her, 'and I'm stuck with you. Ain't it nice?'

'Yes,' she said, sighing and turning over to tan her back. 'It's nice, pop.'

'I'll pop you,' he said in mock anger, but she just smiled and closed her eyes.

Is there anything new you can say about a splendid July afternoon on the seashore? Warm lassitude. Lulling sound of the surf. A kissing breeze. The comfort of quiet broken by children's shouts. So relaxing that you think your bones are going to melt.

'I suppose,' I murmured to Al, 'if we did this every day, it would get to be a bore.'

'You believe that?'

'No. Al, I've got to say something that's really going to shock you.'

'What's that?'

'I'm hungry.'

'I am, too,' Sally yelled, leaping to her feet. 'Let's eat!'

We moved the beach umbrella so it shaded the blanket, and we all sat on that. We gnawed the fried chicken Al had made (delicious!), spooned potato salad, and munched on celery stalks, radishes, and cherry tomatoes. Al had even remembered the salt and paper napkins. The man was a treasure.

When we were finished, Sally surprised me – and her father – by cleaning up and taking all our refuse to the nearest trash can.

'Oh-oh,' Al said. 'She wants something.'

'Don't be a goop,' she said crossly. Then, in a grand manner: 'I may take a walk down the beach. By myself. Just to relax – you know?'

'Just to meet boys,' Al said. 'You know?'

'Father, sometimes you can really be gross!'

We watched her stalk away. She hadn't been down at the water's edge more than a minute before we saw two boys about her own age circle about her and draw closer.

'Will she be all right?' I asked anxiously.

'Don't worry about Sally,' Al advised me. 'She can take care of herself.'

'I hope so.'

'She'll stay close enough so I can keep an eye on her,' he said. 'You'll see.'

She did exactly as he predicted. It was a joy to watch the young flirt at work. Running into the ocean up to her knees, dashing out with whoops of feigned horror at the chill. Laughing and hugging her elbows. Flinging her long blonde hair about. The boys were enchanted.

'Is your ex really going to get married?' I asked Al.

He opened a second bottle of rosé. It was warmish, but we didn't care.

'Probably,' he said. 'She's got this regular guy. I've never met him, but from what I've heard from Sally and her mother, he's solid enough. I mean he's got a good job and all that. An accountant.'

'How do you feel about it?'

He shrugged. 'It's her life. The only thing that bothers me is that Sally will have a new father. Well, a stepfather. Maybe she'll forget all about me.'

'No way,' I told him. 'She loves you; she's never going to let you go.'

'You really think so?'

'Absolutely. Besides, you don't wear a toupee.'

He smiled. 'Yeah, there's that. I don't know what I'd do if I lost

217

that kid. My life is rackety enough as it is. Without her, I'd really be drifting.'

'No chance of getting back together with your ex?'

'Oh, no,' he said immediately. 'She doesn't want to be a cop's wife, and I can't blame her for that. It's what came between us: the job, the damned job. Lousy hours. And her worry. It's not that dangerous, but she thought it was. Every time a cop got killed, she'd cry for days. I'd tell her the percentages weren't all that bad, but she couldn't get it out of her head that some day an Inspector would show up on her doorstep and give her the bad news. A lot of cops' wives drink – did you know that?'

'No, but I can understand it.'

'Still,' he said, 'it's my life. If I wasn't a cop, what would I be? A night watchman? Bodyguard for a rock star? Not president of General Motors, that's for sure.'

We were back in our chairs under the umbrella. The sun glare bouncing off the sand was all I needed. I could feel my skin beginning to tingle. Pretty soon, I vowed, I'd wrap myself in denim.

Al's hand moved sideways. He held my fingers loosely. 'What about you, Dunk?' he said. 'Ready to settle down?'

'I don't know,' I said, embarrassed and confused. 'I really don't know what I want. For the time being I'm just floating. I figure if I'm that unsure, I better wait awhile until I'm more certain of what I want to do.'

'Yeah,' he said, 'that's wise. But don't wait too long. Time goes so *fast*! I remember when I was a kid in grade school, I thought vacation would never come. Time went so slowly. Now it whizzes by. Weeks, months, years. And then you wake up one day and say, What the hell happened? Where did it go?'

We sat awhile in silence, holding hands, watching Sally frolic on the beach with her two beardless lovers. They were tossing a Frisbee back and forth. Lucky kids. Little did they know that they were going to grow up and have troubles.

'By the way,' Al said, 'we finally got into Orson Vanwinkle's bank account. He had over a hundred thousand. Not bad for a secretary – wouldn't you say? Particularly when you consider how well he lived.'

'I would say. Did he leave a will?'

'No sign of one – the idiot. He had no close relatives. Just some cousins. I guess eventually it'll go to them, but meanwhile it'll be a lawyer's delight.'

'What about Dolly LeBaron?'

'She had about five thousand. No big deal. I guess Orson was paying her food bills and maintenance on the apartment and cash for her clothes – stuff like that. But apparently he wasn't laying heavy money on her. Not enough so she could build up a nest egg.'

'That's odd,' I said. 'He seemed to have enough money for a lot of other people.'

'Yeah,' Al said, turning his head to stare at me. 'Like Akbar El Raschid. Why didn't you tell me about that, Dunk? You knew, didn't you?'

'I knew,' I admitted. 'But there are a lot of things you don't tell me, aren't there?'

'Maybe,' he said grudgingly. 'Little, unimportant things.'

'Besides,' I said, beginning to resent this, 'I was the one who told you Orson swung both ways, wasn't I? I figured you'd find out about his connection with Akbar. And you did.'

'After a lot of work,' he said. 'You could have saved us time.'

I dropped his hand. 'That's not my job,' I said angrily, 'to save you time.'

He groaned. 'Jesus,' he said, 'what the hell are we doing? A beautiful day on the beach and we're squabbling about a couple of homicides. Now do you understand why my wife dumped me? I can't forget the job. I'm sorry, Dunk. Let's not even mention it for the rest of the day. Okay?'

'Fine with me.'

'Truce?' he said, taking up my hand again. 'You're not sore at me?'

'How could I be sore at a guy who makes such scrumptious fried chicken?'

'The hell I did,' he said. 'I bought it at Sam's Chicken Chuckles around the corner from where I live.'

I howled. 'You're a bastard,' I told him. 'You know that?'

'Oh, sure,' he said. 'But I could have made it if I had wanted to. I just didn't have the time.'

'Uh-huh,' I said, 'that's your story. I'll never believe you again.'

'I only lie about unimportant things,' he said. 'Here comes Miss America of ten years from now.'

Sally came dashing up to us. How come kids of her age never saunter? They always run at top speed. All that energy . . . I wish I had some.

'Any lemonade left?' she demanded.

'Shake the thermos,' her father said. 'It's your jug.'

219

She drained it and got about a half-cup that she gulped down.

'So tell us, Cleopatra,' Al said, 'did you give them your phone number?'

'They live in Jersey,' she said. 'Can you imagine? Who needs that?'

'Better luck next time,' he said.

We got about another half-hour of sun, then decided we better start back to beat the traffic. We packed up and moved to the parking lot. The car was an oven, and we had to leave the doors open awhile before we could get in. I sat in the back with Sally.

'What am I?' Al demanded. 'A chauffeur?'

'Do a good job,' I told him, 'and we might give you a tip.'

'A small one,' Sally said.

We hadn't been on the road more than ten minutes when she slowly slumped sideways against me. I put my arm about her shoulders, and she snuggled in. She was asleep almost instantly, breathing deeply with just the tiniest snore. She smelled of suntan oil, salt, and youth. Lovely.

Al noticed all this in the rearview mirror and grinned. 'Conked out?' he asked softly.

'She's entitled,' I said.

'You want to? Go ahead.'

'Not me,' I said. 'I just don't feel like it.' Which was a fib. I swore the moment I got home I'd take a hot shower and flop into bed.

We drove back to Manhattan in almost total silence, except when Al cursed at someone who cut him off. He pulled up outside my brownstone and I gently disengaged my arm from around Sally. I had to massage it.

'I didn't go to sleep,' I said, 'but my arm did.'

I moved away from Sally and she slid down until she was lying on the seat.

'Let her snooze,' Al said, turning around. 'I'll wake her up when I get her home.'

I leaned across the front seat, took his face in my palms, kissed him on the lips. 'Thanks for a wonderful day,' I said. 'It was super.'

'It had its moments, didn't it? Do it again?'

'Just whistle,' I said, 'and I'll come a'running.'

'Dunk . . .' he said.

'What?'

He had a strange expression, all twisted. I couldn't tell what he was thinking.

220

'Nothing,' he said. 'It'll go for another time.'

'Whenever you say.'

'Sally likes you; I can tell. You're two of a kind: a couple of nuts.'

'You need women like us in your life.'

'Tell me about it,' he said. 'You think I don't know? I'll wait here until you're inside.'

I paused at my door to turn and give him a wave. He blew a kiss to me.

Old-fashioned. But nice.

27

I slept for about four hours that Sunday evening, completely whacked out from the fresh air and the sun. Then I woke, staggered into the kitchen, drank about a quart of water, and peeled and ate a chilled tangerine. Then I went back to bed – what else? I think the expression is 'plum tuckered'.

When I looked at myself in the mirror on Monday morning, I could see the sun lines of my maillot, but the burn was just a gentle blush. It didn't hurt, and I didn't think it was going to peel – which was a blessing. Just to make sure, I rubbed on some moisturizer. I hated to shed skin, like some old snake.

All in all, I was feeling pretty frisky. I made notes in my journal about what Al had told me of the money left by Orson Vanwinkle and Dolly LeBaron. Then I went out to pick up the morning paper and a brioche. Back home, I sliced open the brioche and slathered it with cream cheese and blackberry jam. That's living!

It became a busy day, which suited my mood exactly. I wanted to be *doing*. When the phone rang, I grabbed it up, thinking it might be Al Georgio, thanking me for the most exciting, memorable afternoon of his life. But it turned out to be Archibald Havistock – which was okay, too.

'Miss Bateson,' he said, 'I must apologize. With the confusion following my secretary's death and my daughter's, ah, recent incident, I fell behind in my personal accounts. I now see that I owe you for two weeks' employment. I am sorry for the oversight. I have written out the check. Shall I mail it to you or would you prefer to pick it up?'

'I'd like to pick it up, sir,' I said promptly. 'Mostly because I'd like the opportunity of talking to you for a few minutes. Would that be possible?'

'Of course,' he said in that deep, resonant voice. 'I expect to be in all day. Come over whenever you wish.'

'And Ruby Querita,' I said. 'May I talk to her, too?'

A brief pause, then: 'Yes, she'll be here.'

'Thank you, Mr Havistock,' I said. 'See you shortly.'

I dressed with deliberate care: a high-necked, long-sleeved white blouse with a calf-length black skirt, not too snug. If I had put my hair up in a bun and stuck a pencil through it, I figured I could have passed as J. P. Morgan's secretary. That was the impression I wanted to give Mr Havistock: a sober, industrious, dutiful employee. Little would he know that I had wolfed three frozen Milky Ways in one afternoon.

I took a final glance in the mirror and wondered if Sally could be right: a short, feathered hairdo might change my entire life. Nah.

I was at the door, ready to leave, when the phone rang again. That *had* to be Al. I dashed back.

'Mary Bateson?' a woman's voice asked.

'Yes.'

'I have a collect call for you from Enoch in Arizona. Will you accept the charges?'

'Yes,' I said. 'Oh, yes.'

'You are Mary Bateson?'

'I am.'

'Thank you. Go ahead, sir.'

'I did it!' he said triumphantly. 'I called collect like you told me to.'

'Bless you, Enoch,' I said, laughing. 'How *are* you?'

'If I felt any better,' he said, 'I'd be unconscious. And you, Dunk?'

'Feeling fine,' I said.

Then I told him about my day at the beach, and he told me that he had been asked to write a monograph on Greek coinage of the Gaulish tribes for a numismatic journal. He sounded chipper – which was a delight.

'Enough of this chitchat,' he said. 'I spoke to my friends in New York who might have handled sales by Archibald Havistock over the past five years. As far as I could learn, he sold mostly through three dealers, which is unusual in itself.'

'How so?'

'Why *three* dealers? Most serious collectors work through one man. You find someone you can trust, someone you like, and you stick with him.'

223

'Not all dealers are like you, Enoch. Maybe he was just shopping around for the best price.'

'Maybe. Anyway, from what I could learn, over a period of five years Havistock unloaded – are you ready for this?'

'How much?' I said eagerly. 'Tell me!'

'Almost half a million.'

'Wow! He must have had some good stuff.'

'He did. The man apparently is, or was, a very dedicated and knowledgeable collector. Not a dog in the bunch. And, of course, the dealers did very well on what they bought from him or handled on consignment. So everyone gained. Still, it's hard to understand.'

'What is, Enoch?'

'You spend a lifetime building up a fine collection and then you sell it off. So maybe he needed the money. But it's sad to break up a collection like that. He's not starving, is he?'

'Far from it.'

'Well, there you are. Dunk darling, do you think this will help you find the Demaretion?'

'I don't honestly know,' I said slowly. 'It's another piece of information to put in my notebook, but what it means, I have no idea.'

'All right,' he said briskly, 'that's taken care of. What's next?'

I cast about wildly for something he could do, knowing how important it was to him to be needed. Then I had an inspiration.

'There's one thing you might do, Enoch,' I said. 'Remember when a new client came into the shop, you always ran a credit check on him.'

'Of course,' he said. 'It's best to know the reputation of the person you're dealing with. Is he trustworthy? Does he pay his bills? Do his checks bounce? Better to know beforehand.'

'Could you run a credit check on Archibald Havistock?'

'Havistock?' he said, shocked. 'He is a wealthy, reputable man.'

'I know,' I said, 'but still, I'd like to learn more about his financial condition.'

This was strictly make-work for Enoch. Al Georgio and Jack Smack had already investigated and told me about Havistock's situation: his income, the fact that most of his assets were in his wife's name. But it wouldn't do any harm to get another opinion.

'I'll try,' Enoch said doubtfully. 'You're wondering why he was selling off all those lovely mintages for the past five years?'

'That's it,' I said gratefully. 'Just a woman's idle curiosity.'

224

'To tell you the truth,' he said, 'I'm curious myself. I'll see what I can do, Dunk dear.'

After we hung up, with vows of love, I started out again. This time I made it.

It was a hazy, dazy day with an odor of sulfur in the air, and I immediately decided against walking over to the East Side. I caught a cab that was mercifully air-conditioned and smelled only of dead cigars.

When I first moved to New York, going from the West Side to the East was like going from Calcutta to Paris, but things had changed and were changing. The city (Manhattan) was becoming one big potpourri of boutiques, antique shops, unisex hair styling salons, and Korean greengrocers. In another five years, I figured, Broadway would have a branch of Tiffany's and Park Avenue would have massage parlors.

Ruby Querita let me into the Havistock apartment. As usual, she was dressed like one of the witches from *Macbeth*, but she gave me a defrosted smile and I touched her arm.

'How are you, Ruby?' I asked.

'Healthy,' she said. 'God be thanked. And you?'

'Hanging in there,' I said. 'Mr Havistock is expecting me. Would you tell him I'm here?'

'I'll tell,' she said, nodding.

'Anyone else home? Mrs Havistock? Natalie?'

She shook her head.

'Well, after the lord of the manor is finished with me, could you and I have a little talk?'

I had never noticed before how piercing her eyes were.

'Yes,' she said. 'All right. I'll be in the kitchen.'

'Your office,' I said, trying a mild jape that fell flat.

Archibald Havistock rose to his feet when I entered the library. He motioned me to the chair facing that enormous partners' desk. It had deep kneeholes, like a tunnel, running through the two linked desks. You could hide a body there.

We exchanged pleasantries, and he gave me a plain white envelope. That was so like him. He preferred not to hand over a naked check. Too crass. Money should be chastely concealed.

'Thank you, sir,' I said, tucking the envelope into my shoulder bag without glancing at the contents. I could be as circumspect as he. 'I wish I felt I was doing more to earn it.'

He sat erect in his leather swivel chair. What a magisterial man! I swear that in a black robe he could have passed for a chief justice. But he was wearing a suit of gray flannel with a silken sheen, light blue shirt with white collar and cuffs, a subdued foulard tie. That silvered hair! Those icy azure eyes! Oh, God, I raved in my mind, if he was only thirty years younger or I was thirty years older.

'No progress?' he asked with a small smile.

'Well . . .' I said, not wanting to admit I was a total dolt, 'I have made progress if that means collecting a great deal of information. But I haven't yet been able to put it all together, see a logical pattern to everything that's happened.'

'I'm sure you will,' he said. 'My wife has great confidence in you.'

His wife did? Did that imply that he didn't? Or was this my day for a paranoia attack?

He swung gently back and forth in his swivel chair. He was wearing a cologne – not Aramis; I know that – but something subtle and stirring. Maybe, on another man, I might have thought it a bit much, but he had the presence to carry it off. My impression was that he didn't give a tinker's damn about what other people might think of how he dressed, talked, lived. He had achieved a kind of serenity.

'Tell me,' he said, 'how do you keep track of everything you've learned? All in your mind?'

'I wish my memory was that good,' I said, 'but it isn't. No, I make notes in a journal. And add everything new I learn.'

'Very wise,' he said, nodding. 'I keep a daily diary of business dealings, telephone conversations, conferences, and so forth. It can be very useful.'

'I hope my notebook will be. Right now I can't make any sense out of it at all.'

A small prevarication. It was beginning to come together.

'You said there was something you wished to speak to me about, Miss Bateson. Something special?'

'Just one question, sir. You may not want to answer it. Could you tell me how much you were paying Orson Vanwinkle?'

He stared at me and didn't answer immediately. Then: 'This is important to your investigation?'

'I think it is.'

'I see no reason why I shouldn't answer. He was paid eight hundred dollars a week. By check. So there is a paper trail if the police or anyone else wants to investigate. Why do you ask?'

'I don't know,' I said fretfully. 'Except that he seemed to be living on a scale far beyond eight hundred a week.'

'I was aware of that,' Mr Havistock said, 'and cautioned him about it more than once. But it did no good. As I think I told you, he was not a solid man. But he was my nephew, and I didn't wish to cast him adrift. And, I must say, he fulfilled his duties. But I warned him about his debts.'

I didn't mention that dear old Horsy left a hundred grand when he shuffled off his mortal coil. Mr Havistock would learn that soon enough – but I preferred he didn't hear it from me. I stood up.

'Thank you, sir. I appreciate your making time with—' Now there was a Freudian slip. But I caught it, I hoped! 'Making time for me,' I finished. 'I'd like to talk with Ruby for a few minutes, if I may.'

He rose and proffered his hand. 'Of course. As long as you like.'

We shook hands and exchanged distant smiles. His clasp was exactly like the man: cool, dry, firm.

When I found my way to the kitchen, I discovered Ruby Querita hunched over the stainless steel sink, snapping string beans and weeping. I put an arm about her shoulders.

'Ruby,' I said, 'what's the matter?'

She shook her head, not answering.

'Your brother?' I asked.

She nodded. 'Life is unfair,' she said.

I wanted to say, 'So what else is new?' but I didn't.

'Ruby,' I said, 'you can be responsible for your own life, but not for other people's. Isn't that true?'

She nodded dumbly, ran cold water over the beans in a colander, and let them drain in the sink. Then she dried her hands on a kitchen towel and we sat down at the table. She had stopped crying.

I hunched forward, keeping my voice low. This was to be a confidential exchange of gossip – just between us girls.

'Ruby,' I said, almost whispering, 'the last time we spoke you hinted that the Havistocks had sinned, that the family was cursed. What did you mean by that?'

'I don't want to talk about it.'

'Please do,' I urged. 'I'm trying to find out who stole the Demaretion. Everyone is under suspicion. That includes you. The police think you may be involved, that you took the coin to finance your brother's appeal. I know that's completely ridiculous, you wouldn't do anything like that, but you've got to help me to find out who actually did it. You can see that, can't you?'

227

She was silent.

'Whatever you tell me,' I went on, 'is strictly between you and me. I have a tight mouth. I'll repeat it to no one. But I've got to find out what's going on in this house.'

'The daughter,' she said. 'Natalie. She runs around with bad people. She steals. Stays out all hours. Sometimes she is gone a day. Two. I think she takes drugs. She is wild. A black boyfriend. She doesn't go to church.'

Nothing new for me there.

'And . . . ?' I prompted her.

'The other one, the older daughter, Roberta, she is married to an evil man. Evil! They do things – I will not tell you. But I hear them talking. Because I am a servant, they think I have no ears. But God will punish them.'

I looked at her, wondering if Roberta and Ross had ever tried to recruit her for their TV spectaculars. It was hard to believe, but with people as flaky as the Minchens, anything was possible. If I learned they had cast a giraffe and a cocker spaniel, I wouldn't have been a bit surprised.

'That's awful, Ruby,' I said, trying to sound shocked and disgusted. 'To think things like that are going on.'

'Oh, yes,' she said. 'But it is true.'

'Do you think Mr and Mrs Havistock are aware of all this?'

She thought a moment. 'About Natalie,' she said finally, 'they know. About their other daughter and her husband, I think they don't know, but they suspect. They have heard things. But how can you reject your children?'

'You can't,' I said.

'No, you can't. So you must suffer. And hope eventually they will see the Light of God that makes a glory of our days.'

'What about the son, Ruby? Luther and his wife. Do they behave?'

'That woman!' she burst out. 'She is a devil! She shows herself – you know? She tempts men, leading them into transgression. No good will come from her. She has sold her soul.'

'I heard,' I said carefully, 'that at one time she made a play for Roberta's husband, and Mr Havistock had to break it up. Is that true?'

She nodded darkly. 'And friends of the family. The men. And delivery boys. She likes to show her devil's power. She will burn in hell!'

I began to get just a little frightened. That kind of religious mania scared me. Keep thinking that way and you might decide to rid the world of evildoers by killing them. It was God's will, wasn't it?

'Ruby,' I said, 'can't Luther control his wife? Make her stop acting like that.'

'He's not a man,' she said scornfully. 'He is a slave.'

'A slave? To what?'

She cupped her two flat breasts under the black bombazine making them jut. Then she reached under the table, and I could only guess that she was grasping her crotch. The gestures were undeniably gross, but there was no mistaking their meaning.

'He is a man possessed,' she said. 'And there is more,' she added, staring into my eyes. 'But so wicked, I cannot tell you.'

And despite my pleading, she would say no more. So I left, needing a breath of even that sulfur-laden outside air to rid myself of the heavier fumes within the Havistock apartment. What a Gothic family that tribe had turned out to be!

I told myself that other than learning Orson Vanwinkle had been making eight hundred a week, I had heard nothing new. What Ruby Querita had related, I already knew, or had guessed. But her fanaticism had given the revelations an ominous weight. I walked quickly away from the Havistock manse before a thunderbolt came down from heaven and destroyed them all. That Ruby was getting to me.

I wondered what was so wicked that she wouldn't speak of it. Then I pondered my next move. I found a sidewalk telephone kiosk in working order (the third I tried), and called Hobart Juliana at Grandby & Sons. Thank God he was in.

'Hobie darling,' I said cheerfully, 'how *are* you?'

'Miserable,' he said. 'All alone and longing for company. *Your* company. When are you coming back to join me?'

'Soon,' I said. 'I hope. Hobie, I'm in your neighborhood, and I'd love to see you. I'd come up, but I'm afraid Madam Dodat might grab me and demand a progress report on my investigation. That I don't need. Could you sneak out for a little while? I'll buy you a drink at the Bedlington bar. How about it?'

'I'm on my way,' he said happily.

It was so *good* to see him again; he really was a sweetheart. We sat in that dim, cloistered cocktail lounge (only one other customer), held hands, and Hobie got me caught up on all the latest office gossip. It was rumored that Felicia Dodat was going to have a tummy-tuck, and it was said that Stanton Grandby was taking pills for flatulence. Fascinating.

'What about you, Dunk?' Hobie said, almost nose to nose with me in the gloom. 'Anything happening on the Demaretion?'

'I think so. I think I'm getting somewhere. But it's taking a lot of digging. Hobie, you've helped me so much, I hate to ask for another favor.'

'Ask away!' he cried. 'What are friends for?'

'Do you like intrigue?'

'Like it? I love it, love it, love it!'

'Well, there's this woman – Vanessa Havistock. She's married to Luther, Archibald's son. She's got this absolutely divine body and doesn't mind showing it.'

'Couldn't care less,' he said, grinning.

'I know,' I said. 'I'm just trying to describe her. Anyway, I suspect she's cheating on her husband. Everyone says she comes on to anything in pants – but that might be just malicious rumors. I mean she's beautiful, and people may resent her for that.'

'Perhaps,' he said. 'Perhaps not. Where there's smoke, there's usually one hell of a fire.'

'What I'd like to do,' I went on, 'is try to prove it out one way or another. She buys her clothes at an Italian boutique on Madison – Vecchio's. You know it?'

'Oh, yes. Bloody expensive.'

'It is that. I think maybe the manager, a guy named Carlo, might be steering tricks her way. You understand?'

'I'm keeping up, sweet.'

'Are you a good actor, Hobie?'

'Good? The stage lost a great star when I decided to devote my life to postage stamps. What do you want me to do?'

'Call her,' I said. 'She's in the book. Phone her and say you're from Wilkes-Barre or Walla Walla or some such place. Tell her you're in town for a business meeting, you're lonely, and would like to take a lovely lady out to dinner. Say that Carlo of Vecchio's suggested you call her.'

'Oh, my God,' Hobie said, 'that's beautiful! Dunk, you're a naughty, naughty woman.'

'I know,' I said. 'I want to get her reaction. If she hangs up on you, that's one answer. If she's interested, that's another.'

'Do it right now,' he said. 'There's a phone in the lobby.'

'She may not be in,' I warned.

230

'Then I'll try later,' he said, slid off the barstool and headed for the lobby. He had a kind of John Wayne sidle, and I never did figure out if it was natural or if he was kidding the world.

While he was gone, I wondered if I should have told him about Vanessa's arrest for loitering for the purpose of prostitution. Then I thought this test would be more legitimate if Hobie knew nothing of her police record.

He was back in less than five minutes, drained his kir, and motioned to the bartender for another.

'Was she in?' I asked.

'She was in, and she's guilty as hell. I told her I was Ralph Forbes – that's the name of my consenting adult – and I was from Tulsa, in town for a bankers' convention. Carlo of Vecchio's had suggested I might call her. Could she join me for dinner at Lutèce, and maybe a night on the town later? Cabarets, discos, piano bars – whatever turned her on. If she was an innocent, she'd have told me to get lost and hung up immediately. But oh, no. Dunk, I could almost hear her ears perk up.'

'She agreed?' I asked eagerly.

'Of course not,' Hobie said. 'She's too smart for that. She gave me some jazz about canceling previous plans and she'd call me back. What she's doing, of course, is checking with Carlo at Vecchio's. Did he give her name to a Ralph Forbes from Tulsa?'

'When she said she'd call you back, what number did you give her?'

'The one on the pay phone I called from,' Hobie said smugly. 'What else?'

I leaned forward to kiss his cheek. 'You're a genius,' I told him. 'But you think if Carlo had confirmed, she would have called back?'

'Absolutely,' he said. 'That lady is hot to trot. She's not the kind you pay in advance. She's the kind you get it off with, and then say, "Oh, darling, you've made me so happy, I want to buy you a gift. But I don't know your sizes or tastes. If I give you money, will you buy yourself something nice and pretend it's from me?" She'll protest and then finally agree. A lot of women are like that – and more men than you can imagine. I've done it myself. It leaves you a small measure of self-esteem. Better than finding cash on the mantel after the guy has gone.'

'Oh, Hobie,' I said, gripping his arm, 'you've been such a big help. When this is all over, I'm going to buy you the greatest dinner at the Four Seasons you've ever had in your life.'

231

He took up my hand to kiss my fingertips. 'I'll nudge you,' he said. 'But the dinner isn't that important. Just come back to share our office again. That'll make me happier than anything.'

We stared at each other. Tender and sad.

'It's a crazy world,' he said, 'isn't it?'

'It is that,' I said.

When we came out of the Bedlington, the air had freshened, and I decided I could walk home without fear of dropping from asphyxiation at the feet of Daniel Webster's statue. The long walk gave me a chance to think. Mostly about Vanessa Havistock.

The way she lived was so inexplicable to me. Married to a guy with a good job. Apartment on Park Avenue. Apparently all the money in the world. So why play the strumpet? Maybe that question contained the answer: she was *playing*. Her strident sexuality was a role. Blessed with sensual flesh, she was using it as a costume.

That began to make sense to me. It had little to do with the disappearance of the Demaretion, but I wanted to understand the people involved. Al Georgio had said Vanessa was actually Pearl Measley from South Carolina. I could extrapolate a lot from that: small-town girl adrift in the big city with nothing to sell but herself.

Then, maybe with memories of a deprived childhood, she gets hooked on *things*: jewelry, ball gowns, paintings, cars, a smart apartment and groovy vacation home – all the panoplies of wealth. But she never forgets where it all comes from – the luscious source.

That was how I saw her: not so much a greedy woman but one terrified by poverty and lack of status. She would, I thought, do anything to maintain her hard-fought and hard-won battle against life. She had vanquished Pearl Measley. Now she was Vanessa Havistock – and don't you forget it, buster!

And when I arrived home, sweated and aching pleasantly from my hike, I emptied my mailbox, and there was a letter from the lady herself: a cutesy invitation to a cocktail party and buffet dinner on Tuesday evening. 'Wear whatever you like – or nothing at all!'

I wouldn't have missed it for the world.

I showered, shampooed, pulled on an oversized khaki shirt I had bought many moons ago at an army surplus store on Forty-second Street. It had been laundered so many times it felt like silk, and was

232

so big it fitted like a burnoose. I padded around the house, wearing that and nothing else, feeling deliciously depraved.

I had just started adding notes on the day's events in my journal when I got a call from Jack Smack. He sounded slightly aggrieved.

'Where the hell you been, Dunk?' he demanded. 'I've been phoning all day.'

'I had lunch with Hizzoner,' I told him, 'and then I had to go down to the Federal Reserve to settle a squabble about interest rates.'

He laughed. 'Okay,' he said, 'I deserved that. How you coming on the Demaretion?'

'As the cops say, zero, zip, and zilch.'

'Yeah,' he said casually, 'me, too. I think maybe my company better pay off. I don't see any happy ending to this thing – do you?'

'You never know,' I said, determined he wasn't going to get anything from me without giving me something in return.

'I did come across one interesting item,' he said. 'Luther Havistock is seeing a shrink. Three times a week.'

'Yes,' I said slowly, 'that *is* interesting. I think the poor man needs it. But it must be expensive.'

'Maybe Daddy is paying the bills,' he suggested, and then paused, waiting for the trade-off.

'That's possible,' I said. 'Perhaps that's why Archibald needed ready cash. Over the past five years he's been selling coins from his collection. Did you know that?'

Silence. Then . . .

'No,' Jack said, 'I didn't know that. Are you sure?'

'I'm sure.'

'Do you know what his total sales were?'

'No, I don't,' I said, surprised that I could lie so easily.

'Maybe I'll look into it,' he said thoughtfully. 'But enough about business; how about dinner tomorrow night?'

'Love to,' I said, 'but I can't. I'm going to a party.'

'Can you take me?'

'I don't think I better.'

'Oh-ho,' he said without rancor, 'it's like that, is it? Well, listen, if the party turns out to be a dud and you decide to split early, give me a call, will you? I'll be in all night.'

'Sure,' I said, 'I'll do that.'

'I'll keep a lamp burning in the window,' he said cheerfully. 'I'd really like to see you, Dunk.'

'I'll try to make it,' I promised. 'I'll give you a call either way.'

'You're a sweetheart – did I ever tell you that?'

'No, and it's high time you did.'

He made a kissing sound over the phone and hung up. A nut. But a nice nut.

28

W HAT A party that was! Almost exactly as I imagined sophisticated Manhattan soirées would be when I was sinking dunk shots in our Des Moines driveway. Elegantly dressed women. Handsome men. Champagne. Exotic food. Everyone saying clever things. The whole bit.

So why wasn't I ecstatic? Because there was something so *forced* about those twittering people. If Vanessa Havistock was playing a role, all her guests were, too. I mean everyone was *on*, flushed, nervy, trying to top each other's gags and put someone down. 'Don't tell me you're still eating *kiwi*!'

I know what my father would have said about that bunch: 'More dollars than sense.'

My first shock came when I spotted Roberta and Ross Minchen standing close to the bar, smiling glassily and chatting animatedly with anyone who came near. Casting a new video classic, no doubt.

Their presence really surprised me. After that snarly standoff at the Russian Tea Room, I would have sworn Vanessa would never again give Roberta the time of day, let alone invite her and spouse to an expensive party. But there they all were, everyone apparently lovey-dovey and not a weapon in sight.

I looked around for host or hostess. I saw Vanessa talking seriously to – guess who? Carlo of Vecchio's, that's who. The Adonis looked splendid in a deep-red velvet dinner jacket, ruffled shirt, gold lamé butterfly bow tie. Too bad he was such an oozy man.

Then I located Luther, all by his lonesome in a corner, working on a drink so big it looked like an ice bucket. I pushed my way through the throng, smiling and nodding at all those sleek strangers. They couldn't have cared less. Finally I planted myself in front of Luther.

'Good evening!' I said brightly.

235

He stared, trying to focus. 'Evening,' he said. Then : 'Oh, it's Miss Bateman.'

'Bateson.'

'Bateson, yes, sorry. Are you having a good time?'

'I just arrived, but it looks like a lovely party.'

'Does it?' he said, looking around with a bleary stare. 'I don't know any of these people.'

'Sure you do. You know your sister and her husband.'

'Oh, *them*. They don't count. But all the others . . . They come here, drink up all my whiskey, eat themselves sick, steal the ashtrays – who *are* they? Vanessa's so-called friends.'

'Surely you know some of them.'

'Don't want to,' he said surlily. 'Bloodsuckers. Leeches. I keep telling Vanessa, but she won't listen. She thinks they're the *in* people. They're in all right. In my house, in my booze, in my food.' He laughed his high-pitched giggle, then thrust his schooner at me. 'Do me a favor?' he asked. 'Please? Get me a refill at the bar. I don't want to talk to the Munchens.'

'Minchens.'

'I call them the Munchens,' he said, with that frantic laugh again.

He was even paler than when I last saw him: a ghost in a rusty tuxedo. But his hands weren't trembling, so I figured he was well on his way. I took his glass. 'What are you drinking?' I asked.

'Gin.'

'With what?'

'More gin. Make sure it's the ninety-four proof. But you don't have a drink. Aren't you drinking?'

'Not yet. But I'll get something for myself.'

'Try the champagne,' he advised. 'Good stuff. Cost a bundle,' he added gloomily.

At the bar, tended by a dwarf in a clown's costume, I was grabbed by Roberta and Ross with effusive joy. They insisted on kissing me – which I could have done without. We exchanged small talk. Small? It was *tiny*! – and I finally got away from them, carrying my glass of champagne and Luther's beaker of gin.

One advantage of being tall is that you have a great view of what's going on in a crowded room. I saw Vanessa moving amongst her guests, patting, hugging, smooching. She was flushed with excitement. Her long black hair was up in a coil, stuck through with two ivory chopsticks. The makeup, I knew, was a professional job. She was wearing the fringed dress from Vecchio's and looked absolutely smashing.

I was wearing my white poet's blouse and a skirt of what seemed to be a brocaded upholstery fabric. I had bought it in a thrift shop, and I loved it. It made me feel like an ottoman. My hair was in its usual wind-tunnel state.

I handed Luther his drink. 'There you are,' I said. 'Double gin on the rocks. Ninety-four proof.'

'Bless you,' he said. 'Do you think I should commit suicide?'

That was a stunner. How do you reply to something like that? Treat it as a joke? Take it seriously?

'I don't think you should,' I said finally. 'Why would you want to?'

'Oh, I don't know,' he said vaguely. 'I'd just like to *do* something.'

He took a deep gulp of his drink. Some of it ran down his chin, and he wiped it away with the back of his hand.

'I like you,' he said abruptly.

'Thank you,' I said. 'I like you, too.'

'You do?' he said, surprised. 'That's odd.'

'What's odd about it?'

'Nobody likes me.'

'Come on,' I said, uneasy with this crazy conversation. 'Your wife, your parents, your sisters, your friends – a lot of people like you.'

He stared at me owlishly. 'I don't think so,' he said. 'I think they endure me. I think I endure me. Hey!' he said, suddenly brightening. 'You're looking for the coin – right?'

'Right.'

'Find it yet?'

'No,' I said, 'not yet. Any idea who has it?'

'Probably Vanessa,' he said with his high-pitched whinny. 'She's got everything.'

I took it as drunken humor. 'Your wife is a very beautiful woman,' I told him.

'Sure she is,' he said. 'Till midnight. Then she turns into a toad.'

'Well, I think I'll wait until midnight. That I've got to see.'

'You'll see,' he said, nodding solemnly. 'You'll see.'

I tried to change the subject. 'Your parents aren't here tonight?'

'They rarely go out at night. They sit at home and stare at each other. Thinking.'

I couldn't cope with this dialogue; it was becoming too unpleasant. 'I think I'll find your wife,' I told him, 'and pay my respects.'

237

'You respect her?' he said nastily. 'That's a switch.'

I touched his arm, smiled, and moved away. The guy was bonkers.

Vanessa gave me a big hug. She smelled divine.

'*So* glad you could make it, Dunk,' she burbled. 'Having a good time?'

'Wonderful.'

'It *is* nice, isn't it?' she said, looking around. 'Don't forget to eat. The buffet's in the other room. *Do* try the caviar on smoked salmon. Yummy! And by the way, you've already made a conquest.'

Fat chance!

'I have?' I said.

'Carlo was looking for you. You remember Carlo from Vecchio's? I think the poor boy is quite smitten. He wanted to talk with you, but you were busy with Luther. What *were* the two of you chattering about for so long?'

She didn't miss much.

'Just laughing up a storm,' I told her. 'Your husband has quite a sense of humor.'

'Does he?' she said dubiously. 'I've never noticed it. Dunk, I've got to circulate and act like a hostess. Promise me you'll be nice to Carlo.'

'Of course.'

She leaned close to whisper in my ear. 'I hear he's hung like a horse.'

Then she laughed and moved away to greet some arriving guests. I slid through the mob into the dining room to inspect the buffet. Talk about your groaning boards! That one was wheezing, presided over by a chef in a high *toque blanche* wielding a long-handled fork and saber.

The pièce de résistance was a steamship roast beef, rare as anything. That platter was surrounded by a million calories in all kinds of side dishes: cold vegetables and fruits, appetizers and nibbles, obscenely rich desserts, and a melting ice sculpture of Leda and the Swan. What the swan was doing to Leda, I don't wish to say.

The chef, an elderly black man who could carve like a surgeon, prepared a plate for me with little bits of almost everything. Balancing all this, plus cutlery and a stiff linen napkin, and trying to keep my champagne glass upright, I looked around for a place to sit and eat. I was rescued by Carlo, who came up to me, laughing, and relieved me of my burdens. He led me out to the mirrored foyer where there was

238

a small marble-topped table flanked by two lovely and extremely uncomfortable cast-iron chairs.

'You wait,' he ordered, 'I'll be right back.'

And so he was, bearing his own plate of nothing but very, *very* rare roast beef and a few cold hearts of palm. He also had an unopened bottle of champagne clamped under one arm.

'Now then . . .' he said, seated himself opposite me, and expertly twisted out the champagne cork. He refilled my glass and poured his own. He sat back, crossed his legs, carefully adjusting the crease in his trouser leg. What a dandy!

'I am so happy to see you tonight,' he said, watching me eat. 'Happy to have the chance to speak to you.'

'You are?' I said, concentrating on my food. Vanessa had been right; the caviar and smoked salmon was yummy.

'But of course,' he said. 'The other day at Vecchio's I could not talk. Not with the signora present. You understand?'

I nodded, not certain I *did* understand.

'I have always had this thing for tall women,' he said, showing me a mouthful of white teeth that looked like Chiclets. 'A secret passion.'

I laughed, and he was offended.

'You doubt me?' he demanded.

'Of course not. It's just that I'm – embarrassed.'

'That is natural,' he said generously. 'But I speak the truth. Dunk – may I call you Dunk?'

'Sure,' I said. 'Aren't you going to eat? The beef is delicious.'

'Later,' he said. 'I think you and I could be – you know? Good friends. Very good friends.'

'That's nice,' I said. 'You can't have too many friends, can you?'

He was puzzled. 'I mean special friends,' he said. It sounded like *speciale*.

I had a Swedish meatball on my fork, halfway to my mouth, but I paused, looking at him. I never doubted for a minute that Vanessa had put him up to this *seductio ad absurdum* – but why?

He took a sip of champagne, then stared at me over the rim of the glass with widened eyes. God, he was good! All I could think of was Rudolph Valentino in the tent, sex-crazed eyes glittering.

'We can see more of each other?' he whispered. 'Dunk?'

'If you like,' I said. 'Why not? But it will be difficult. I'm very busy.'

'Ah, yes,' he said. 'You are a detective – no?'

'Amateur,' I said. 'I really don't know a great deal about it.'

He daintily cut up his rare beef into postage stamp slices. He had beautiful hands. The nails manicured, of course. Al Georgio's were bitten.

'I would like to be a detective,' he said, keeping my champagne glass filled.

'Another secret passion?' I asked.

He looked at me sharply to see if I was ribbing him, but I kept my expression serious and interested.

'Yes,' he said. 'Another dream. I would wear an elegantly tailored trench coat – British, of course – and a black Borsalino turned down on one side. Very mysterious. Very menacing.'

We both laughed, and I began to think he wasn't such a schlemiel after all.

'Tell me,' he said, reaching across the table to spear one of my smoked oysters on his fork, 'how does a detective work? You go around, ask questions, try to catch people lying?'

'Yes,' I said, 'something like that. You collect as much information as you can.'

'But how do you remember it all?' he persisted. 'What people have said, what they have done. Do you keep it all up here?' He tapped his temple with a forefinger.

'Nobody's memory is that accurate,' I said. 'Professional detectives file reports. I keep a notebook, just to make sure I don't forget anything. I write it all down.'

'Ahh,' he said sadly, 'then I cannot be a detective. I am very bad at writing. My poor mother in Tuscany complains bitterly. Why don't you write? she asks. But I am too concerned with other things.'

'You could find the time,' I told him.

He shrugged. 'Some people write, some people live. Dunk, I saw some tiramisu at the buffet. It is made with mascarpone. A dreamy dessert. Have you tried it?'

'No, I haven't. Good?'

'*Delizioso*,' he said, kissing his fingertips. 'Let me get us some.'

'Small portions,' I pleaded. 'I'm stuffed.'

'Very, very small portions,' he said, standing up. He patted his flat stomach. 'I must keep myself in condition,' he said with a lewd smile.

I had been wrong; he *was* a schlemiel.

The tiramisu was heavenly – but so rich! The dry champagne helped, and so did Carlo – by dropping the hard-on role and becoming very amusing, telling me outrageous stories of some of the customers who came into Vecchio's, including a transvestite who spent a fortune on sequined cocktail dresses.

'A fantastic body,' Carlo reported. 'All silicone, of course. But still, she, he, it, is beautiful. Shall we join the party?'

I stood up – a bit unsteadily, I admit. Carlo grabbed my arm. 'All right?' he asked.

'Fine,' I said. 'It's the tiramisu.'

'But of course,' he said. 'It has brandy in it. Did I not mention that?'

Back in the mob scene, Carlo excused himself and drifted away, not to return. Whatever happened to his secret passion? I looked around for Luther Havistock. No sign of him. The Minchens were sticking close to the bar. Vanessa was still circulating, urging people to move to the buffet.

I went looking for a telephone. There seemed to be one in every room, but they were all in use – by guests calling friends in Hong Kong, no doubt. Finally, driven by need, I went into a bathroom, and there was a lovely mauve Princess phone. I called Jack Smack, called him three times, in fact, waiting for the other freeloaders at the party to get off the line. Finally I got through.

'Hey there, Dunk,' he said genially. 'Good party?'

'Good,' I said. 'Not great, but good. Champagne and super food. I'm a wee bit disoriented.'

'A wee bit disoriented,' he repeated, laughing. 'You mean you're dead drunk.'

'I am not dead drunk,' I said indignantly. 'And I resent the— What do I resent?'

'The accusation? The implication?'

'Yes,' I said, nodding at the phone, 'I resent the implication. Is your invitation still open?'

'Of course. Do you want me to come get you?'

'I am quite capable,' I said loftily, 'of navigating by myself.'

'Of course you are,' he said. 'Promise to take a cab?'

'I promise.'

'Promise not to talk to the driver?'

'Can I say "Good evening" when I get in, and "Good night" when I get out?'

'Only that,' Jack said, 'and nothing more. Promise?'

'Go to hell,' I said, giggling, and hung up.

In my foggy state I still remembered that, as my dear mother had taught me, I must seek out the hostess and thank her for a lovely

241

evening. But it was such a madhouse in the apartment – people sitting on the floor and gobbling from their buffet plates, a few passed-out drunks, two couples dancing to no music that I could hear – I decided to steal away like a mouse and write Vanessa a thank-you note the next day.

At the doorway, I turned and looked back, towering over the *walpurgisnacht*. In a corner behind the bar I noticed Vanessa, Roberta Minchen, and Carlo huddling together, thick as thieves. They were speaking seriously, not chattering, not smiling, and I suddenly had a sinking feeling that I had talked too much that night to Carlo, the demon lover.

Following Jack's instructions, I cabbed down to his loft in silence, sobered and thoughtful.

29

'I want a quart of ice water,' I told Jack. 'Immediately.'

'Water?' he said. 'Cheap date.'

But he brought me a pewter tankard of ice cubes and a glass pitcher of water. He filled the mug, waited while I gulped it down, then filled it again.

'Feeling better?' he asked.

'I drank too much, ate too much, talked too much.'

'Welcome to the club,' he said. 'Who threw this shindig?'

'Vanessa Havistock,' I told him.

'Oh-ho,' he said. 'And I wasn't invited? I better change my deodorant. Learn anything?'

'Yes,' I said. 'I learned that Luther Havistock is a ding-dong, right on the edge. May I take off my shoes?'

'Whatever turns you on,' Jack said.

He was wearing sandals on bare feet, flannel bags, and a dress shirt with the sleeves rolled up and the tails hanging outside. What a casually handsome man! He made Carlo look like a mannequin. I mean Jack moved like a premier danseur. He could pick his nose and it would be a work of art.

'I know what you need,' he said.

'Don't be so sure of yourself,' I said.

'Do what Daddy tells you. Have exactly one ounce of cognac. Sip it very, very slowly. In twenty minutes you'll be a new woman, ready to run the four-forty. Trust me.'

'Never,' I said, 'but I'll try the cognac.'

He was right. The first sip burned, but after that it lulled, soothed, smoothed, and I began to get back to what I laughingly call normal.

'How was Vanessa acting tonight?' Jack asked. 'Coming on to every guy in sight?'

'She was doing all right. If I was a man, I'd be interested.'

243

He shook his head. 'A barracuda,' he said. 'She scares me. I think I talked to her twice, and each time, after I left, I patted my hip to make sure my wallet was still there.'

I laughed. 'Don't tell me the great Romeo is frightened of a poor little old female?'

'Who said she's a female? Not a human female. She's an animal, and this Romeo never learned to work with a chair and a whip. Anything else happen at the party?'

I knew he was pumping me, but I felt so mellow I didn't care.

'The Minchens were there,' I said. 'Which surprised me. I went to lunch with Vanessa and Roberta, and it was a shouting match. I thought they were sworn enemies, but tonight was like old home week. Maybe they all starred in the same video porn flick.'

He stared at me. 'Dunk,' he said, 'what are you talking about?'

'I thought I told you,' I said confusedly. 'Or maybe I told Al Georgio. He just laughed. You might as well know about it.'

So I related the story of my evening at the Minchens', and their efforts to recruit me into their circle of videocassette stunt men and women.

'And the Minchens were in them?' Jack said. 'This wasn't commercial stuff you saw?'

'They were in them,' I assured him. 'It was homemade.'

'Son of a bitch,' Jack said thoughtfully. 'Who would believe it? They look like Mr and Mrs Square. I've got a VCR, but I don't have any porn tapes. I never think of sex as a spectator sport. Want to watch *The Sound of Music*?'

'No, thanks.'

'Good. I haven't got it. How about the original *King Kong*?'

'I never think of sex as a spectator sport. Jack, why are we wasting time talking about videocassettes?'

'Beats the hell out of me,' he said. 'I guess I was trying to be a gentleman.'

'That'll be the day,' I said.

He was *such* a lover. He turned me upside down and inside out. After he kissed my breasts, I said, 'Now you must marry me.' He laughed. A hollow laugh, I thought.

'Hey,' he said, 'you're free, white, and twenty-one.'

'At least,' I told him. 'What comes next?'

'Probably me,' he said, groaning and going back to work.

What a frolic that was! The tap dancer was so loving and funny and knowing. He knew just which switches to flick and buttons to press. I didn't want to think of how he had learned all that.

He was all over me. A wicked tongue. And absolutely no inhibitions. Which made me respond in kind, of course. When you're in a foreign country, you try to adopt the customs of the natives, do you not? But he had some nerve calling Vanessa an animal; this kid was a tiger.

Later, when it was over, my heartbeat and respiration slowing, I was reasonably certain I wouldn't have to be admitted to Intensive Care. Jack was clever enough to hold me in a nice, warm, horizontal hug. He didn't miss a trick.

'So tell me,' he said, 'what do you think of the International Monetary Fund?'

I laughed and punched his arm. 'I wish I could hate you,' I told him, 'but I can't.'

'Why would you want to hate me?'

'Because you're no damned good.'

'That's true,' he acknowledged, 'but then I never claimed to be a Boy Scout, did I? You know what I'm going to do now?'

'I'm afraid to ask.'

'Have a beer,' he said. 'Be right back.'

When he returned, he put the cold can of Pabst on my stomach.

'You bastard!' I gasped.

'Dunk, you said Luther Havistock was right on the edge. What did you mean by that?'

Just like Al Georgio. Neither of them could forget the job.

'I think there's a potential for violence there,' I said. 'He was somewhat smashed, but *in vino veritas*. He was talking wildly. About suicide, amongst other things. Including some disagreeable stuff about his wife, Not exactly what I'd call a healthy situation.'

'He's hurting,' Jack said. 'Moneywise, I mean. You think that's why he's boozing?'

'That may be part of it. But there's more to it than that. Vanessa is leading him a merry chase and he just can't keep up.'

'Yeah,' Jack said, 'that's my take, too. You think he swiped the Demaretion?'

'No. I don't think the poor man's capable of deciding what he wants for lunch, let alone engineering a clever caper. Jack, the guy is falling apart.'

245

He looked at me strangely. 'Bright lady,' he said. 'Dunk, I've got to apologize. When I first met you, I thought you were just another pretty face. I know differently now. You've got a brain.'

'Is that why you lured me onto these crazy futons?'

'No,' he said, laughing, 'that had nothing to do with your brain. It was your belly button.'

'My *what?*'

'It's an outsy,' he explained. 'Haven't seen one in years.'

'You're a stinker,' I said. 'An A-Number One, dyed-in-the-wool stinker. May I have a sip of your beer?'

'A little one,' he said, holding the opened can up to my lips. I got a small swallow. Then he carefully poured a few drops over my boobs and licked them off.

'Yum-yum,' he said.

'Talking about brains,' I said, 'if you had one, you'd be dangerous.'

'I happen to be a closet intellectual,' he told me. 'But there is a time and a place for everything. Dunk, I hate to make this shameful confession, but I think you're nice people.'

'I can endure you, too,' I said. 'Jack, do me a favor?'

'If I can.'

'I forget whether it was you or Al who told me, but one of you said Ross Minchen has been making some hefty withdrawals from his bank account over the past few years. Could you find out where it's going?'

'Oh, boy,' he said, 'that's a tough one. If he wrote a check to someone, maybe I could trace it. If he took it in cash, it'll be practically impossible. I'll see what I can do. Why do you ask?'

'Money,' I said. 'That seems to be the thread running through everything: the theft of the coin and the murders of Vanwinkle and LeBaron. Admittedly some very heavy human passions were involved, but money looks like the motive.'

'Speaking of heavy human passions . . .' he said, looking at me.

'Yes?'

'I have a heavy human passion.'

'What a coincidence!' I cried.

It was bliss. He taught me so much. And in all modesty, I think I can say I improvised a little on my own. It was all so mindless and delightful. Fun and games, I suppose you'd call it, but it seemed to me there was more to it that that. There was a kind of wild, joyous, childish primitivism. Instead of a high-tech loft in SoHo, we could have been in a jungle or on a desert island. I mean we behaved like we were the last people on earth.

I lost all sense of time. I do remember that at one point, early in the morning, Jack roused long enough to say, 'No way am I going to get up and drive you home.'

'No way am I going to go,' I said drowsily.

'See you at breakfast,' he said, and we went back to sleep on the futons.

In the morning we showered together – and that was a giggle. Then Jack donned a terry robe, and I pulled on his white dress shirt with the rolled-up sleeves. He thawed some frozen croissants and we had those with lime marmalade. And lots of strong, black coffee – not instant or decaf. We didn't talk much. Mostly we just looked at each other and grinned.

It was almost eight o'clock before we shook off our dopey lassitude and were able to get dressed. Then Jack drove me uptown in his Jaguar. He double-parked outside my building.

'What can I say after I say I'm sorry?'

'Sorry about what?' I demanded.

He put a palm to my cheek, kissed me on the lips.

'Not a goddamned thing,' he said.

'I concur in your opinion,' I said, got out of the car, then turned back. 'Jack, you'll check on Ross Minchen's bank withdrawals?'

'Sure.'

'You're a darling.'

'I'd be the last to deny it,' he said, winking at me, then pulling away with a squeal of the Jag's tires.

I had two locks on my apartment door (plus an interior chain latch). The lower lock had a spring tang and the upper was a dead bolt. I never, but *never*, left the apartment without locking the bolt and double-locking the spring latch. It was a habit, and I always locked up, even before running down to the corner to mail a letter, to be gone for no longer than a minute.

Now, when I inserted my keys, I discovered the dead bolt was already unlocked and the spring latch not double-locked. I stood staring at the faceplates, unable to believe I had been so careless. I leaned closer to inspect locks and door. No nicks, scars, or gouges. I remembered what Al Georgio had said of the Vanwinkle and LeBaron homicides: 'No signs of forced entry.'

I knew very well what I should do; the police had issued enough warnings. If you suspected there was an intruder in your home,

247

do not enter. Call the cops or, at the very least, summon a burly neighbor to escort you inside. Every single woman living alone in New York knew that.

But, fearing the open locks were merely the result of my own stupidity, I opened the door a few inches and called, 'Hello?' How's that for the acme of silliness? If there was a crook inside, did I expect him to carol back, 'Hi, there!' But there was no answer. Just silence.

I cautiously ventured inside, then turned and locked, bolted, and chained the door behind me. Another idiotic mistake. If there was a thief on the premises, what good would locking the door have done? I should have left it wide open in case I had to beat a screaming and hysterical retreat. I just wasn't thinking clearly.

I moved slowly through the apartment, checking every room. Nothing. Then I tried the back door to my minuscule garden. It was still locked and chained, and, looking through the window, I could see no one lurking outside.

I went back to open closet doors, peer under the bed, and draw back the shower curtain. All clear. But, standing in the middle of the living room, hands on hips, looking around, I had a definite feeling that someone *had* been there. The door of the cabinet in my little sideboard was slightly ajar. I always made sure it was tightly latched to help keep out dust.

And other things weren't precisely in the position I had left them. The cushion on my armchair, for instance, had been flopped over; I could have sworn to that. And there was just something in the air of the place: a faint, strange scent signaling an alien presence.

The television set was still there. My two radios, my poor little jewel box, almost a hundred dollars in cash in the drawer of the bedside table – all untouched. Then I smacked my forehead with a palm, gave a groan of dismay, and went galloping into the kitchen to search the cabinet above the sink.

Dolly LeBaron's package was still there. Thank God!

I went back into the living room, flopped on the couch, and tried to make sense of it all. I knew, absolutely, that I was not being paranoid; someone *had* been in my apartment – but for what reason? Sighing, I gave up trying to figure it out, and decided to take my mind off the puzzle by entering all the things I had learned the previous evening in my spiral notebook.

Of course it was missing.

30

I CALLED Al Georgio, and this time I was in luck; I got him on the first try.

'Al,' I said, 'I've got to see you right away.'

He must have caught something in my voice because he immediately said, 'Dunk, you okay?'

'I'm all right, but I've got to see you.'

He didn't say any bullshit things like 'Is it important?' or 'Can't it wait?' He just said, 'I'll be right there,' and hung up. The man was a tower of strength.

I still wasn't thinking clearly. If I had been, I'd have peeled off my fancy party duds – poet's blouse and long, brocaded skirt – and pulled on jeans and a T-shirt. But it never occurred to me. So when Al arrived and looked me up and down, I was sure he guessed I had been out all night; he didn't carry a detective's gold shield for nothing. But he never mentioned my costume.

'You all right, Dunk?' he asked anxiously.

'I think so,' I said. 'I'm not sure. I made some coffee. Have a cup?'

'Love it,' he said. 'What happened? You look spooked.'

We hunched over the cocktail table, sipping our hot coffee, and I told him all about it. He got up, went to my front door, and inspected it. Then he came back.

'Dunk,' he said, 'those locks are cheese. I could crash this place with a hairpin, a nail file, and a plastic credit card.'

'What should I do?' I said desperately.

'Get Medeco locks with big pry-plates around the face. Get a long jimmy shield for the jamb of the door. No guarantee, but it's better than what you've got. You say nothing was taken but your notebook?'

'That's right.'

'What was in the notebook?'

'Everything,' I said despairingly. 'Everything I learned about the Demaretion robbery. Everything about the Havistock family. About the murders of Vanwinkle and LeBaron. Everything you and Jack Smack told me. Al, that notebook had everything I've been doing since this whole thing started. I'll be lost without it.'

'Can you remember what was in it?'

'I'll try. I think I can, but there was so *much*. I needed those notes.'

'I know,' he said sympathetically. 'I go back over my reports again and again, trying to find something I've missed.'

'Can you do anything?' I asked hopefully.

'Like what? Have the place dusted for prints? A waste of time. Whoever grabbed your notebook was probably wearing gloves, and in and out of here in fifteen minutes. Where did you keep it?'

'In the upper drawer of the sideboard.'

'Locked?'

'No.'

He sighed. 'It's gone, Dunk. And I doubt if you'll ever get it back. I can ask neighbors if they saw or heard anything, but that's the best I can do.'

'Forget it,' I said. 'You're right; it's just gone.'

'You think it happened last night?'

'Yes,' I said, 'I was out.'

'Lucky you,' he said casually. 'Better than being home asleep when the guy broke in. Dunk, who knew you were keeping a notebook?'

I held my head in my hands, trying to think. 'I told Enoch. That's Enoch Wottle, my friend in Arizona. You can scratch him as a suspect. I mentioned it to Archibald Havistock, and he could have repeated it to his wife.'

'Yeah,' Al said, 'at the dinner table where Natalie and Ruby Querita might have heard.'

I nodded miserably. 'And I told a friend of Vanessa's last night. So she could have known about the notebook. And that means Luther, too. Also, the Minchens.'

'Jesus Christ, Dunk, why didn't you take out a full-page newspaper ad to let everyone in New York know you were keeping notes on the Demaretion robbery.'

'I talked too much,' I agreed mournfully. 'But who could have figured anyone would be interested enough in the stupid thing to steal it.'

'Obviously someone who felt threatened by your investigation and wanted to find out exactly what you knew. Who's this friend of Vanessa's?'

'Carlo. He's the manager of a Madison Avenue boutique where Vanessa spends a bundle.' Then I decided to come clean. 'Al, I went to a party at Vanessa's last night. That's where I got a mite smashed and shot off my mouth about the notebook. I didn't get home until early this morning, so anyone at the party could have popped over here and grabbed it.'

Thankfully, he didn't ask me where I had been 'until early this morning.' Maybe he knew – or guessed.

He finished his coffee and sat back on the couch. 'No use brooding about it, Dunk. You'd do better trying to remember your notes and figuring out what you might have had that drove someone to breaking-and-entering. Learn anything at the party?'

I told him what I had told Jack Smack, that Luther Havistock had been in a pitiable condition and, in my opinion, was close to violence. Also, that the Minchens had been present, to my surprise, and seemed to be palsy-walsy with Vanessa.

'I have no idea what that means,' Al said. 'Do you?'

'Haven't the slightest,' I said, not yet ready to tell him about my crazy theory. And unwilling, at the moment, to confess I had a mysterious package that belonged to Dolly LeBaron in my kitchen cabinet.

We sat in silence awhile. He seemed in no hurry to leave – which was fine with me. After what had happened, it was nice to have a big, husky cop on the premises.

'Anything new on the homicides?' I asked.

'What?' he said, coming out of his reverie. 'No, nothing new. We're up against a stone wall. Unless we get a lucky break, I'm afraid the whole thing will have to be put on the back burner.'

'You can't do that,' I said hotly.

'No?' he said with a sour grin. 'You know how many killings there have been in this town since Vanwinkle got snuffed? It's a problem of time and manpower, Dunk. We can't work one case for months or years. Besides, Vanwinkle and LeBaron are the homicide guys' headache. It's not mine. I've got enough to worry about, wondering if I screwed up on the Demaretion thing. My bosses aren't exactly enthusiastic about the way I've handled it – or mishandled it.'

'Jack Smack hasn't done any better,' I pointed out. 'And neither have I. It's not your fault, Al.'

He gave me his slow, charming smile. 'Thanks for your loyalty;

I appreciate it. Dunk, I talked to Sally on the phone last night. She said to say hello.'

'And hello to her. How is she?'

'Doing great in school. Getting good marks. And she's in a play where she gets to sing a song. She's all excited.'

'I can imagine.'

'You like her, Dunk?'

'Like her? What a question! I love her. She's a marvelous kid.'

'Yeah,' he said, 'I think so, too. I just wanted to find out how you felt.'

Then he was silent again, sitting there like a slack giant, rumpled as ever. What he needed, I decided, was a loving wife who would wind him up every morning and send him off to work with a pressed suit, shined shoes, and a straight part in his hair. He needed sprucing and the knowledge that someone cared. He was beginning to show a hermit's disrepair. I didn't think he was a man who enjoyed solitude.

'Something on your mind, Al?' I asked him. 'You seem awfully quiet.'

'Yeah,' he said, leaning forward with his elbows on his knees. 'I've got something on my mind. Dunk, will you marry me?'

I used to believe it was a literary figure of speech to say someone's jaw dropped in amazement, but I could feel mine go *kerplunk*! I had just been thinking he needed a wife to straighten him out and give his life meaning. What a shock to learn I had been nominated.

'My God, Al,' I said, 'you can't be serious.'

'Never more serious in my life. Hear me out, Dunk, before you laugh at me.'

'I'd never do that, and you know it.'

'Well, I'll give it to you straight. I've been thinking about it a long time. Since I met you and drove you home – remember? Let me give you the minuses first. I told you why my wife dumped me. She couldn't stand the pressures of my job. That's all right; I can understand that. But if you married me, the pressures would still be there. The job would come first. Lousy hours. Meals where I don't show up. Maybe gone for a day or two and all you get are phone calls. Not exactly what you'd term a storybook romance. Plus the possibility that some weirdo might blow my head off. A remote possibility – but still it's there. Also, I admit, I can be stubborn. You know – the Italian macho syndrome. I try to control it, but sometimes it gets away from me.'

'You do okay,' I told him.

'Do I?' he said. 'Well, I try. And then there are a lot of little things that might drive a wife bananas. Like I think I'm such a hotshot cook and could be supercritical of what I'm given to eat. And I guess I'm not the neatest guy in the world. I'm trying to give you all the drawbacks, Dunk.'

I smiled and took his hand.

'Now for the pluses,' he said. 'Such as they are. I make a good buck. Not great, but good. Maybe someday I can make lieutenant. Chancy, but it's a possible. The pension is better. If my ex gets married, which I'm praying for, then I'll be saving the alimony. I've got a few CDs – nothing to brag about. I'm in good health. Overweight, but healthy. I really can cook, and don't mind helping with housework if I've got the time. But the most important plus, Dunk, is that I love you. I really do. If we got married, I would never cheat on you. I wouldn't even *dream* about it. I would be with you always.'

This was my first proposal of marriage, and I didn't know how to handle it. I was so confused that my best reaction, I figured, would be to delay, temporize, put off a decision until I could determine how I felt. But Al, bless him, made it easy for me.

'Look,' he said, 'I don't expect an immediate yes or no. You're a brainy lady and I know you'll want to think about it and weigh the pros and cons. I just wanted to make my pitch and let you know how I feel. Take your time. If you say no, I'm not going to stamp my foot and pout. It's your decision. If you say yes, I'll be the happiest son of a bitch in New York. But don't let the way I'm going to feel affect what you decide. You do what you think is best for you.'

I had to kiss him. He was so honest, forthright, and solid. I never doubted his integrity for a moment. He was exactly the man he appeared to be. No sham. No playacting. What you see is what you get.

'Al,' I said, 'first of all, I thank you for even thinking about me that way. First time it ever happened to me, and it's great for a girl's ego.'

'Listen,' he said, 'if you've got any questions, don't be afraid to ask them. You know, like my finances, bank balance, debts, and all that. Religion. I'll answer everything. Also, what about children? Do you want your own kids or don't you? These are things we'd have to work out if you decide to say yes. But let's put all our cards on the table first. I think that's the best way, don't you?'

'You bet,' I said. 'Al, just as you figured, I'm not going to give you an answer right now. I've got some heavy thinking to do.'

'But you're not giving me a fast no?'

'You're right; I'm not.'

'That's good enough for me,' he said, rising. 'And remember what I told you: Do what you think is best for you.'

We embraced and I hugged him tightly. I tried to keep from weeping. I don't know why I felt like crying; a woman's first marriage proposal is hardly a reason for melancholy. I think it was just that, at the moment, I felt so tender and loving towards him.

When he was gone, and I had imprisoned myself with those cheesy locks, I finally got out of my party clothes and pulled on something more informal and comfortable. While I was doing this, moving as dreamily as a somnambulist, I thought of Al's offer and tried to imagine what my life would be like as Mrs Al Georgio. Mrs Mary Lou Georgio. Mrs Dunk Georgio.

I couldn't see myself clearly in the role of a wife. I could easily see Al as a husband. Other than his rackety job, he seemed to have all the attributes of a good, solid, faithful mate. I knew he'd take the marriage vows seriously, especially that part about 'till death do us part.'

But what kind of a spouse would I make? I decided, sighing, that I'd never know until I gave it a go. I might have the best intentions in the world, but chance and circumstance have a way of fouling up the most sincere resolves. I guess, when you got right down to it, marriage frightened me. The big unknown. Who could predict if it would be a benediction or a curse? Not me.

So I tucked *that* decision into the back of my mind, letting it percolate awhile, and turned my attention to more immediate demands. How was I going to replace my missing notebook? I could do something about that, and started by running out to buy a yellow legal pad at our neighborhood stationery store. I also stopped at the deli to pick up a cold six-pack of Bud. I still had a thirst that wouldn't quit.

Back home, sipping from an opened can, I made brief jottings on the pad of everything I could recall that had been included in the stolen journal. You know, I think the attempted duplication of my original notes was a blessing in disguise. Because I'm sure I forgot a lot of meaningless details. Red herrings flopped at the wayside. There apparently was a kind of mental selection involved here: The things I remembered and scribbled down seemed to be significant and to have a logic and pattern I hadn't seen before.

My crazy theory didn't appear so demented after all. It was now a rational and verifiable explanation of everything that had happened. It took all the events into account and supplied motives and reasons for the puzzles that had been bedeviling me.

It even gave me a very good idea of what was in the late Dolly LeBaron's mysterious package, now nestling amongst pancake mix and instant rice in my kitchen cabinet.

31

'I'm sorry, Dunk darling,' Enoch Wottle said apologetically, calling from Arizona. 'What I found out about Archibald Havistock's finances you could put in your eye and it wouldn't hurt a bit.'

'That's all right, Enoch,' I said. 'I know you tried, and I appreciate it.'

'The dealers I talked to made credit checks maybe four or five years ago. At that time his reputation was A-OK. They had no trouble with him whatsoever. So they saw no reason to investigate again.'

'Of course not,' I said. 'Why should they? Enoch, thank you again for your help. I couldn't have done it without you.'

'Done what?' he said sharply. 'Dunk, you sound like you know something.'

'Do I?' I said, wondering if Al's marriage proposal had given me confidence. 'I'm not sure I know anything definitely, but I'm making some guesses that I think are on target.'

'And you'll get the coin back?'

'I hope so.'

'I hope so, too. However it comes out, you'll let me know?'

'Of course, dear. Thank you for calling.'

He hadn't told me what I wanted to hear, but there was more than one way to skin a cat.

It was Thursday morning, and I was filled with vim and vigor, planning how I would spend a day that would, inevitably, end up with the total triumph of Dunk Bateson. It didn't turn out exactly that way.

I dug an old shopping bag out of my closet – a brown paper job with twine handles. I filled it with catalogues, books, a folding umbrella, a pouched plastic raincoat, a box of Alka-Seltzer, and my office coffee cup. Then I set out for Grandby & Sons, stopping off at a liquor store en route to pick up a gift for Hobart Juliana: a bottle of Irish Mist, which he dearly loved.

He was delighted to see me, and even more delighted when I began to stow my belongings back into my desk and onto my bookshelves.

'Ma and Pa Kettle are back together again!' he shouted.

We celebrated by having a cup of black coffee and opening Hobie's gift to have a wee taste. A nice way to toast my homecoming.

'I've got to call Felicia,' I told him. 'Listen to this, Hobie. I think it's the first time I'm going to lie with malice aforethought.'

'Welcome to the real world,' he said, smiling.

I punched out Madam Dodat's intraoffice extension and waited impatiently while her snooty secretary put her on the phone.

'Dunk, darling!' she caroled. 'How *nice* to hear from you. Do you have good news for us?'

'I think so,' I said. 'I'm downstairs in my office and I'd like to meet with you and Mr Grandby if that's possible.'

'Oh, dear,' she said, 'I'm afraid not. Stanton isn't in. It's his day for squash and a sauna.'

The thought of god sitting naked in a sauna was more than I could bear. That glistening penguin!

'Is this a progress report, Dunk?'

'Something like that,' I said.

'Then there's no reason why you can't tell me. I'll repeat it to Stanton just as soon as I hear from him.'

'I don't think so,' I said decisively. 'I want him to be there. And it wouldn't hurt to have the lawyer present. Lemuel what's-his-name.'

'Whattsworth.'

'Yes. I'd like him to be there. Can you arrange it?'

'Well . . .' she said, obviously offended by my peremptory tone, 'I'll see what I can do. How long will you be here?'

'About fifteen minutes.'

'I'll try to get back to you before you leave,' she said. 'If not, I'll call you at home. Is it important?'

'Very,' I said, and hung up, glorying in my boldness.

'What was that all about?' Hobie asked curiously.

'I need some information from them,' I explained. 'But if I told them what I wanted, they'd turn me down cold. So I implied that I have a progress report to deliver. That'll bring them running, hoping to learn something that might forestall a lawsuit by Archibald Havistock.'

He laughed. 'Dunk, you're becoming a *very* devious lady.'

'I'm learning,' I said. 'Hobie, let's have another sip of that glorious elixir.'

'As many as you like,' he said, pouring into our coffee mugs. 'It's like old times again, Dunk.'

We parked our feet on our desks and raised our cups to each other. 'Hobie,' I said, 'one more favor? Please? The last, I swear.'

'The *last*?' he said. 'You mean this thing is finally unraveling?'

'I think it is. Keep your fingers crossed.'

'I shall. What's the favor you want?'

'Just your opinion. When you were asking around about Orson Vanwinkle's activities, did you get the idea that he might be a man who would engage in – ah, how can I put this delicately? – in group sex?'

'Orgies, you mean?' Hobie said, grinning. 'Oh hell, yes. Dunk, from what I heard, the guy was an absolute *freak*. He probably got it off with Doberman pinschers, for all I know. He was a wild one.'

'Thank you, Hobie,' I said gratefully. 'When I write a novel about all this, you're going to get the biggest credit line in the book.'

'Could you refer to me as Rodney instead of Hobart?' he said wistfully. 'I've always fancied the name Rodney. Hobart sounds like a collapsed soufflé.'

We laughed, and chatted of this and that. I was standing, ready to leave, when Felicia Dodat called back. She said she had arranged a conference with Stanton Grandby and Lemuel Whattsworth – and herself, of course, – for 1:00 PM on the following day, Friday. Would that be satisfactory?

'It'll have to be,' I said shortly, in my new assertive role. I was really beginning to enjoy throwing my weight around.

'So long, dear,' I said, embracing Hobie. 'I shall return carrying my shield or on it.'

He gave me a look spangled with love. 'Lots of luck, Dunk,' he said.

'And I think Hobart is a perfectly marvelous name,' I told him. 'Live with "Dunk" for a while, and you'll be thankful for what you've got.'

I cabbed home, practically feverish with anticipation because I knew what I had to do next. I rushed into my apartment, closed the venetian blinds and drew the drapes – like an idiot! – and hauled Dolly LeBaron's package down from the top shelf of the kitchen cabinet.

258

I turned it over and over in my hands, inspecting it, hefting it. Then I fetched a pair of manicure scissors and started cutting all those windings of Scotch tape. I finally got the brown paper bag sliced open. Within was a shoebox, as I had suspected. The stamping on the end read: 4-B, RED.

I opened it as cautiously as if I had been defusing a bomb. Please, God, I prayed silently, let me be right.

Inside were wrappings and paddings of purple tissue paper. I peeled everything away slowly and carefully. Then I held the contents. The secret. I didn't know whether to shout with joy or weep with sadness.

But I *had* been right.

I didn't even want to think about it. I didn't want to ponder or question or analyze. Action was the name of the game. Full court press. Up and in. Dunk shot. Crowd roaring. The satisfaction of completing a class act. Nothing like it.

I started making phone calls. It took me almost a half-hour to get it set up, but I pushed it through, insisting.

When I got hold of Jack Smack, he said:

'Is this about Ross Minchen's bank withdrawals, Dunk? Forget it. He took out cash. There's no way to trace what he did with it. Blew it on slow horses or fast women – who knows?'

'That's not important now,' I said impatiently. Then I told him what I wanted.

'Why does it have to be my place?' he complained. 'I've got a million things to do here at the office.'

'It *has* to be,' I said. 'At three o'clock. Trust me.'

'All right,' he said resignedly, 'I'll be there.'

Al Georgio was easier. 'What's up, Dunk?' he said.

'Something interesting,' I said. 'It's going to help make you a lieutenant.'

'Oh?' he said. 'That I've got to hear. Okay, I'll be there. Give me the address.'

So, a little after 3:00 PM, we all met at Jack Smack's loft in SoHo, me carrying Dolly LeBaron's package, hugging it tightly as if it contained the plans for an atomic bomb, which, in a way, it did.

Both of the men looked at me like I was some kind of a nut.

'Dunk, what *is* this?' Al said gruffly.

I didn't answer him. I said, 'Jack, you mentioned once that you own a videocassette recorder. Is that right?'

He looked at me, puzzled. At least he was smart enough not to say,

259

'You know I do, Dunk. I wanted to play *King Kong* for you the other night when we made nice-nice.' *That* would have raised Al Georgio's bushy eyebrows!

Instead, Jack said, 'Yeah, I've got a VCR.'

'Play this for us, will you?' I asked him, unwrapped the package, and handed him Dolly LeBaron's videocassette.

He inspected it. 'What is it?' he said. 'A travelogue of the Children's Zoo in Central Park?'

'If it is,' I said, trying to laugh and not show my nervousness, 'I'm going to spend the rest of my life wiping egg off my face. Just show it, will you?'

He warmed up the set, slid in the cassette, and we settled back. The videotape started. The colors were sharp, everything in focus, sound clear. It had played for about five seconds when Al Georgio shouted, 'Holy Christ!' After that, we watched in silence.

It was what I had guessed: a sexual *pas de quatre* starring Roberta and Ross Minchen, Orson Vanwinkle, and Dolly LeBaron. It wasn't pretty, but it was explicit. The knowledge that two of the performers had been brutally murdered gave all those grunts and groans a surrealistic quality. But it was still an X-rated film. More foolish than exciting.

When it ended, Jack rewound the tape, slid the cassette out, and handed it to Georgio. 'I think you'll want this, Al,' he said. Then we sat there, saddened and depressed I think, staring at each other. Finally . . .

'Where did you get it, Dunk?' Al asked quietly.

I explained how Dolly LeBaron had come to my apartment shortly before she was killed and left the sealed package in my care.

'She made me promise to destroy it if she didn't come back for it,' I said. 'After she was murdered, I didn't know what to do, so I didn't do anything. But then I put a lot of things together and decided I better see what she had left with me.'

I had thought that Al Georgio would scream at me for withholding evidence, but he didn't. 'What things did you put together, Dunk?' he said.

'Vanwinkle was living high off the hog, spending much more than the eight hundred a week he was making as Mr Havistock's secretary. So where was he getting it? He had the reputation of being a wild freak, a drunken sensualist. Even poor Dolly admitted they did crazy things.'

'Okay,' Al said, 'I can take it from there. Orson and Dolly go to one of the Minchens' skin extravaganzas, and a tape is made of their gymnastics together.'

'Blackmail,' Jack Smack said. 'Orson swipes the tape, the night it was made or maybe at a later session, and he begins to lean on the Minchens. That would account for Ross's bank withdrawals.'

'Mr and Mrs Havistock were involved in estate planning,' I added. 'Rewriting their wills. Can you imagine what would have happened if Vanwinkle took the tape to Mabel and Archibald? As far as inheriting goes, Roberta and Ross would have been down the drain. So they paid Orson to keep his mouth shut. What else could they do? He had the tape.'

Al Georgio rose and began to pace back and forth, hands in the pockets of his polyester slacks. 'It listens,' he said. 'I like it. I like it very much. A scumbag like Vanwinkle isn't going to let up. Blackmailers never do. He increases the pressure. Finally, Ross Minchen decides he can't take any more of this; he's got to end it, once and for all.'

'How's this for a scenario?' Jack chimed in. 'Vanwinkle ups the ante and Minchen agrees. He goes to Orson's apartment. Vanwinkle lets him in, expecting payment. Instead, he gets two slugs in the head. Exit Orson. Then Minchen searches the apartment for the tape.'

'But he can't find it,' I said, putting in my two cents' worth, 'because Vanwinkle had given the cassette to his girlfriend for safekeeping.'

'You think Minchen finally figured that out?' Al asked me.

'Probably,' I said. 'Dolly told me she was getting threatening phone calls. Or maybe she decided to go into the blackmailing business on her own. With Orson dead, how was she going to pay for that apartment, the bikinis, and all her other swell stuff? However it happened, Ross Minchen, frantic now, went up to her place, killed her, and tore everything apart, looking for the tape. Again he didn't find it. Because it was in my kitchen cabinet.'

Al nodded with satisfaction. 'Better and better,' he said. 'This is something I can take to the brass. Thank you, Dunk. You'll have to make a sworn statement of how you came into possession of the tape and what Dolly said to you. Okay?'

'Of course,' I said.

'Fine. Then I'll be on my way to get the wheels rolling.'

'Arrest warrant?' Jack asked.

Al thought a moment. 'It may not be necessary. With Minchen's bank withdrawals and this' – he held up the videocassette – 'I think we can prove probable cause, considering the gravity of the crimes. But that's for the Department's legal eagles to decide. I'll let you both know how it turns out.' He paused at the door. 'Jack, do me a favor, will you?'

'What's that?'

'The next time you show a film, try to have some buttered popcorn.'

After he was gone, Jack brought an opened bottle of chilled Soave from the refrigerator and poured us each a glass. We sat there, sipping, regarding each other without expression.

'You're really something,' he said finally. 'You saved Al's ass today – you know that? He was getting nowhere on the Demaretion case, but breaking the homicides will take the pressure off. How the hell did you do it?'

'I had the videocassette.'

'Sure you did, but you didn't know what was on it. As for the rest of the stuff, Al and I both knew as much as you did, but we didn't have the brains to put it together. You're really a wonder.'

'Thank you.'

'Now how about saving my ass?' he said. 'What have the killings got to do with the disappearance of the Demaretion?'

'Nothing,' I said. 'Not directly. They were two different crimes.'

'Vanwinkle didn't steal the Demaretion?'

'No.'

'Then who did?'

I thought a moment. 'Tell you tomorrow,' I said.

He stared at me. 'You're kidding.'

'I'm not. I've got one more piece to fit into place, and then I'll know.'

'What time tomorrow?'

'Ohh . . . how about three o'clock? At the Havistocks' apartment.'

'I'll be there.'

'It may turn out to be a waste of time, Jack. But if I can't sew it up, I'll tell you what I do have.'

'That's good enough for me. How about dinner tonight?'

'No, thank you. I've got to get home and do some things. I'll take a rain check.'

He accepted that. It was one thing I admired about him: he endured rejection and failure as calmly as success and triumph. But maybe he just didn't care.

I looked around at that big, spacious loft. Twelve-foot ceilings and a huge skylight. It was about twice the size of my pad. Everything was so open and airy. The Russian Ballet could do *Swan Lake* in there and never touch a wall.

'Like it?' Jack said, guessing what I was thinking.

'I sure do,' I said.

'Want to move in?'

'I'd love to,' I said. 'When are you moving out?'

'I'm not,' he said. 'I want you to move in with me. Plenty of room. I'll even buy a regular bed.'

I gawked at him. I couldn't believe I had heard correctly – but I had. He was looking at me intently, no smirk, and I wondered how I was going to handle this. Slap his face? Stalk out in injured silence? Break into girlish giggles?

'Jack, is this a joke?' I asked him.

'No joke. I like you, Dunk. I like being with you. If you feel the same way about me, why don't we try living together?'

'For how long?'

He shrugged. 'As long as it lasts. Who can predict? You may want to move out after two days. I may want to evict you. But let's give it a try.'

'What's the point?' I said.

'Does everything have to have a point? Don't you ever act on impulse, and damn the consequences? I do – all the time. And it turns out good more often than it turns out bad. I'll pay the rent and utilities. We'll go fifty-fifty on the food and booze. You can keep your apartment if you like. In fact, it would probably be smart. A safety net. But you'd be living here.'

'Until you got bored,' I said.

'Or until you did. This would be a two-way street. If you want to leave or I want you to leave, that's it – no explanations necessary. No excuses, no complaints. But I think we could have a hell of a time together – for as long as it lasts. I don't foresee any big arguments. We haven't had any yet, have we?'

'No,' I said faintly, 'not yet.'

'I told you I like you, and I do. And I think you like me. Do you like me, Dunk?'

I had to nod.

'So it makes sense,' he said. 'It's really no big deal. But I'm tired of tomcatting around. And I imagine you'd like someone to come home to. Wouldn't you, Dunk?'

Again he forced me to nod. He knew me.

'Well, then,' he said, 'why don't we give it a try? What have we got to lose? You'll keep your apartment, keep your job. I'm not saying that living together will be all peaches and cream, but it might turn out to be something great.'

'But not marriage?'

He looked away. 'A little early to be talking about that. They used to call it a "trial marriage." That's what I'm suggesting. What do you think?'

'You want an answer right now?'

'Oh hell, no,' he said. 'Take your time. Think about it. I do admire you. You're a very mental lady. And you're sensational in the sack. I think we're sexually compatible, don't you?'

I nodded again, thinking that if I kept this up, my head would come off.

'Consider it,' he urged. 'You'll be able to live your own life just as you have been doing. I will, too. We'll have our jobs. But we'll also have each other. A lot of laughs. That's something, isn't it?'

He was a good salesman. Also a handsome salesman. A charming, rakish salesman.

'I'll consider it,' I agreed, shocked to realize that after all my drought years, I had a sudden deluge: two proposals (one legal, one illegal) in as many days.

'Sure,' he said, 'you do that. I'm not going to pretend to be anything but what I am: footloose and fancy-free. But if you can accept that, I think you and I could climb clouds.'

'For a while,' I said.

He shrugged again. He did a lot of shrugging. 'Nothing's forever, is it?' he said. 'Grab what you can: that's my philosophy. Am I wrong, Dunk?'

I glanced at my Snoopy watch and stood up. 'I've got to get going.'

'Drive you home?'

'No, thanks, I'll take a cab. I'm still billing Archibald Havistock for expenses.'

'You'll think about it? Moving in with me?'

'Absolutely,' I said. 'I can guarantee I'll think about it.'

'That's good enough for me,' he said, and gave me a chaste kiss on the cheek before we parted. He was wearing Aramis again.

What an evening that was! I wanted to do some heavy thinking about the Demaretion investigation, but my personal problems kept intruding. Finally I gave up and wallowed in self-analysis, trying to face up to the decisions I had to make: accept Al's proposal or Jack's proposition. Or neither. I was determined to be very logical.

I thought I knew the two men well enough to make a rational choice. They were total contrasts: Al heavy, serious, solidly dependable. He would always be a hard worker and good provider. Jack was a lightweight, elegant and debonair, a man to whom irony was a way of life and commitments a curse.

Al needed a wife. Jack didn't need anyone. Al was a devoted father. Jack was a social chameleon. Al drove a spavined Plymouth. Jack drove a shiny Jaguar. Al wanted to legalize our relationship. Jack wanted a handy bed-partner. Al said he loved me. Jack said he liked me. Both men could cook.

You can see what a state my mind was in. Nutsville! I suppose I had something to eat that night, but I don't remember what it was. Probably bits and pieces of this and that. I do remember I did a lot of pacing, hugging my elbows and pondering about who I was and what kind of life I wanted. No easy answers to those questions.

I went to bed early, spent a sleepless hour wrestling the sheets, and then got up, sighing. I pulled on a robe, moved back into the living room, and took up my knitting. That was usually a sure cure for insomnia, but this time it didn't work. My brain kept churning, and I wished someone – mother, father, Enoch Wottle, anyone! – would appear and *tell* me what to do.

I looked up from my clicking needles, and the apartment had never seemed so empty, and I had never seemed so *alone*. I think it was at that moment I came to my Great Decision.

Then I could sleep.

32

I DO remember what I had for breakfast on Friday morning because
it was special. I figured it was going to be a momentous day in my
life so I followed my mother's dictum: 'When there's work to be
done, it's best done on a full stomach.' A debatable opinion – I can't
see a trapeze artist loading up on spaghetti and meatballs before a
performance – but nevertheless I believed it.

So I went to our local deli and treated myself to a double tomato
juice, scrambled eggs, kippered herring, and home-fries, and
English muffin with apple butter, and two cups of black coffee. Then
I walked back to my apartment with the morning *Times*. I searched
for some mention of the arrest of Ross Minchen, but there was
nothing.

I put the paper aside to read later and began to scribble the day's
schedule on my yellow legal pad. The timing of everything seemed
right. The first thing I had to do, I decided, was to contact Al
Georgio and get him over to the Havistocks' apartment for what
might or might not be the grand dénouement.

But he called me before I could call him. He sounded absolutely
awful.

'Al,' I said anxiously, 'what's wrong?'

'I've been up all night,' he said in a growly voice. 'Well, I did have
about two hours' sleep on a cot with a mattress as thin as a stale
pancake, but then they got me up and it started all over again.
There's good news and there's bad news. Which do you want first?'

'Oh, God,' I said, 'I hate that stupid question. All right, I'll
take the good news first. Maybe it'll give me strength for what's
coming.'

'Okay,' he said. 'We lowered the boom on Ross Minchen. He's
behind bars right now, with his lawyer fighting to get him out. He
hasn't admitted a damned thing, but we found a choice library of

porn videocassettes in his apartment – all home movies. Plus a .22 revolver with two slugs missing from the cylinder. The idiot didn't even clean and reload – can you imagine? The DA's man is very high on this one. He says if ballistic tests prove out, he'll go for Murder One on the Vanwinkle kill. Even if Minchen plea-bargains – because he was being blackmailed, you know – he's still going to do time. Does that make you happy?'

'What about Dolly LeBaron?' I demanded.

'Well, that'd be a tough one to prove. If we can put him away for one homicide, won't that satisfy you?'

'I guess,' I said, thinking of silly Dolly. Even her murder seemed of no interest to anyone.

'Now for the bad news,' Al Georgio said. 'A real shocker.'

'Let's have it.'

'I told you, didn't I, that if we waited long enough, everyone connected with this case would get knocked off and we could all go home. Well, it's happening. Vanessa Havistock is dead.'

'Dead?' I said, beginning to tremble. 'Al, I can't believe that.'

'It's the truth, kiddo,' he said. 'I saw the body – and wish I hadn't. It happened early this morning. Four or five o'clock, the ME's man figures. She was murdered, but there's no mystery about it. Hubby Luther pulled the plug on her. Then he called nine-eleven and reported what he had done. He was sitting there, waiting, when the blues arrived. They read him his rights, but he didn't care; he admitted everything. I think the guy is cuckoo, and his lawyers will probably plead the same thing.'

'How did he kill her, Al?'

'You don't want to know that, Dunk.'

'I *do* want to know,' I said fiercely.

'He beat her to death. With his fists and his feet. He destroyed her. You were right about him being on the edge. He finally went over.'

'Ah, Jesus,' I said, sickened and saddened. 'The poor woman. The poor man. Poor us.'

'Yeah,' Al Georgio said, 'I know what you mean. I hate to turn the day rancid for you, Dunk, but you'd have heard about it anyway, and I wanted to tell you the good news about Ross Minchen.'

'Sure, Al,' I said, 'I understand. Thank you for calling. Are you going home now?'

'Nah,' he said. 'Wish I could, but I'm sitting in on the interrogations of the Minchens and Luther Havistock, so I'll be around and semi-awake all day.'

'Good,' I said. 'Can you meet me at the Havistocks' apartment at three o'clock?'

He was silent a moment. Then:

'Got something good, Dunk?'

'I think so.'

'On the Demaretion heist?'

'If all goes well. If I fall on my face I'll give you everything I do have. Jack Smack will be there, too.'

'Hey,' he said, 'we're becoming like the Three Musketeers.'

'More like the Three Stooges,' I said.

'See you at the Havistocks' at three,' he said, laughing, and hung up.

Al was familiar with violent, bloody death and could accept it stoically. But I wasn't and couldn't. So I shed tears for Vanessa Havistock. Not a lot, but some. I knew there was quality in life, and I supposed there was in death, too. I knew I had mourned more for Dolly LeBaron. Mindless Dolly had been a true victim. Vanessa had engineered her own destruction.

The two were contrasts, in looks, intelligence, life-styles. But there was something of each in the other. When I thought of it, Dolly was Vanessa when she was Pearl Measley and first came to the Big City from South Carolina to make her way. And Vanessa still had the wants and appetites of a country girl bedazzled by wealth and opportunity.

Now they were both dead, all their hopes and ambitions and greeds brought low. There was a moral there, I supposed, but I couldn't see it. All I could grieve was the waste: two lives ended too soon, annihilated by passions that went out of control and became sins.

Vanessa's murder by Luther Havistock added credibility to my theory of what had happened and increased my hopes of bringing the whole thing to a screeching halt. But I found no satisfaction in that. If I had been sharper, smarter, faster, perhaps I might have prevented the bloodbath. A sobering thought, and one I didn't wish to dwell on.

I tore all the annotated sheets from my pad, folded them up, and stuffed them into my shoulder bag. I started out for my appointment at Grandby & Sons, in no mood to be lied to, stalled, or bullied. I was determined to have my way.

We gathered in that funereal conference room. Felicia was wearing one of her 'simple black frocks' that looked like it had been

268

sprayed on her. Stanton Grandby wore his penguin's uniform. And Lemuel Whattsworth wore his usual earth-colored three-piece suit that seemed ready to mold. All three wore expressions of frozen interest in what I had to say.

'Well, Dunk,' Felicia said with her chintzy smile, 'I hope you have some good news for us.'

I ignored her. 'Mr Grandby,' I said, 'has Archibald Havistock brought suit for the loss of the Demaretion?'

God looked to his attorney. 'Litigation has not actually commenced,' Whattsworth said cautiously. 'However, the possibility still exists. We are, in my opinion, legally vulnerable for the loss of the coin since you, Miss Bateson, an employee of Grandby and Sons, signed the receipt.'

He had to remind me of that – the wretch!

'But Mr Havistock hasn't made any claim as yet?'

'Not at this point in time,' the lawyer said.

I took the folded notes from my shoulder bag and made a great pretense of shuffling through them, pausing occasionally to read. All flimflam, of course. I knew what was in them and what wasn't.

'Mr Grandby,' I said, 'do you have any plans to auction the Havistock Collection minus the Demaretion?'

'No,' the penguin said. 'Not until this thing is cleared up. Under the contract we have a year before the collection goes on the block.'

'So, as of this date, Mr Havistock has received nothing, and his collection is still in Grandby's vaults?'

'That is correct.'

'Dunk,' Felicia said, 'what *is* this all about?'

Again I ignored her. How I loved it!

'Mr Grandby,' I said, 'I know that it is standard operating procedure when someone comes to us with valuable property to be auctioned – be it furniture, paintings, coins, stamps, or whatever – a credit check is made to determine the reputation and trustworthiness of the client. I presume such an investigation was made of Archibald Havistock. Could you tell me what the results were?'

'That is confidential information,' Lemuel Whattsworth said in his thin voice.

I stood up, jammed my notes back into my shoulder bag, and faced them defiantly.

'You're paying me to investigate the disappearance of the Demaretion,' I said, in what I hoped were steely tones. 'If you refuse to cooperate, that's your problem, not mine. I've asked you for information. If you refuse to divulge it, then I tender my resignation as of now, and you can face the possibility of paying for the Demaretion's loss on your own.'

Stanton Grandby groaned. 'For heaven's sake, Lemuel,' he said, 'tell her.'

'I advise against it,' the attorney said.

'Then I'll tell her,' Grandby said. 'Please, Miss Bateson, sit down. The credit check on Archibald Havistock was satisfactory. He was – is a rich man. But most of his wealth is in unimproved land which is in his wife's name. The only section of his credit report that gave us pause was that he was not in a very liquid condition. That is, he did not have a great deal of cash in relation to his total assets.'

'I know what "liquid condition" means,' I said. I wasn't going to let him patronize me.

Now that the cat was out of the bag, the lawyer took over. 'However,' he said, 'that is hardly an unusual condition of people seeking to auction property. Invariably they wish to convert their collections to cash. I fail to see how Mr Havistock's shortage of liquid resources relates to the theft of the coin. If the Demaretion had been included in the auction, he would have gained more.'

'That's true,' I agreed. 'A great deal more.'

I think I had them thoroughly befuddled at that point – which suited me just fine. Let them suffer awhile. I thought I'd bring them out of their misery soon enough, but meanwhile I enjoyed their discomfiture. Such *stiff* people!

'Let me get this straight,' I said. 'If the Demaretion is not recovered, Grandby and Sons will have to recompense Mr Havistock for its loss. But actually, your insurer, Finkus, Holding, Incorporated, will pick up the tab.'

'That, essentially, is correct,' Whattsworth said. 'Minus the deductible, of course. Which I may say, without fear of contradiction, is a considerable sum.'

'All that doesn't amount to a row of beans,' Stanton Grandby said impatiently. And from that moment I began to like him – almost. 'The dollar loss isn't going to kill us. What does hurt is the damage to our reputation. Grandby's has never had a scandal of this magnitude in our long and honorable history. People entrust valuable property to our care in the expectation that it will be guarded as if it was our own. If we are forced to admit carelessness or incompetence, the result will be similar to a run on a bank: people will simply lose confidence in our house. That I will not allow.'

270

Then all three looked at me as if I was to be their savior, the Joan of Arc who would solve all their problems, temporal and spiritual.

'We'll see,' I said, standing up again. 'I thank you for your cooperation.'

'Dunk!' Felicia Dodat wailed. 'Don't you have *anything* to tell us?'

'Not at the moment,' I said. 'Things are moving too swiftly. I'm sure you are aware of the murder of Orson Vanwinkle, Mr Havistock's private secretary. Last night, Ross Minchen, Mr Havistock's son-in-law, was arrested and charged with committing that homicide. And early this morning Mr Havistock's son, Luther, confessed to the brutal slaying of his wife. So you see, there is more to this than just the disappearance of an ancient Greek coin.'

I left them stunned and shattered.

I had plenty of time to walk over to the Havistocks' apartment; it wasn't far. I hadn't called for an appointment because I thought I'd be put on hold; they'd be distraught and concerned only with the imprisonment of their son. But I was resolved to wait there until I could see Mabel or Archibald, or both. I owed them that.

It was a murky kind of day, the sky a swamp and the air as thick as pudding. No breeze at all; the poor, dusty leaves on the street trees weren't moving, and everyone seemed to go shuffling along, conserving their energy to breathe. Which was no great treat.

I had expected to find a gaggle of reporters outside the Havistocks' door, and perhaps a TV crew. But the hallway was empty. I rang the bell and waited. The door was opened cautiously a few inches, the chain still on. Ruby Querita peered out.

'Ruby,' I said, 'it's me. Can I come in, please?'

She let me enter, then hurriedly relocked, bolted, chained the door. 'Lots of people come,' she said. 'I don't know who they are.'

I nodded. 'I can imagine. Big trouble, Ruby. More and more trouble.'

She took a deep breath. I could see that she had been weeping. That dour face was creased with damp folds and wrinkles. All her features seemed drawn down, everything sagging with sorrow. I realized then that, despite her imprecations and predictions of doom, she loved this family and felt their hurts. I put an arm about her shoulders.

'Are you all right?' I said.

'I live,' she said. 'I try to understand God's justice.'

We spoke in whispers, as if a corpse was laid out in the next room.

'Is anyone home?' I asked her.

'Natalie is in her room. She won't come out.'

'Good. Make sure she stays there. Mr Havistock?'

'He is at the lawyer.'

'And Mrs Havistock?'

'She is here. In the living room. She sits and stares. She will not eat.'

'Ruby, would you tell her I'd like to talk to her? I'll wait here. If she doesn't want to see me, I'll go away.'

The housekeeper drifted away. I had never before noticed how silently she moved. She was back in a few moments.

'She says to come in,' Ruby reported. 'Please, be very good to her. She is broken – like this.' Ruby made a twisting gesture: two closed fists moving in opposite directions. 'She tries to live – but I know.'

'I'll try not to disturb her. Ruby, there are two men coming at three o'clock. Will you tell me when they get here? One is a police officer.'

She stared at me. 'Oh,' she said. 'Ah. Then it is the end?'

'I think so,' I said. 'I think it is finished.'

I left her weeping, tears slowly dripping down those dark furrows in her cheeks.

When I entered that fusty living room, Mabel Havistock was seated on a severe ladder-back chair, pressed into it as if to support the rigidity of her spine. Her broad shoulders were square, the long jaw lifted. I saw no outward signs of that twisting motion Ruby had made; this woman had not been broken.

'Miss Bateson,' she said with just the faintest hint of a wan smile, 'thank you for coming by.'

'Ma'am,' I said, totally incapable of commiserating adequately, 'I am sorry for your troubles.'

She gave a sharp nod, but that heavy, corseted body did not relax for an instant. As usual, she was groomed to an inch, the blued hair precisely in place, the dress of flowered chiffon unwrinkled. Her eyes were as cold as ever, showing no signs of the strains she was enduring. How solid and craggy she was! She could have been right up there on Mount Rushmore.

'Please,' she said, gesturing, 'do sit down. Would you care for a cup of tea? Coffee? Anything?'

'No, thank you, Mrs Havistock,' I said, touched by her effort to act the gracious hostess. I sat in one of those obese club chairs facing her. I found myself at a lower level, looking up at her – which, somehow, seemed right. 'Actually I came to see your husband, ma'am, but Ruby tells me he's out.'

'Yes,' she said, 'he is consulting with the attorneys regarding our son Luther. I believe – we believe the boy was temporarily deranged and in need of, ah, professional help.'

'I agree completely,' I said. 'The last time I saw him, I thought he was close to the breaking point.'

She stared at me. 'All my children,' she said bleakly, but I didn't understand the significance of that. She shook her massive head slightly as if to clear her mind. 'What was it you wished to see my husband about?' she asked.

The question made me acutely uncomfortable. I could have faced Archibald Havistock and told him the truth without flinching. But this woman – nephew murdered, daughter an attempted suicide, son-in-law arrested for homicide, son a confessed killer – surely I could not add to her sorrows; it would be too painful, for her and for me.

She must have guessed what I was thinking because she raised her heavy chin a trifle and said, 'I am stronger than you think.'

She gave me such a keen, shrewd look that, at that moment, I was certain, absolutely, positively, that she knew why I had come and what I had discovered.

'Mrs Havistock,' I said, feeling my face suddenly flushed with confusion and embarrassment, 'you've known all along, haven't you?'

'Not known,' she demurred, raising a cautionary finger, 'but suspected.'

I took a deep breath. What a family! Wheels within wheels.

'When I accepted your offer of employment,' I said, 'I agreed that if I discovered a member of your family was involved in stealing the Demaretion, I would come to you first before going to the authorities.'

'I am aware of that,' she said calmly.

'Then why in God's name did you hire me?' I cried out.

She touched that beehive of bluish hair. 'I insisted on it because I thought you were an intelligent, persistent young woman. And perhaps because I considered that you might serve as a kind of avenging angel who would set right a wrong.' She was silent a moment. Then: 'A wrong that I didn't have the courage to set right.'

How I admired her! What a blunt, honest woman. I could

understand her conflicting feelings. Suspecting but not knowing, and not really wanting to know because the final realization might mean the end of her life as mother, wife, and dutiful matriarch of this dissolute family.

'I am not an angel,' I told her. 'As for avenging anyone or anything, I really have no interest in that. My initial motive for beginning the investigation was to clear my name. It was purely selfish. But then, I admit, I got caught up in the challenge of the search.'

'And now it's at an end?' she said.

'Yes, Mrs Havistock,' I said, 'it's at an end. I have asked Detective Al Georgio of the New York Police Department and insurance investigator John Smack to join me here. When they arrive, and when your husband returns, I think we better finish all this.'

'Yes,' she said, sighing, 'it's time. When did you begin to understand what had happened?'

'Not for quite a while. There were too many loose ends, too many false leads. Then I got this crazy idea I could scarcely believe myself. But as time went on, it began to seem more and more logical. Not logical, perhaps, but understandable.'

'Irrational!' she thundered. 'Totally irrational! I should have told you my suspicions from the start. I acted like a weak woman.'

'Not weak,' I said. 'Never. But you *are* a woman, wanting to protect your family, your marriage, your home. I don't blame you. No one can blame you.'

There was a slight cough from the doorway. We looked up. Ruby Querita.

'Those two men,' she said. 'They're here.'

'Please show them in, Ruby,' Mrs Havistock said as serenely as if she was inviting the entry of dignitaries.

Al Georgio and Jack Smack came in, bobbing their heads at us. I stood up.

'Ma'am,' I said to Mabel Havistock, 'I must talk to these gentlemen, explain to them what has happened. Perhaps it would be best if I spoke to them in the hallway or another room.'

'No,' she said decisively, 'you may talk to them here, in my presence. I assure you I shall not be shocked or insulted.'

'As you wish,' I said.

I waited until Al and Jack got seated, side by side on one of those awful brown velvet couches. I turned sideways in my armchair so I could address them and still not ignore Mrs Havistock. I wanted to note her reactions to what I had to say. I spoke as directly and concisely as I could.

'For the past five years,' I said, 'or perhaps more, Archibald Havistock had been having an affair with Vanessa, his son's wife. They met in that apartment on East Sixty-fifth Street, leased by Lenore Wolfgang, Mr Havistock's attorney. I am sure he paid Vanessa for her sexual favors. I suppose they called the payments "gifts," but whatever you call them, she was getting a great deal of money out of him.'

I paused to glance at Mabel. Her naturally florid complexion had paled, but her lips were tightly pressed, and she made no effort to interrupt my recital.

'I have good reasons to believe,' I continued, 'that Vanessa was also entertaining other men, and receiving cash "gifts" from them as well. Whether Archibald was aware of those activities, I don't know. I suspect he was, but so sexually obsessed that he could not bear to give her up. The same was true of her husband. Luther must have known where all the money was coming from, but he was in thrall to his wife and endured her unfaithfulness. But he drank heavily; it was, literally, driving him out of his mind.'

Al and Jack glanced at each other, both expressionless. Then they turned back to me. I had no idea how they were taking all this, but I supposed, being detectives, they would have a lot of questions to ask later.

'Now we come to Orson Vanwinkle,' I went on. 'He came to work as private secretary to Archibald about five years ago. Being the kind of man he was, it didn't take long for Orson to discover his boss was involved in an adulterous relationship with his daughter-in-law. So Orson began to blackmail him. To come up with the payments, Archibald had to sell off coins from his collection. The cash drain must have been horrendous. Not only was he paying Vanessa for those afternoons on East Sixty-fifth Street, but now he was paying Orson to keep his mouth shut. Do you wish to comment, ma'am?' I asked, turning to Mrs Havistock.

'No,' she said. 'I have no comment.'

I think that impressed Georgio and Smack more than anything: the wife was making no objections to this sordid tale of her husband's adultery. They began to believe it could all be true. I could see their increased interest in the way they leaned forward, waiting for more revelations.

'And then,' I said, 'Vanwinkle and his sappy girlfriend, Dolly

275

LeBaron, went to one of the Minchens' filming parties, and Orson saw the opportunity to enlarge his blackmailing business. He stole the videocassette, put the arm on Ross Minchen, and had another source of income. No wonder he was living so well and throwing money around like it was going out of style.'

'The Demaretion,' Jack Smack said in a low voice.

'All right,' I said, 'now we come to the Demaretion. I think what happened is this: Orson decided to extort a final big payment from his two blackmail victims and then move abroad with Dolly to live happily ever after on the French Riviera. But that required a lot of loot, so you can imagine what he demanded. It proved to be too much for Ross Minchen, which led to his murdering Orson and Dolly. But Archibald Havistock is no killer; he concluded the best way to get rid of that devil Vanwinkle who was sucking him dry would be to pay him off and get him out of the country. The only way Archibald could come up with that kind of cash would be to put his coin collection up for auction. Then he could pay off Orson and have enough left to continue his liaison with Vanessa. Al, are you with me so far?'

'So far it listens, Dunk,' Georgio said. 'You're on a roll. Keep going.'

'Well, now it gets a little heavy,' I said, 'but bear with me. First of all, you have to understand the psychology of true collectors. They don't buy things for investment or profit, but because the objects are rare or beautiful or both, and they love them. Mr Havistock was – is – a true collector. It must have hurt him to sell off coins over the past five years, even if they were only duplicates or lesser items from the really fine collection he had put together. But now he had to sell off everything including the Demaretion. Surely it was anguishing for him to put on the block all those glorious mintages he had spent a lifetime amassing. But he went ahead with the auction contract. Then, at the last minute, he decided to hold out the Demaretion. He *couldn't* let it go, it was the gem of his collection. In his eyes it was priceless. And he figured that if he kept the Demaretion, he could collect on the insurance.'

Jack Smack looked at me with astonishment. 'Dunk, are you telling us that Archibald Havistock stole the Demaretion?'

'How can a man steal his own coin?' I asked. 'What I'm saying is that Archibald prepared a sealed empty display case, properly taped inside a Styrofoam box and marked as package thirteen. Then he switched boxes. Who else could have done it? Not Orson Vanwinkle.

276

He was with the guards from the armored van. Not anyone else in the family because they couldn't have known how the display case was sealed with wax imprinted with the signet ring, and how the outside box would be taped and numbered. No, Mr Havistock made the switch.'

'And what did he do with the original box thirteen?' Al asked.

I shrugged. 'Probably shoved it into that deep kneehole under his desk where he had kept the empty case. He made the switch, then strolled into the living room for a couple of minutes to chat with his family. Styrofoam box thirteen was loaded into the van, and it was only after I signed the receipt for the collection at Grandby's that we discovered the Demaretion was gone. Mrs Havistock, do you agree that's the way it happened?'

'I don't know,' she said stonily. 'I cannot say if the details are correct. I do know my husband loved his coins. Especially the Demaretion. It is quite possible it happened as you described.'

'Wait a minute,' Jack said. 'Suppose Havistock did keep the Demaretion, then who wrote the letters to my company offering to make a deal?'

'Orson Vanwinkle,' I said promptly. 'When the coin disappeared, he knew immediately that only Archibald could have switched cases. He was smarter and faster than I was. But then he had a criminal mind and assumed everyone was as crooked as he. So he went to Mr Havistock and demanded part of the insurance on the loss of the Demaretion. It meant nothing to Orson that Archibald loved that coin and wanted to keep it. So he wrote the letters to your company, Jack, to raise cash as quickly as possible, and he wrote that drop-dead letter to me.'

'So who was dealing in Lebanon?' Al Georgio asked.

'Archibald,' I said. 'After Vanwinkle was killed, the letters to the insurance company stopped, and the Beirut dealer offered the coin. Mr Havistock would know about him and his sleazy reputation. After all, Archibald had been involved in the collection of antique coins for many years; he probably knows everyone in the field. And if you're wondering why he tried to peddle the coin through the Beirut dealer, the answer is simple: he needed the money. Orson was dead, but there was still Vanessa and her "gifts." And Grandby's postponed the auction of the Havistock Collection in their vaults. And the insurance companies were dragging their feet on the payoff for the missing coin. A lawsuit might take years. So, in a word, Mr Havistock found himself broke. Or at least cash-poor. He had to sell the coin if he wanted to keep Vanessa happy. It came down to a choice between a splendid treasure of ancient Greek mintage and the woman who obsessed him. Vanessa won – for a while.'

Then we were all silent, looking at each other. Mabel Havistock had remained stern and erect through much of my narrative, but now I noticed she was beginning to slump. Not slump so much, perhaps, as soften. No longer so hard, so unyielding. Hearing what she had feared spoken aloud had taken something out of her. I had hit her like a tabloid headline, and I knew it hurt.

'A nice story,' Al Georgio said finally, 'and I believe every word of it. But you know what we've got, Dunk?'

'Zero, zip, and zilch,' I said, sighing.

'Right,' he said. 'Jack?'

'Nothing. His insurance company hasn't paid him a cent, and my company hasn't reimbursed Grandby's. So how can we scream fraud? At the moment we just can't nail him.'

'Hasn't he suffered enough?' I said.

'No,' Mrs Havistock said. 'Not enough.'

Al Georgio stared directly at her. 'Ma'am,' he said softly, 'you know a wife cannot be compelled to testify against her husband. But if she volunteers, her testimony is judged just like that of any other witness.'

'I volunteer,' Mabel Havistock said grimly.

'Volunteer for what?' a resonant voice asked from the doorway, and we all looked up.

Archibald Havistock stood planted, regarding us with his ice-cube eyes. Al, Jack, and I stood and confronted him.

'Sir,' Al said, 'could we have a private talk with you, please?'

Havistock bristled. 'By what right,' he demanded, 'do you invade my home and disturb my wife? I must ask you to leave at once.'

'Mr Havistock,' Al said pleasantly, 'cut the bullshit. You'll either talk to us here and now or I'll take you down to the precinct house and we'll talk there. Is that what you want?'

The two big men locked stares, and it was Archibald who blinked. 'Very well,' he snapped. 'Come into my library. Please keep it short.'

'It will be,' Al promised. 'And sweet.'

We all moved out into the hallway and down to the library. Mrs Havistock watched us go, her eyes filmed with tears. And for the first time I thought Ruby Querita had been right: she *was* broken.

Al took my arm and held me back for a moment. 'Who swiped your notebook?' he asked in a low voice.

'I think it was Carlo, one of Vanessa's pimps. She probably had them all over the East Side.'

'What a woman,' he said, shaking his head. 'She should have gone public and sold shares.'

In the library, without invitation, the three of us pulled up chairs in a semicircle facing Archibald Havistock as he sat in the swivel chair behind his desk. I took a good look at him.

He was impeccably dressed as ever, all pressed, creased, starched, and shining. The only sign of disarray was a single lock of his silvered hair that had fallen over his right temple. He kept brushing it back with his palm, but in a moment it would flop down again. I know it sounds fanciful, but that errant lock of hair symbolized for me the man's disintegration.

'I trust this won't take long,' he said, speaking to Georgio.

'That depends on you,' Al said. 'I'll start off by telling you what we've got.'

Then, a lot blunter and harsher than I had been, he repeated everything I had just recited in the living room. He kept it brief and toneless, making it sound like an official police report. I was impressed, but other than continually brushing his hair back with his palm, Mr Havistock showed absolutely no signs of dismay. The thought occurred to me that I might be totally wrong. Oh, my God!

'So,' Al Georgio concluded, 'I think the best solution to this whole thing would be if you turned the coin over to me. If you do that, I think it's safe to say there will be no arrest, no prosecution. Jack?'

'Not from our end,' Jack Smack said. 'All we want is the return of the Demaretion.'

Archibald Havistock leaned back in his chair and regarded us with what I can only describe as a benign smile.

'A fairy tale,' he said in his rich, boomy voice. 'Not a word of truth in it. Do you have any evidence at all to support this farrago?'

'You deny what I just told you?' Al asked.

'Utterly and completely,' Havistock said, leaning forward over his desk. 'If this nonsense was what you wanted to talk to me about, then I must ask you again to leave.'

Al sighed. 'Mr Havistock, I know you've got heavy troubles. Your son and son-in-law are going to be charged with homicide. Your nephew and daughter-in-law are dead. Your daughter attempted suicide. Enough problems for any man. But if you keep jerking me around, I'm going to have to add to your troubles. I'll give you one last chance: Where's the Demaretion, Mr Havistock?'

Archibald looked at him warily, seemed to consider a moment, but then shook his head. 'I assure you,' he said, 'I do not have the Demaretion and I do not know where it is.'

'You want me to get nasty?' Al said. 'I can get nasty.' Then he gave me a lesson on what a professional detective can do with the resources of the NYPD behind him. 'Here's the program: First, I'm going to bring a photograph of you over to the super of that apartment on East Sixty-fifth. I'll lean on him, and no matter how much you paid him to keep his mouth shut, he'll admit that, yeah, you were there two, three, or four afternoons a week with Vanessa.

'Then I'm going to get copies of your cables to that coin dealer in Beirut. How else would you communicate with him – by postcard? Maybe you phoned. If you did, New York Telephone will have a record of the calls.

'Then I'm going to get a search warrant and tear this place apart. Even if I don't find anything, the neighbors will learn about it. Won't that be nice?

'Then I'm going to have another talk with poor, confused Luther, just to make sure that he knew his father was shtupping his wife.

'Then I'm going to pull in Carlo and any other pimps who delivered johns to Vanessa. The tabloids will eat it up.

'Then I'm going to ask the District Attorney to take a close look at the activities of Lenore Wolfgang, especially in leasing that love nest of yours. I don't know whether or not what she did was unethical, but it might be enough to get her disbarred.

'Then I'm going to ask the IRS to audit your returns – did you report the sale of those coins over the past five years? – and the returns of Vanessa, Luther, and everyone else in your family.

'And finally, just to add to your troubles, I think I'll have a long chat with Mrs Havistock. That lady is ready to talk, and after what you've done to her and the family, I believe she'll tell the truth.

'See how nasty I can be, Mr Havistock? Now do you want to keep insisting the whole thing is a fairy tale?'

Throughout Georgio's discourse, Archibald sat stiffly upright, propping himself with his two palms pressed onto the desktop. I saw no change of expression as Al heaped stone upon stone. But that lank lock of hair now hung across his forehead, almost covering one eye, and he made no effort to brush it back into place.

It was so quiet in that library that I could hear traffic noises on the street below, thought I heard the hoot of a tugboat on the East River, and did hear the drone of an airliner letting down for LaGuardia. No one spoke. We all waited.

Mr Havistock, who had been staring stonily at Al Georgio, now turned his gaze to me. He looked at me a long time.

'Congratulations,' he said finally with his wintry smile. 'I tried to convince my wife not to hire you, but she insisted. I knew you were aching to find the coin. Someone had made a fool of you, and you wanted revenge.'

'I would have given anything if it had turned out differently,' I told him. 'I admired you.'

'Did you?' he said. Then, forlornly: 'I wish I did.'

'The Demaretion, Mr Havistock,' Al said impatiently.

He opened his top desk drawer, found a small key, then swung around in the swivel chair, his back to us. He leaned forward, unlocked a cabinet under those handsome bookshelves. He brought out a Styrofoam box, stood, and placed it on his desk. The tape had been removed, but I recognized it at once: box thirteen.

Mr Havistock slid out the sealed teak display case with the glass cover. Then we all rose and bent over the desk. There it was.

That gorgeous, cursed coin! It loomed like a silver sun. So crisp, so strong. We all stared, mesmerized, and I thought of all the people who had owned it, even briefly. The loves, murders, treacheries, the sorrows and ecstasies – all that the Demaretion had seen and come through unclipped, unscratched, shining and complete.

'Is that it, Dunk?' Jack Smack asked.

'Yes,' I said huskily, 'that's it. It's beautiful, isn't it?'

I looked up at Mr Havistock, but he would not meet my eyes and turned away.

'Thank you, sir,' Al Georgio said briskly. 'We'll take it along now.'

He slid the display case back into the Styrofoam box, tucked it under one arm, and started out, motioning us to follow. He paused at the doorway and turned back for one final oratorical flourish.

'I leave you to the tender mercies of your wife, Mr Havistock,' he said. 'Lots of luck.'

It wasn't until we were down on the sidewalk in front of the apartment house that we stopped to grin at each other.

'Dunk,' Al said, 'you're a genius.' And he leaned forward to kiss my cheek.

'A double-genius,' Jack said, kissing the other cheek. 'A triple-genius! Al, how do you feel about this female-type detective making us look like a couple of klutzes?'

'I love it,' Georgio said. 'I'm going to take all the credit at the Department for closing the file. Aren't you going to take all the credit with your company?'

'You bet your sweet ass,' Jack said. 'The coin has been returned; that's all we were interested in. Al, Havistock is going to walk, isn't he?'

'Sure he is,' Al said. 'What could we charge him with? All those things I threatened – so much kaka. I could have done all that, but it wouldn't have convicted him of anything. Just made his life more miserable than it is now. Let him walk; I've got the coin.'

'If you're not going to arrest him,' I said, 'what do you need the Demaretion for?' And I whisked the box from under Al's arm. 'It belongs to me. I signed for it.'

He looked at me a moment, startled. Then he laughed. 'You're right, Dunk, it's yours. Want us to escort you back to Grandby's?'

'Nope,' I said, 'I'm going to do this my way. If someone tries to mug me, you'll have another homicide to investigate. Not mine; the mugger's.'

'Be careful, Dunk,' Jack warned.

'Talk to you guys later,' I said, and went breezing away.

It was late in the afternoon, and I knew my chances of getting a cab were nil. So I practically ran back to Grandby & Sons, hugging the Demaretion to what I laughingly call my bosom and trying not to shout with triumph.

I dashed up the stairs to my old office and banged on the door, then started kicking it. Hobart Juliana peered at me through the peephole, then unlocked.

'Dunk,' he said, bewildered, 'what on earth . . . ?'

'Look!' I yelled. 'Just look at this!'

I slid the display case from the box and placed it on Hobie's desk. He bent over to inspect that single coin nestled on velvet in the middle compartment. Then he straightened and turned to me.

'Oh, my God,' he said. 'The Demaretion. Dunk, it's glorious!'

'Yes,' I said, wanting to laugh and cry at the same time. 'It's so lovely, so lovely.'

He gave a whoop of delight, grabbed me, and we went dancing around the office, banging into tables and desks, holding each other and so excited and joyous I didn't think I could stand it.

Hobie stopped suddenly. 'Let's go,' he said. 'We've got to impress Madam Dodat and god with your incredible victory.'

So, with me carrying the display case, we sped into Felicia Dodat's office, barging by her indignant secretary. Felicia looked up, shocked by this sudden intrusion. I plunked the display case down on her desk.

'There it is,' I said. 'The Demaretion.'

She stared at it a moment. 'Oh, Dunk,' she said, 'isn't that *nice*! I must call Mr Grandby. He'll be so *pleased*.'

Within ten minutes there must have been a dozen people crammed into Felicia's office, all bending to examine that old Greek coin and laughing, kissing me, or shaking my hand. God was there, but all he could say was, 'Well, well, well.' He kept repeating it: 'Well, well, well.' Everyone wanted to know how I had recovered it, but I just smiled mysteriously and winked. A great moment in my life. Dunk shot.

Finally Madam Dodat shooed everyone out of her office except for Mr Grandby, Hobie, and me.

'All right, Dunk,' she said, giving me her toothy smile, 'now tell us how you did it.'

I had my story ready. I told them that Archibald Havistock was an impassioned collector and, at the last minute, just couldn't let go of the Demaretion. I told them nothing of his relationship with his daughter-in-law or of his being blackmailed by his nephew. If the tabloids got hold of the story, everyone would know the details soon enough, but they weren't going to hear them from me.

They accepted my version readily enough, and we all agreed that true collectors were infected with a mania that could never be cured. Then the four of us formed a triumphal procession down to the vaults, god carrying the display case, and saw it safely locked away.

'Well, well, well,' Mr Grandby said, beaming, 'I think this calls for a celebration. Will you join me for dinner?'

So we did, adjourning to the Bedlington dining room where we all had Chateaubriands with the best Béarnaise sauce I've ever tasted. And two bottles of champagne. My employer was acting in a most unpenguinlike manner. He even leaned over to whisper in my ear that I could expect a salary raise for my 'remarkable efforts' on behalf of Grandby & Sons.

We parted about eight o'clock. God and Felicia Dodat went off together – to an apartment on East 65th Street, I wondered? Hobie and I embraced on the sidewalk, and I swore I would be in to work first thing Monday morning. Then he left to return to his consenting adult. I cabbed home alone.

There was nothing interesting in my mail – just bills and junk. So I kicked off my shoes and sprawled on the couch, beginning to feel a letdown after all the day's excitement. There was no reason I should have felt depressed – I had won, hadn't I? – but I did.

Then I realized what was saddening me was the fate of Archibald Havistock. I had thought of him as a statue, but now he was overturned, broken, and crumbling. I tried to understand how that could have happened. He was an intelligent and rational man; how could he have acted as stupidly as he did?

Perhaps it was male menopause. Perhaps it was nothing more than lust for a young, lubricious body. But I thought it was more than that. He was a deep man and must have known exactly how foolish it was to become enthralled by his son's wife, a doxy, and risk the happiness of his home. But he could not resist.

Suddenly it occurred to me that he might actually have been in love with her. It was possible. That reserved, magisterial, *complete* man may have, for the first time in his life, felt an overwhelming passion that gave new meaning to his life. He surrendered to that surge, not caring, because it was new to him and he had never learned to cope with such fervid emotions.

But whatever his motives or obsessions, nothing could excuse his illogical conduct.

I sighed and went into the bedroom to phone. I had two calls to make. The first to Al Georgio, telling that estimable man that no, I would not marry him. The second to Jack Smack, telling that flighty tap dancer that yes, I would move in with him.

You can be logical about other people's lives, but never about your own.